Mindful Self-Care for Clinicians and Caregivers: A Group Facilitator's Guide

Water Lily Flourishing

This water lily, rooted deep in the earth, lifts its blossomed head to flourish in the sunlight. It is a vivid symbol of the nourishing connections between nature, body, and senses made readily apparent by bright, intimate awareness. Our book extols this way of earthbound, sunlit presence as a path to self-care, nourished during gathering with others while caring. As self-care flourishes, it makes way for the rewarding gift of presence during the powerful dynamic between a caregiver and the person who makes this privilege possible.

Footnote:
The photograph *Water Lily Flourishing* was taken at the Dallas Arboretum and Botanical Garden, Dallas, Texas, by Robin B. Jarrett.

Mindful Self-Care for Clinicians and Caregivers

A Group Facilitator's Guide

Martin Lumpkin, PhD
Psychologist, Dallas, Texas, United States

Marielle H. Collins, PhD
Clinical Health Psychologist, Assistant Professor of Psychiatry, Cleveland Clinic Lerner College of Medicine, Ohio, United States

Robin B. Jarrett, PhD, ABPP
Professor of Psychiatry, University of Texas Southwestern Medical Center, Department of Psychiatry Dallas, Texas, United States

ELSEVIER

ACADEMIC PRESS
An imprint of Elsevier

Academic Press is an imprint of Elsevier
125 London Wall, London EC2Y 5AS, United Kingdom
50 Hampshire Street, 5th Floor, Cambridge, MA 02139, United States

ISBN: 978-0-443-29821-9

For information on all Academic Press publications visit our website at https://www.elsevier.com/books-and-journals

Publisher: Stacy Masucci
Acquisitions Editor: Simonetta Harrison
Editorial Project Manager: Billie Jean Fernandez
Production Project Manager: Vijayaraj Purushothaman
Cover Designer: Miles Hitchen

Typeset by TNQ Tech

Dedications

We dedicate *Mindful Self-Care for Clinicians and Caregivers: A Group Facilitator's Guide* to all those involved in the caregiving process and especially:

To my wife, Janet, who walked with me hand in hand on the path of mindfulness and caregiving; my mother, Margaret, who taught me how to give care; and all my teachers of Mindfulness-Based Stress Reduction, who elevated my meditation practice to the level of self-care.

Martin Lumpkin, PhD

To my mother, Rev. Mary Anne Collins-Stauffer, and my father, Dr. John J. Collins, who embody selfless caregiving as a minister, a doctor, parents, and grandparents. To my husband, Kyle Gooderham, whose unwavering support has meant everything. And to my precious son, Rhone Matthew, who fills my heart with light and joy.

Marielle H. Collins, PhD

To mentors, clinicians, and caregivers

including my husband: J Wesley Norred,
my parents: Rev. Richard Bailey Jarrett and Mrs. Barbara Lee Palmer Jarrett
and the clinicians and caregivers at:
the University of Texas Southwestern Medical Center in Dallas, Texas, and
Friends Homes in Greensboro, North Carolina

who lived the powerful, sustained dynamic within giving, receiving, and caring.

Robin B. Jarrett, PhD, ABPP

Contents

How to Use This Guide

Mindfulness Self-Care for Caregivers (MSCC): A Group Facilitator's Guide includes descriptions of eight intervention sessions organized into the following sections:

- A Quick Guide gives a session summary and overview. Marked with:
- An Introduction provides the rationale, format, and useful notes. Marked with:
- The Session Guide describes the aim, content, and guides. Marked with:
- The Participant Summary, often handed out at the beginning of each session, provides a brief session summary and space for notes. Marked with:
- Participant handouts for review and reference in between sessions. Marked with:

The authors and publisher give book purchasers permission to reproduce the worksheets to promote mindful self-care, assuming that the reproduction and use include the references to the author and publisher therein.

In addition, you will find an online portal of audios, videos, and photos associated with (https://shop.elsevier.com/books/book-companion/9780443298219). The authors and publisher give book purchasers permission to use materials at the portal, assuming use includes the references to the author and publisher therein.

You will also find Author Reflections that are set apart in bolded boxes and Facilitator Contemplations for self-reflection (set off in smaller boxes). Additionally, you will find vignettes that are italicized to convey the perspectives of both Facilitators and Participants. These symbols form a map and provide guideposts for our readers as they discover their way on this mindful journey.

Foreword

The crusty senior attending psychiatrist had just come off a long night of call and was chatting with some of the nurses before heading home. "*I just can't believe what residents expect these days*," he grumbled. "*My call schedule has me doing an 18-hour shift once a month and my resident is asking for time off so that he can attend a hospital-sanctioned Spa Day for his mental health.*" I overheard this conversation in the early 1990s and one of the reasons it stuck with me was how well it illustrated the generational divide in attitudes toward self-care for clinicians. It captured the stark contrast between putting your needs in the background so that you can grind out demanding clinical activities versus taking a preemptive stance on self-care in order to avoid burnout. To be fair, the recognition of burden and strain on healthcare workers and caregivers has grown over the past two decades and was brought into sharpest relief during the pandemic, but it is one thing to recognize a problem and quite another to have scalable resources for addressing it. *Mindful Self-Care for Clinicians and Caregivers: A Group Facilitator's Guide* is exactly such a resource.

Caregiving is defined by many religious traditions as an act of virtue and as the North American population ages, it is becoming ubiquitous. Statistics bear this out. Formal caregivers, such as healthcare workers, are instrumental in ensuring the physical and emotional needs of the people they look after with an additional one in five Americans describing themselves as providing informal care, defined as unpaid and often family-focused.

With such high levels of participation in the enterprise of caregiving, it does beg the question of why it took so long to recognize that the needs of caregivers deserve attention. There are plenty of other domains in which the burdens faced by those in the workplace are recognized as cumulative and in need of intervention. Take "Startup Founder Burnout" as a recent example. People now accept that the toll of endless hours, financial instability, unrelenting pressure, and high expectations can lead to founders becoming detached and ineffective in running their companies. Perhaps the lag in awareness of the stresses associated with caregiving is rooted in the beliefs about the focus needing to be on the receiver, and not the provider of care...that there is something selfish about thinking that a caregiver's needs count in the equation as well. But when the all too real stresses of caregiving swamp the meaning and purpose of providing care, then burnout and disengagement is a real possibility.

Mindful Self-Care for Clinicians and Caregivers: A Group Facilitator's Guide addresses this problem directly by implementing an evidence-based solution for the management of stress and difficult moods that features mindfulness meditation at its core. Mindfulness practice has been shown to reduce reactivity and offer a sense of wholeness and grounding. By expanding the capacity for well-being, caregivers can find their way back to the purpose and meaning and provide care through a lens that is less transactional and more relational.

The book itself, it seems to me, was written with this meta-goal in mind—how best to support facilitators of MSCC in delivering the six to eight session group program. As is increasingly the case with other structured mindfulness-based programs, MSCC pays equal attention to structure—providing session outlines, rationales, handouts, and transcripts alongside more unstructured elements related to embodiment, practice, and inquiry. This is a signal strength of MSCC. It messages very clearly that while the reader holds in his/her hand a session by session outline of the program, the way that it is delivered is critical. Teaching MSCC from a place of practice, compassion, and curiosity is paramount; in fact, some might say that this is the curriculum itself. By combining these two emphases into an accessible, comprehensive, and compelling framework, the authors have done an excellent job in allowing clinicians and caregivers to draw nearer to the wellness resources they very much deserve.

Zindel Segal, PhD
Distinguished Professor of Psychology in Mood Disorders
University of Toronto Scarborough

Preface

Why Did We Write Mindful Self-Care for Clinicians and Caregivers: A Group Facilitator's Guide?

We authors have been touched—both professionally and personally—by the joys and challenges of caring for others, especially those living with illness or vulnerability. In our work and personal lives, we have also witnessed the profound impact caregiving has on those who give it. We wanted to find a way to honor these experiences by shining a light on the care of the caregiver.

This *Guide* was given birth during and after the era of the COVID-19 global pandemic, war, violence, and continued global and political unrest. Today, the effects of these intense calamities and upheaval remain. Caregiving is central to sustaining life and to coping with illness, death, grief, and separation. The strain of caregiving was apparent as we all tried to adapt to the requirements of a global pandemic and war amid inter/national political divides. We wanted to find a way to support caregivers, both unpaid (informal) and paid (formal). We aspire to disseminate the power of mindful practice in an accessible and helpful way. So, we set out on our own journey to offer and to disseminate effective evidence-based practices to promote self-care in supporting and nurturing caregivers in their daily work.

Caregiving can be joyful when it meets the needs of a vulnerable person and increases purpose and meaning for the caregiver. Because we are unaware of a better term, we refer to the person receiving care as the care person. In so doing, we hope to underscore the human dynamic of caring between the persons receiving and giving care. In the best of circumstances, this dynamic is a vital relationship and not merely a rote role. We emphasize this interpersonal dynamic, as it is powerful within caregiving.

Care persons entrust caregivers with a unique and special privilege. They entrust parts of their physical and emotional well-being to another person, implicitly giving the message, *"I trust that you will do your best for me."* The nature of caregiving, while potentially rewarding, however, can be physically and emotionally challenging or exhausting when it is continuous across a career or the long phase of a relationship. Caregiving can last for hours, months, years, or a lifetime. Interruptions in caregiving can become rare. In order for caregivers to approach each new day with resilience and resolve, the caregiver needs time for reflection, self-care, and calm.

A potent resource for increasing self-care, calm, and enriching daily living is the state and skill of mindfulness. Jon Kabat-Zinn, a founder of the contemporary mindfulness movement in the West, defines mindfulness as "paying attention in a particular way: on purpose, in the present moment, and nonjudgmentally" (Kabat-Zinn, 2013). He elaborates on the blend of focused attention and broad awareness with a grounding in body and sensory experiences he sees as skills that can be cultivated through stationary and moving meditation practices, as well as brief, informal everyday exercises (Kabat-Zinn, 2013). As Farb and Segal (2024) demonstrate, these practices rely on highlighting sensory experiences to access mindfulness.

Mindfulness practices are recommended to promote self-care. Such practices have been shown to effectively decrease stress, depression, anxiety, and pain, as well as to promote a state of general well-being (Goldberg, et al, 2022; Lomas et. al., 2018; Kriakous et. al., 2021; Li et. al., 2022). This well-being is what we aspire for caregivers to experience. In *A Guide*, we provide a full complement of tools to qualified facilitators to help caregivers practice mindful self-care. We hypothesize that not only will caregivers reap the benefits, but also, due to the interpersonal dynamic between the caregiver and their care person, the care person will also benefit. *Mindful Self-Care for Clinicians and Caregivers (MSCC): A Group Facilitator's Guide* is a mindfulness-based intervention (MBI) that aims to provide caregivers with the skills to access the privileges and benefits of giving care, while also coping with the inherent challenges of consistently providing outstanding care, whether for brief or long periods of time, frequently unconditionally and without external validation.

Written for facilitators skilled in mental health care, our aim is to consolidate tools and resources to evoke experiences of mindful self-care and reinforce the skills that sustain them. In Part A, we ground MSCC squarely in theory and the evidence available to support its use and dissemination. We noticed there is not a comprehensive guide that combines science, theory, processes, tools, lived experience, and art forms that activate all the senses (seeing, hearing, tasting, moving, touching, movement, and balance) to promote caregivers' mindful self-care. This *Guide* supports professionals who can facilitate group processes to promote mindful self-care in both formal (professional) and informal (lay) caregivers. In Part A of *A Guide*, we provide the evidence and theoretical basis for mindful self-care, which describes the concepts. In Part B, we offer suggestions for setting up and facilitating MSCC groups. We created an earlier version of the MSCC *Guide* (Lumpkin and Jarrett, 2015). This version was used in an initial feasibility and acceptability study which showed that MSCC was valued, acceptable, safe, and feasible for caregivers (parents) of youth with autism spectrum disorder (Bellone et al., 2023).

In Part B, we provided the aims and structure of each session, while also providing materials and tools (e.g., handouts, practices, audio and video recordings, poems, and photographs) for facilitators. The *Guide* appendix includes listings of the resources and supplemental materials which are available through a portal available to readers at https://shop.elsevier.com/books/book-companion/9780443298219. Our aim is to make available a ready-to-go guide for qualified facilitators to develop groups for caregivers seeking greater resilience as they care for others, often in social systems that feel unresponsive to their needs. In this *Guide*, we sought to incorporate images that illustrate the nature of experience inherent in both mindful living and in caregiving.

We developed *Mindful Self-Care for Clinicians and Caregivers (MSCC): A Group Facilitator's Guide* to respond to the psychological needs of formal or informal caregivers of persons with acute or chronic illnesses or those who require care due to their stage of life, whether infants, young children, or frail elders. By design, our concept of caregiving is quite broad, and the interventional protocol we provide is flexible.

In *Mindful Self-Care for Clinicians and Caregivers (MSCC): A Group Facilitator's Guide*, the psychosocial intervention defined is a six- to eight-session mindfulness-based intervention (MBI), usually experienced weekly, inspired by *Mindfulness-Based Stress Reduction* (MBSR; Kabat-Zinn, 2013) and *Mindfulness-Based Cognitive Therapy for Depression* (MBCT; Segal et al., 2013). We are grateful to these colleagues for their contributions and acknowledge that we are standing on their shoulders. In Part B, describing each MSCC session, we integrated, adapted, and innovated basic MBI interventions for the busy and demanding context of caregiving.

We have developed MSCC to shepherd professional facilitators as they design and facilitate group sessions that can be in person or remote, using secure telehealth and best, confidential virtual practices. Ideal facilitators have some training in mental health and some previous experience background in MBCT, MBSR, or basic MBIs and training in mindfulness meditative practices. This book includes concepts, processes, and tools to promote the facilitation of mindful self-care in caregivers, using the power of group dynamics. Additionally, we operationalize MSCC to encourage researchers to explore its best indications and its most robust mechanisms of actions.

We note that informal caregiving is frequently experienced and societal support is often sorely lacking. Society and institutions are often not sensitized to the contexts and supports that formal caregivers need to perform at optimal levels and sustain excellence. We offer MSCC in the hope that the social context will evolve to meet these basic human needs of all involved in the caregiving process.

Who are Our Readers? MSCC Facilitators

Facilitators for the MSCC groups may include skilled and developing psychologists, social workers, nurses, guidance counselors, pastoral clergy, or other professionals who are experienced in the basic concepts from mental health and mindfulness meditation. While trainees may use the MSCC *Guide* as a text, its implementation is for professionals already trained and experienced in guiding people as they learn mindfulness skills in groups. A more detailed description of the role of facilitators can be found in Part A—Chapter 2 under "What is the role of the facilitator."

Who Are Formal and Informal Caregivers Who Would Benefit from Participating in Mindful Selfcare Groups?

Formal caregivers are paid professionals providing medical care, psychological care, or social support for ill and vulnerable persons. Formal caregivers include, but are not limited to, healthcare workers, mental health clinicians, clergy, and teachers at all levels in all settings. Informal caregivers, such as family or significant others, are those caring for ill or vulnerable persons needing acute or ongoing caregiving. The informal caregiver tends to provide their caregiving without pay.

The informal or formal caregivers who participate in MSCC are likely to be:

a) adult females and males, aged 18 or more,
b) have responsibility for caring for persons who are vulnerable or ill, requiring ongoing assistance from the caregiver,
c) able to provide informed consent for participating in an MSCC group,
d) able to commit to attend MSCC sessions,
e) willing to maintain confidentiality and privacy, both verbal and environmental, for fellow participants, and
f) willing to use a computer or smart device to access tools and materials of MSCC when the group is held virtually rather than in person.

This Guide was developed in order to:

a) guide facilitators to use MSCC in a consistent manner,
b) provide tools for MSCC facilitators to effectively offer the intervention,
c) provide caregivers with tools to learn MSCC,
d) disseminate MSCC, seeking to promote psychological well-being for clinicians and caregivers, and
e) promote research by providing an operational definition of what MSCC really is.

Facilitator's Contemplation

In *A Guide*, we hope to speak directly to you, as a person and a facilitator of mindful practice in clinicians and caregivers. We recommend that you have some experience as a participant in a group focused on learning the skills and process of mindfulness, as well as a personal practice. To integrate these recommendations with your own mindful practice and preparation for each group session, we offer you—a ***Facilitator's contemplation***, located at the end of PART A Chapters 1 and 2 and at the end of each Session (1–8) in PART B. The idea is that you can reflect on the question (contemplate) as part of your preparation for facilitating a given session. The questions are formed to help you facilitate with a "presence" of open curiosity, acceptance, and awareness of all that clinicians and caregivers will create as they gather together, and with you.

Why Mindful Self-Care for Clinicians and Caregivers?

A formal caregiver—such as a mental health clinician or other healthcare professional—may be trained in the technical and emotional aspects of care, yet still accumulates stress, emotional burdens, and painful memories over the course of their education and career. Despite professional boundaries and clinical training, formal caregivers often witness suffering, confront moral dilemmas, and absorb the emotional weight of their patients' experiences. Over time, this exposure can lead to compassion fatigue, burnout, or a quiet erosion of their own well-being. In our conceptualization and writing, we use the term caregiver to also include clinicians. Self-care is essential for healthy longevity in helping professions.

Similarly, an informal caregiver of an ill or vulnerable person lives in a world that can be filled with profound responsibility, self-sacrifice, and often loss. The burdens may include making difficult, often solitary decisions; managing the logistics of care; and consistently advocating for their loved one's needs. Self-sacrifice often means putting one's own needs last. Loss can come in the form of losing the care person as they had been anticipating the end of life of the care person and losing the former life of the caregiver as it used to be.

Mindfulness-Based Stress Reduction, as developed by Jon Kabat-Zinn and his colleagues (MBSR; Kabat-Zinn et al., 2013), has an evidence base of more than 30 years, bringing self-care into the medical community. This intervention teaches mindfulness as a set of attitudes and skills that people can practice directly into their lives as ways of reducing stress. For the informal caregiver of persons with illness or vulnerability, mindfulness offers practices that can result in renewal and stability in the midst of life's storms.

The mindfulness interventions of *Mindfulness-Based Stress Reduction* (MBSR; Kabat-Zinn, 2013) and *Mindfulness-Based Cognitive Therapy* (MBCT; Segal et al., 2013) have strong research support in the field of psychosocial interventions (Creswell, 2019). *Mindful Self-Care for Clinicians and Caregivers (MSCC): A Group Facilitator's Guide* takes its vision from these two mindfulness-based interventions, adding a focus on the context of formal and informal caregiving. Like MBSR and MBCT, MSCC shares the following characteristics:

(1) a developmental skill structure over a number of sessions,
(2) facilitator commitment to their own mindfulness practice,
(3) a mix of formal and informal mindfulness practices,
(4) inquiry-based learning facilitation,
(5) home practice,
(6) participant sharing of experiences,
(7) use of metaphor and poetry, and
(8) emphasis on mindful attitudes alongside mindfulness practices.

In summary, MSCC is a psychosocial intervention delivered through a six- to eight-week group format with weekly hour-and-a-half sessions, with a strong emphasis on mindfulness practices outside of a session. *A Guide* offers 6–8 sessions to build flexibility depending on the needs of the participants and setting. *A Guide* is timely in that it is built on the emerging, promising findings that mindful practices enhance the wellbeing of both informal and formal caregivers alike, as discussed in Part A.

Where Will Mindful Self-Care Groups Gather?

Mindful self-care groups can gather anywhere privacy and safety are available. Settings may be inside, outside, in-person or remote, at work, home, school, church, mosque, synagogue, clinic, nursing home, retirement home, or anywhere a caregiver frequents or rests.

Overview of Mindful Self-Care for Clinicians and Caregivers (MSCC) Sessions

Mindful Self-Care for Clinicians and Caregivers (MSCC) is close enough to the styles of MBSR and MBCT that the following references might be of use to facilitators in search of more resource material on facilitation, descriptions of formal and informal practices, the art of inquiry, and the incorporation of mindful attitudes. A good introduction to the MBSR format and principles can be found in *The Heart of Mindfulness-Based Stress Reduction: A MBSR Guide for Clinicians and Clients* (Rosenbaum, 2021). For MBCT, there is *Mindfulness-Based Cognitive Therapy for Depression* (MBCT; Segal et al., 2013). MBCT, unlike MBSR, organizes its approach to specific conditions, such as depression, relapse prevention, or context.

The specific context MSCC is that of caregiver stress and self-care. In terms of formal practices, MSCC makes use of gentle stretches and Qigong movements (Cohen, 1997) instead of yoga because there is less risk for injury than usual yoga practices. The sessions offer themes that build on each other. Participants are exposed gradually to formal practices, beginning with the most accessible and moving to those that are more challenging. From the beginning, brief informal practices are encouraged as participants pause in their everyday lives to reset toward ways of releasing stress and finding emotional nourishment. Once participants understand the general concept of mindfulness, they learn how stress is generated by automatic ways of avoidant coping and how mindfulness can be an alternative response to stress. In the latter phases of the sessions, participants examine caregiver stress and self-care strategies.

Each session follows the same basic structure. First, there are *Check-ins* to encourage group member sharing of experiences with mindfulness practices in the context of daily life, particularly as a caregiver. The sessions include a *Guiding question* to prompt discussion. Very often, participants inspire and teach each other from these shared experiences. After *Check-ins*, *Mindful pauses* are brief mindfulness exercises that ground the session early in a guided experience, suggesting ways one can informally practice mindfulness in everyday life.

Next, there is a highlighting of the *Session theme*. In this section, the facilitator introduces the theme of the session with a guiding question, a primary image or metaphor, and a discussion clarifying the theme. The facilitator will pose a question for discussion and prompt shared experiences in caregiving.

Formal experiential practices follow. The first is a moving meditation and the second is a stationary mediation. Often participants find stationary meditation less difficult when preceded by the movement exercise. Most all parts of the session include an inquiry that evokes, clarifies, and validates participant responses to the mindfulness exercises. The session ends with a *Summary and invitation to explore* the various practices over the time in between sessions. Rather than create homework in a top–down fashion, exercises and meditations are presented and "tasted" in class and then offered as options that can be chosen based on interest and curiosity. Resources are made available at the end of the class for home practice, such as audio files, videos, outlines, and poetry.

Session guides are not meant to be rigid, mechanical scripts, but rather a foundation flexible enough for adaptation. The atmosphere of the class and the facilitator's personal connection with the themes and practices are vital. Each MSCC session structure and process will be an effective blend, like a musical score brought to life through the facilitator's expression and professional style.

Given the demands of caregiving, there will be times when participants will miss one or more sessions. Participants will be encouraged to attend sessions whenever possible and review the resources and handouts from each session. Furthermore, they are encouraged to practice mindfulness in daily life as we hypothesize that experiential learning is a key mechanism in the effectiveness and benefits of MSCC.

Below summarizes the title and focus of the 6–8 sessions as further described:

Session	Title and Focus
1	What is Mindfulness?
2	Mindful Observing
3	Mindful Responding
4	Self-Care and Self-Nourishment
5	Mindfulness and Relationships
6	Mindfulness in Daily Life
	Additional Booster or Make-Up Sessions that may be provided
7	Discovering Your Way to Mindfulness
8	Minding Your Own Care

Using the Mindful Self-Care for Clinicians and Caregivers (MSCC) Guide

The following guide for facilitators supports the delivery of 6–8 sessions.

Using the Mindful Self-Care for Clinicians and Caregivers (MSCC) Guide group experience. Each session includes the following items:

- Quick Guide, *shorthand prompts as reference for the facilitator during the group process.*
- Introduction *of themes, concepts, and questions to be introduced in a group.*
- Facilitator's Guide, *which expands on the methods to be used in a group.*
- *The* Participant's Summary *handout is designed to prompt and review session concepts and experiences.*
- *Handouts,* the audio, video, visual aids, and handouts for use between sessions.

The session *Quick Guide* provides the facilitator with session snapshots that can be referenced to remind the facilitator what to consider next.

Introductions for each session create a vision to hold in mind as the facilitator guides caregiver participants in the development of mindfulness perspectives and skills. The facilitator plays a vital role in helping these special individuals learn to support themselves by moderating the stress of caregiving and in finding ways for improved self-care. There may be teaching moments based on group members' reports. The art of facilitation goes beyond the mechanics of the session structure. This is where you—as facilitator—most come in with your knowledge and classroom mindfulness. You will need to decide, as the session process unfolds, what to stay with and what to shorten or alter. All session parts are given time estimates for a total of 1 hour and 30 minutes. This time length was chosen because of caregivers' time pressure in their lives. Many find it easier to commit to these shorter sessions rather than struggle with "yet something else to schedule." Videos and audios allow people to practice session exercises at home as well as in class. We ask facilitators to be time-conscious but not time-driven. As long as the participants feel stirred excitement for learning, learning will surely happen.

The *Session Guide* provides the facilitator with the procedural details for each session.

The *Participant's Summary* is both a summary and a worksheet for each session.

The *Resources* section also includes handouts and summaries to promote skill development in the participants. Digital images as well as audio and video recordings are included to enhance the process and spark the joy of experimenting and are listed in the Appendix. The audios and videos demonstrate various stationary and moving forms of meditation or mindfulness exercises.

Session *Handouts,* listed in the Appendix and available on the portal, are included to be used to help caregivers learn MSCC and highlight the key points organized by session. These are found after each session's *Introduction* and the *Session Guide.* They are provided online by the publisher with the purchase of this book.

Audios and Videos are listed in the Appendix and are available on the portal.

Poems and Art for use during sessions are listed in the Appendix and are available on the portal. They are offered to facilitate a participant's learning of mindful self-care. The photographs for each session are provided in a format that the facilitator can use to set the mood or tone as the group begins to gather for the session. Facilitators may consider what art forms best match their participant population and setting.

A Note about the Authors

As we collaborated on this book and reflected on the dynamic between informal caregivers, formal caregivers, and care persons, we realized each author had occupied all these roles, at various timepoints throughout our lives. We know that caregivers (informal and formal) are frequently managing their own health concerns of health maintenance or illness amid giving care. We hope to bring the authenticity of our lived experience to how we describe and illustrate the various roles. We incorporate these lived experiences to illustrate not only what we have learned as academic clinicians and researchers, but also what we have come to understand as humans who have cared for family and loved ones. Just as importantly, we have been shaped by the experience of receiving care ourselves. In each role, we are aware of the power of mindful practice inside the interpersonal experience of giving and receiving care. There are reflections of some of our lived experiences set off in bold boxes within the *Guide.*

We offer this *Guide* as a path forward to empower caregivers during their journey to accept and embrace their experiences with acceptance, curiosity, and flexibility, all the while benefiting from gathering with other caregivers. As we wrote, we reflected on the full experience of mindful practices during caregiving, and we gathered in our own small group and reflected on the powerful application of mindful practice.

Acknowledgments

From All Authors

Each author acknowledges the contemplative traditions that have been and are practiced over the globe and through the ages. We note that behavioral traditions have the capacity to help people, and they have survived the test of time. These traditions are our roots.

We acknowledge John Kabat-Zinn for his pioneering work in facilitating mindful practices in Western culture. *Mindful Self-Care for Clinicians and Caregivers (MSCC)* grows from his earlier work, as well as the work of Zindel Segal, Willem Kuyken, and colleagues, and others too numerous to list who contribute to the field of contemplative neuroscience. We are but a branch on the great tree they planted and nourished.

We wish to thank our spouses for their interest in and support of this project. They had to patiently extend to us time and space away from family life to bring this book to fruition. Thank you, Janet, Kyle, and Wes.

We are particularly grateful to Janet Lumpkin for her sensitive reading of our manuscript and the editing suggestions that strengthened our book. We appreciate the Jerry H. Lewis, M.D. Mental Health Research Foundation for funding a preliminary research project supporting the fundamental model and feasibility of Mindful Self-Care for Clinicians and Caregivers. Further, we appreciate the support of the numerous Elsevier staff who helped us publish this book.

From Martin Lumpkin, PhD

So many people to thank for my journey into mindful self-and-other care. My heartfelt gratitude to my wife, Janet, for her loving and energetic support of all the trails and byways I took to find my way to mindfulness practices and study. To my teachers in the Insight Meditation Society and the Center for Mindfulness at UMass Medical Center in Worcester, I bow in amazement at how their seeds germinated. The Division of Psychology faculty and students at UT Southwestern at Dallas allowed me, a fledgling facilitator, to try my hand with an unfamiliar approach called mindfulness, which was largely unknown in our part of the country.

To my partners in the book, Marielle and Robin, thank you for your words and insights—and human presence during times each of us needed a bit of caregiving. We shared the highs of writing breakthroughs, the anxiety of health crises, and the birth of a child. Now there is a journey.

And so much gratitude to those who trusted me as a teacher and caregiver: those in my mindfulness groups taught me so much, and my parents at the end of their lives taught me the heart of caregiving.

From Marielle H. Collins, PhD

I am deeply grateful to the many people who have supported me throughout this journey. To my mother, Rev. Mary Anne Collins-Stauffer, thank you for being the first person to believe in my calling to become a psychologist. I am grateful to my father, Dr. John J. Collins, who inspired my passion for working with medical patients in the acute hospital as a health psychologist.

To my sisters, Johanna Collins-Wood and Madelena Collins, and my brother-in-law, Benjamin Collins-Wood, thank you for being my steadfast support team and for the countless ways you have been by my side over the years. Thank you to my husband, Kyle Gooderham, who has loved and supported me through his actions as much as his words and who has championed my career in the midst of building our family. I love you with all my heart. Thank you to my precious son, Rhone, who made me a mother for the first time while I was writing this book. Caring for you and loving you is my greatest joy.

I am endlessly grateful to my mentors, clinical supervisors, and colleagues who have guided, taught, and shaped me into the clinician I am today. I would like to acknowledge all the outstanding caregivers at the Cleveland Clinic; it is an honor to care for patients alongside you.

To my patients and clients, thank you for the great privilege of bearing witness to your stories, your resilience, and your strength. To my fellow authors, Marty Lumpkin and Robin Jarrett, thank you for your mentorship, encouragement, and friendship. I am forever grateful.

From Robin B. Jarrett, PhD, ABPP

I would like to acknowledge my mentors and teachers who helped to develop any skill I may have in analyzing complex information, innovation, or writing about it. I am grateful to primary mentors, including Richard B. Jarrett (my father), who taught me the value of service, the necessity of critical analysis, and the power of learning in transformation. He shared the meditations of the heart with great acceptance. I am grateful to Barbara Lee Palmer Jarrett (my mother), who taught me how to write, valued my drive to explore, and encouraged me, through her words and then daily perseverance, as we wrote *A Guide*. I thank Rosemery O. Nelson Gray, PhD, who taught me not only how to explore science via experimentation but also how to write about clinical psychological science.

I recognize each clinician and caregiver who has held my hand (literally or figuratively) during the dynamic of teaching about and giving care.For clinicians and caregivers, I hope that *A Guide* will make self-care more accessible and will facilitate the connection available in small groups bound by caregiving.

I thank my many patients and students who have given me the great privilege of listening and being present during their growth; their examples have challenged me to grow as well.

I am indebted to my co-authors Martin Lumpkin and Marielle Collins, who made writing this book a joyful experience and propelled mindful growth. Without them, *A Guide* would still be an idea rather than a reality.

Most importantly, I am grateful for J Wesley Norred (my husband), whose loving support nurtures me and propels our explorations, past, present, and future.

Part A

Theoretical, Empirical and Practical Foundations for Mindful Self-Care for Clinicians and Caregivers

In PART A, we give facilitators a broad conception and empirical foundation for providing Mindful Self-Care for Caregivers, along with a glimpse of our journey as we developed MSCC. We hope to inspire our readers' next steps and to ignite curiosity about MSCC as an intervention to use in groups and to investigate through research. In Part A Chapter 1 (Section 1), we identify who caregivers are (i.e., informal and clinician [formal] caregivers), what caregivers and care persons experience dynamically, and why mindful self-care is a helpful skill and process. We highlight the privilege of caregiving and the problem of burnout for clinicians (formal caregivers) and informal caregivers alike, showing why effective strategies to combat burnout and stress are needed. In Part A Chapter 1 (Section 2), we introduce the MSCC model and evidence base for Mindfulness-based Interventions (MBIs). We categorize Mindful Self-Care for Clinicians and Caregivers (MSCC) as a member of that family. The aim of MSCC is to help caregivers access the privileges and benefits of giving care while also coping with the inherent challenges. Here we provide the theoretical and empirical foundation that facilitators need to effectively teach mindfulness and facilitate MSCC in groups. Similarly, we write for scholars, trainees, and researchers who see MSCC as part of their agenda.

In Part A Chapter 2 and Part B, we describe the practical and logistical processes involved in facilitating MSCC.

After each major section, we offer you a Facilitator's Contemplation that may help you prepare for and meditate upon MSCC and its sessions.

Chapter 1—The Rationale, Concepts, and Research Underlying Mindful Self-Care for Clinicians and Caregivers

Abstract

In Part A Chapter 1 we give facilitators a broad conceptual and empirical foundation for providing Mindful Self-Care for Clinicians and Caregivers, along with a glimpse of our journey as we developed MSCC. The aim of MSCC is to help caregivers access the privileges and benefits of giving care, while also coping with the inherent challenges. We provide the theoretical and empirical foundation that facilitators need to effectively teach mindfulness and facilitate MSCC in groups. We hope to inspire our readers' next steps and to ignite curiosity about MSCC as an intervention to use in groups and to investigate through research. We identify who caregivers are (i.e., informal and clinician [formal] caregivers), what caregivers and care persons experience dynamically, and why mindful self-care is a helpful skill and process. We highlight the privilege of caregiving, and the problem of burnout for clinicians (formal caregivers), and informal caregivers alike, showing why effective strategies to combat burnout and stress are needed. We introduce the MSCC model and evidence base for mindfulness-based interventions (MBI's). We categorize Mindful Self-Care for Clinicians and Caregivers (MSCC) as a member of that family.

Keywords: Burnout; Effectiveness; Mindful Self-Care for Clinicians and Caregivers (MSCC); Mindfulness-based Interventions (MBIs); Models; History

Mindful Self-Care for Clinicians and Caregivers. https://doi.org/10.1016/B978-0-443-29821-9.00001-7

"Rainbows and Rain"—This photograph was taken on the road from Santa Fe to Taos, New Mexico in 2024 by Robin B. Jarrett. For her, it reflects the joys and challenges of caregiving and care receiving.

Section 1—An Overview of Mindful Self-Care for Clinicians and Caregivers

Mindfulness for Clinicians and Caregivers: Who, What, and Why?

Mindful Self-Care for Clinicians and Caregivers (MSCC) has the potential to help caregivers, of all types, access the positive aspects of caregiving and cope with the inherent and often intense challenges of the role. *Mindful Self-Care for Clinicians and Caregivers aims to cultivate mindfulness skills in caregivers through their focused attention, curiosity, and full awareness and acceptance of their senses and experience, without judgment.* These mindfulness skills allow caregivers of all types to approach their privilege and challenge with a new lens which fosters resilience and mitigates burnout. MSCC, derives its evidence-base from the family of interventions called mindfulness-based interventions or MBIs, defined below. In this Chapter, we define and describe the who, why, and what of mindful self-care. In short: Who are the intended recipients of MSCC? They are caregivers in a mixed world of fulfillment and stress. Why MSCC? Because MSCC has the potential to reduce caregiver stress and burdens. What is MSCC? Below we describe the model underlying MSCC, its forerunners, and research support. The how of MSCC follows in later sections or chapters which detail a format for facilitating mindful skills through specific practices.

The Face of Caregiving and Care Receiving

Like the National Institute of Health (NIH), we define caregivers as people who provide care to someone else who needs assistance with taking care of themselves (NIH, 2020). The care recipient or care person may need assistance due to physical, emotional, or developmental conditions or other states.

Formal caregivers are paid professionals providing medical care, psychological care, or support, social or otherwise, for ill and vulnerable persons. Formal caregivers include but are not limited to: medical and mental health professionals or clinicians, healthcare workers, clergy, and teachers at all levels in all settings.

Informal caregivers (i.e., family or significant others) are those caring for ill or vulnerable persons needing acute or ongoing care. Many Americans serve as caregivers, providing uncompensated care that has a great economic value. Estimates, summarized by the Family Caregiver Alliance, suggest that about 53 million caregivers have provided unpaid care to an adult or child and about 34.2 million Americans have provided unpaid care to an adult age 50 or older (AARP, 2020). In the US, 5.1 million caregivers cared only for a child, 38.9 million cared only for adults, and 9 million cared for both children and adults (AARP, 2020). Approximately 39.8 million US caregivers provided care to adults (aged 18+) with a disability or illness (Coughlin, 2010). About 15.7 million adult family caregivers are giving care to someone suffering from Alzheimer's disease or some other form of dementia (Alzheimer's

Association, 2015). The estimated economic value of informal caregivers has increased from $600 billion in 2023 to $470 billion in 2013 (AARP, 2023).

Most caregivers (89%) provide care for an adult relative; 50% care for a parent or parent-in-law; 10% for a friend, neighbor or another nonrelative; 14% for a child; and 8% for a grandparent or grandparent-in-law. Most caregivers are female with the average age of a caregiver at 49.4 (AARP, 2020). We recommend to our readers the in-depth reports on informal caregivers by the AARP for 2020 and 2023 (AARP, 2023; AARP, 2020). These reports provide rich statistics and descriptions of multiple aspects affecting the lives and functioning of caregivers.

From henceforth, we include clinicians under the term caregiver. While we use the terms "caregiver" and "care recipient or care person" to refer to distinct roles, it is not uncommon for a caregiver to also receive care from another caregiver, informal, and/or formal. Thus, this dichotomy is only a heuristic and dependent upon the role and/or setting.

Why Do Caregivers Need Self-Care?

Caregiving is physically and emotionally challenging. For some, chronic caregiving can lead to an increased sense of burden and the risk of burnout. The model underlying MSCC posits that mindful practice can reduce the stress, burden, and burnout associated with caregiving. Further, if such distress is managed, caregivers are better positioned to access the positive emotions and privileges associated with their unique role. Also, the practices within MSCC help caregivers foster attention to balancing the caregiver role with other vital parts of their life and remain fed and nourished in all areas. This balance is one of the keys to effective and healthy caregiving.

More than 1 in 5 Americans are informal caregivers. Each year, the numbers grow. (These numbers increase when we add in formal caregivers.) About 36% of these informal caregivers reported high levels of emotional stress or strain, while around 28% rated their role stress as moderate (AARP, 2020).

When the stress of caregiving overwhelms the positives of the caregiving experience, there is a risk of experiencing this responsibility as a burden. If the perceived sense of burden intensifies, the caregiver may experience burnout. The sense of burden may be variable or constant, acute or chronic, moderate or intense; however, problems arise when burden begins to negatively impact caregivers' lives and functioning. In the caregiver literature, burden has three aspects: it is based on self-perception, multifaceted strain, and occurs over time (Liu et al., 2020). In other words, it is the embodied experience of one's judgments and feelings which are influenced by social, financial, physical, and/or emotional strains as they bear on the person over time. The outcomes of caregiver burden include decreased care provision, decreased quality of life, and breakdown of psychological and physical health (Liu et al., 2020). Stress from unbroken, intense, and chronic caregiving demands can lead to burnout. According to information provided by The Cleveland Clinic regarding caregiver burnout, "Caregiver burnout is a state of physical, emotional and mental exhaustion. Caregivers who experience burnout may feel tired, stressed, withdrawn, anxious and depressed" (Cleveland Clinic, 2023, para. 1). In a state of burnout, a person often feels depleted of internal resources for positive coping and external resources for support.

The price of many caregivers' stress loads can be high. Schultz and Sherwood (2008) summarized research on this cost and declared caregiving a major public health issue. Some of their conclusions are as follows: Though about one third of informal caregivers cite the primary experience of their role as positive and meaningful, a significant number of caregivers fit the model of chronic stress experiences. With even more dire results, Krämer and Bleidorn (2024) studied more than 28,000 Australian, Dutch, and German caregivers and found that becoming informal caregivers had negative effects on mental health and psychosocial well-being. These results worsened for women and the longer a person was in the caregiver role. These studies suggest that when caregiver stress becomes chronic rather than episodic or acute, it gradually depletes internal coping resources over time. When inner and outer resources are depleted under the impact of unrelenting stressors, there is an increase in physical and psychological strain. Later stages of this chronic stress pathway become characterized by high levels of unpredictability and uncontrollability. Exhaustion and stress spread to other life areas like work and relationships, and high levels of sustained vigilance are present. Research has found that various stressors, common to caregiving, are tied to psychological distress, physical ailments, poor self-care behaviors, and even death. Caregivers who witness their care person's suffering and sense of helplessness or despair are at greater risk for depression. For many caregivers, the price of caregiving can be high, long lasting, and life altering.

Yet not every caregiver is susceptible to deterioration under chronic stress. What makes some vulnerable and others less so? Research on caregivers sheds some light on this issue. Though external stressors like financial burdens, a care person's difficult behavior, or a lack of social support play a role in what a caregiver experiences as challenging, it seems that the caregiver's subjective judgments mediate the relationship between stressors and health or well-being outcomes (Son et al., 2007; Aneshensel et al., 1995). One large study found that caregivers' perception of strain was a major risk factor for mortality (Schultz & Beach, 1999). It is in the zone of subjective awareness, appraisal, and emotional reactivity that interventions like mindfulness training aim to impact. Mindful self-care helps caregivers become more aware of their internal states, how these states impact stress levels, and the importance of engaging in intentional self-care.

The Privilege of Caregiving

We write about the costs of caregiving, the stress of its responsibilities and its challenges. Yet, for many, the rewards of giving care are central and a kind of ballast in the sea of its demands. It is when the balance of reward and cost is lost, or begins to falter, that caregiving can create a turbulence that results in burden and even burnout, as mentioned above. Around 51% of the more than 1 in 5 Americans who are caregivers report that this role has given them a positive sense of purpose or meaning (AARP, 2020). Nevertheless, these positive feelings coexist with feelings of stress or strain (AARP, 2020). The following caregiver quote captures this complex dynamic: "I am so grateful to have this time with my family, and I truly believe that caregiving is a calling. Unless you live this, you have no idea how tolling it can be physically AND mentally" (AARP, 2023). Nevertheless, these positive feelings coexist with feelings of stress or strain (AARP, 2020). The following caregiver quote captures this complex dynamic: "I am so grateful to have this time with my family, and I truly believe that caregiving is a calling. Unless you live this, you have no idea how tolling it can be physically AND mentally" (AARP, 2023).

Emerging research has demonstrated that relationship quality between caregiver and care recipient can influence the caregivers' ability to identify rewards and positive aspects of the caregiving role (Yu et al., 2018). Importantly, when caregivers can identify positive aspects of meaning and purpose and feel effective in their role, this may assist in reducing caregiver burden (Cheng et al., 2013). It also has the potential to improve the quality of the care received as well as the length of time the caregiver can sustain the caregiver role (Cheng et al., 2013).

Given the critical role of positive feelings for caregiver resilience, let us consider possible rewards of caregiving. Some of these rewards are extrinsic, that is, dependent, in part, on what the care person gives back. For example, the caregiver may be given gifts of gratitude, trust, and deepened intimacy. The giver may be the care recipient or family members or associates of the care recipient, or even the institution in which the care is received and provided. The rewards of being appreciated, counted on, depended upon are meaningful to most caregivers.

Caregiving can call forth a sense of shared vulnerability that opens caregiver and care person to moments of deepened love and sharing. Beyond the duties and decision of caregiving lie times of laughter and playfulness, times of mutual tears, and poignancy. For there is the patient or care person being treated/cared for and the person within the patient, at times, eager, willing, and ready to engage and connect. Contributing to this dynamic of connection and the rewarding relational elements of caregiving is the overarching component of the relationship quality between the caregiver and care person. Studies looking at premorbid relationship satisfaction of informal caregivers have found that caregivers who report lower premorbid relationship satisfaction perceive higher burden than caregivers who report higher premorbid relationship satisfaction (Steadman et al., 2007). Additionally, research has found that the motivation and meaning that caregivers attach to their caregiving role can also impact their wellbeing (Quinn et al., 2010). Being aware of these factors and attuned to the dynamics and complex interactions at play during caregiving can create opportunities for a caregiver to bring intentionality, insight, and awareness to this role. In practice, this may involve recognizing and appreciating rewarding moments of connection while also acknowledging and observing challenging aspects of the caregiver–care recipient relationship with understanding, awareness, and without judgment or self-criticism.

In addition to rewards received within the caregiving dynamic, there also may be more intrinsic rewards derived through the caregiving experience. Regardless of what the care person gives back, some caregivers can find in themselves an over-riding sense of calling (mentioned in the above quote). While the opportunity to give care may create for some a sense of being burdened by an unwanted or unexpected obligation, it may also inspire valued purpose. The work of caregiving can be an opportunity for personal growth, a way to give back, and a way to meaningfully live out and embody strongly held values. The latter sense might be called the heart of caregiving ….caring and giving.

Another intrinsic reward of caregiving is the opportunity to develop knowledge and skills. Caregivers taking on a new and challenging role may initially experience uncertainty related to a perceived sense of inadequacy and deficient knowledge and skills within an atmosphere of anxiety. Over time, however, one's experience in reading needs, finding resources, and making the best decisions under the circumstances may help the caregiver evolve, gain confidence, and develop a feeling of expertise. A study looking at self-efficacy among caregivers found that family caregivers who reported high levels of self-efficacy in various domains related to their roles, also reported more positive gains and reduced burden (Cheng et al., 2013). A caregiver's perception that they make a difference, effectively respond to challenging situations and can cope with these conditions appears to play an important role in mitigating stress and burden. Informal caregiving may initially start with a sense of believing that resources are in others (healthcare professionals, etc.) rather than oneself and the relationship with the care person. With experience, however, this perspective can shift into a deepened sense of becoming the "expert" in the unique individual (s) cared for, fostering increased meaning.

Professional caregivers who develop confidence in their skills and decision-making are less likely to experience the strain of caregiving. Many clinicians feel a deep sense of calling to their profession, which gives their work meaning beyond just earning a pay check. Collaborating closely with a team of clinicians in a professional role can foster social connectedness and provide a sense of purpose, helping individuals feel they are contributing to something greater than themselves. This can be particularly meaningful when combined with the fundamental reward of seeing one's impact on the relief of suffering, improved health, and emotional well-being in the patients under one's care. Knowing about and appreciating caregiving rewards is an important part of mindful self-care. What comes naturally at first may fade to the background when caregiving challenges and stressors expand and persist. Taking time to recall and re-vitalize one's core values has the potential to keep caregivers fed in ways that sustain their efforts.

The Interpersonal Dynamics Between Caregivers and Care Persons

Caregiving is not unidirectional. The caregiver and care person impact one another, influencing the emotional well-being and physical health of each in a continually flowing stream of interactions. Each respond to the other's mood and outlook, with or without awareness. The emotional atmosphere can brighten or darken, sometimes based on the extent to which each one is being valued, being seen, making a positive or negative impact, and sensing the way stress and suffering is borne in the other. Caregiving is more like a dance than a linear assembly line.

Both informal and formal caregivers, although working in different contexts, can experience satisfaction when contributing to the welfare of the people in their care. For the informal caregiver, particularly if a friend or family member, the emotional and physical stakes are quite high as we have seen in the section on caregiver stress and burden. The *dance* of caregiver and care person highlights the *mutual* impact of both partners on each other. Studies on informal caregivers indicate that there is more circular than linear influence. Exchanges of support positively aided care persons, while reciprocity of support decreased caregiver burden.

Relationship satisfaction best predicts positive caregiver role experience, with lower relationship satisfaction linked to depression and lower self-reported health, for both caregiver and care person (McPherson et al., 2011). In a kind of vicious circle, a care person's depression has been demonstrated to lower relationship quality for caregivers (Monin et al., 2019). Other studies have found that caregiver anxiety evokes anxiety and depression in care persons. Care persons are more likely to be depressed or anxious when they perceived a negative relationship with their caregiver (Hwang & Kim, 2024). Additionally, research has found the chances that care persons experience depression increases when caregivers perceive caregiving in a more negative light (Hwang & Kim, 2024). Health systems have opportunities to consider this dynamic in the processes they create that affect the quality and safety of caregiving.

Formal caregivers are subject to compassion fatigue and burnout when overloaded with more than they can competently do and witness patient suffering they feel helpless to alleviate. Over a career, these stressors can have a cumulative effect. In a circular way, patients experience greater distress when their caregiver is emotionally exhausted (Gustafson & Hemberg, 2021). Studies show that physicians who are experiencing a high level of burnout score lower on patient satisfaction ratings (Weng et al., 2011). More than many healthcare professionals realize, patients tend to want greater back-and-forth communication and sense of partnership (Kennedy et al., 2017). The mutuality of caregiver and care person is further underscored by findings indicating caregiver burden can be alleviated by reciprocity or balance in the give-and-take of the caregiving relationship (Reid et al., 2005).

Why is this circular relationship important to the aims of MSCC? Self-care skills directly and positively impact more than the formal or informal caregiver; they impact the well-being and health of the care person as well. Sensitizing the caregiver to their own internal reactions helps them monitor both themselves and the immediate quality of their relationship with the care person. Through this awareness, the caregiver can learn to avoid being triggered into mindless negative reactions, altering the mutual dance. An understanding and awareness of this mindful dance elevate the caregiver role beyond necessary duties to include the healing influence of positive presence. Cultivating a mutual appreciative dynamic with the caregiver-care person dyad, affects the sense of meaning, significance, and health of these partners in care.

What Is the History of Mindfulness-Based Interventions (MBIs) and How Are MBIs Defined?

In 1908, Ebbinghaus remarked that while the field of psychology has a long past, it has a short history (Ebbinghaus, 1908). The same observation applies to the field of mindfulness-based interventions (MBIs) today. The practice of focusing attention on present-moment experiences has long been a part of the contemplative traditions of major religions, where it has served to manage distractions and prepare the mind and heart for spiritual connection. Buddhist teachings on mindfulness and meditation began over 2000 years ago in India with Siddhartha Gautama, known as the Buddha. It is primarily from Buddhism that contemporary, secular understandings of mindfulness and meditation have emerged (Feldman & Kuyken, 2019). In Western contexts, mindfulness is now recognized in multiple forms: as a state of mind, a process, and a practice. Each involves intentional awareness and is supported by attitudes such as kindness and curiosity, with core elements including focused attention, open awareness, and a strong sense of ethical sensitivity (Feldman & Kuyken, 2019). This rich foundation reflects the long past of mindfulness practice.

The short history of mindfulness can be seen as one jewel in the crown of Buddhist practices and teachings, carefully extracted, refined, and separately cultivated. The principles, attitudes, and practices of secular mindfulness are no longer couched as ways to find God or to reach some ultimate enlightenment. Instead, mindfulness becomes a way to flourish in this modern world through the aliveness of savoring present experiences and self-regulation of internal stress. It can be argued that deep and sustained mindfulness practices may lead to large inner transformations related to Buddhist enlightenment or theistic divine communion, but the way of contemporary mindfulness does not actively or strategically promote such agendas. Thus, the more spiritual aspects of mindfulness are left open to individual interpretation, while its attitudes and awareness skills are spotlighted and continue to grow as accessible and somewhat universal pursuits.

The short history of mindfulness within the Western culture began with Jon Kabat-Zinn (2013) when he developed in 1979 mindfulness-based stress reduction or MBSR at the University of Massachusetts Medical Center. Kabat-Zinn practiced yoga and Buddhist meditation. Seeing a wider potential of these practices for the non-Buddhist population, he started teaching *formal* meditation and *informal* everyday ways to evoke mindfulness to patients referred to him by physicians at the University of Massachusetts Medical Center. These were generally patients suffering from severe depression, anxiety, and chronic pain that were at the ends of their medical ropes, with no more treatment alternatives. Kabat-Zinn removed the language and references to Buddhism, shaping a secular intervention with mindfulness skills at the center for the primary purpose of alleviating, so called, self-generated stress people unwittingly create in their reactions to their conditions of suffering. Mindfulness was seen as a pathway to reducing suffering, as well as evolving enhanced states of aliveness, joy, and calm.

Kabat-Zinn created a group-based learning format of 8 two-hour sessions that included home practice with or without taped guided meditation and written descriptions of the way of mindfulness. The secular program was designed to pose no conflict with participants' religions or nonreligious beliefs and affiliations. The foundation of MBSR included a perspective on how the mindfulness process works, These include attitudes like nonjudging one's experiences, formal practices like mindfulness of breath, body scan, walking meditation and yoga), and informal practices that "seed" one's day with simple shifts into periods of greater mindful attention.

The teacher was more of a facilitator, immersed in his or her own mindfulness practice, and serving as a guide by nonverbally communicating the spirit of mindfulness to others. Teaching, aside from some technical instruction, was participant-centered, that is, it was unforced and invitational, with self-care and experiential learning prioritized. Participants were invited to share their experiences of mindfulness exercises while the facilitator validated and, nonjudgmentally reflected what was heard, at times, gently inquiring about aspects of the experience to highlight session themes. From the beginning of MBSR, Kabat-Zinn initiated research into its effectiveness. Since 1979, there have been hundreds of studies of MBSR (Kabat-Zinn, 2013). Kabat-Zinn also began training others including formal caregivers, those wishing to be facilitators, and nonclinically distressed persons interested in the life enhancing elements of mindfulness.

Mindfulness-based stress reduction inspired other mindfulness-based therapies and interventions usually developed by mental health professionals. Often, these were group contexts of 8 sessions or less. One example that has helped shape MSCC is mindfulness-based cognitive therapy for depression or MBCT (Segal et al., 2013). This solidly researched approach adapted the application of mindfulness training to target and treat special conditions, including depression relapse vulnerability, anxiety, addiction, and eating disorders. Mindfulness-Based Stress Reduction by design is open and applicable to a variety of conditions, valuing the inclusion of a mix of individuals over the tailored composition of groups. Specialized or not, most mindfulness-based interventions today see their roots in MBSR and its spirit of teaching. In that tradition, we focus on the role of the facilitator of MSCC as one who teaches mindful skills and practices. MBSR and MBCT have shown broad efficacy. A meta-analysis of the effects of MBSR and MBCT covering 49 studies (4733 people) on nonclinical populations found that these interventions significantly reduced rumination, depression, anxiety, and overall stress while increasing quality of life and well-being (Querstret et al., 2020).

We developed MSCC for caregivers who are not seeking formal mental health treatment and define MSCC as a psychosocial intervention in the family of evidence based-MBIs. In the Preface of this book, we characterize MSCC as having a family resemblance to MBSR in certain keyways. Aside from its 8-session format and focus on formal and informal practices, MSCC embodies the spirit of MBSR and its sibling, MBCT. The session atmosphere, treatment of participants, and requirement of facilitators' own ongoing mindfulness practices and way of life are critical components. The unique part of MSCC is in fact its special focus on caregivers.

Section 2—Development of MSCC and Its Underlying Model

The Development of MSCC: The Authors' Collaborative Journey

Lumpkin has had a long-term, passionate interest in contemplative thought and practices. These interests ran parallel to his study of philosophy and psychology when he was in college. In the 1970s, he was drawn to study meditative states and disciplines, particularly in the various forms of Buddhism. He learned vipassana meditation from Joseph Goldstein, a teacher at the Insight Meditation Society in Barre, Massachusetts, attending week-long silent retreats. Included in Lumpkin's further development of mindfulness meditation were intensive training retreats in MBSR and MBCT. He has offered mindfulness training in various contexts, including the University of Texas Southwestern Medical Center in Dallas, Texas. His interest in bringing mindfulness to caregivers grew from witnessing the effects of mindfulness in his own and others' lives and his immersion in the caregiver role for his mother diagnosed with dementia.

For Jarrett, the emerging evidence base supporting MBIs could not go unnoticed. She participated in experiential seminars on MBIs taught by Zindel Segal, PhD and later by Martin Lumpkin, PhD. With sparks from these seminars and encouragement from Lumpkin, Jarrett became more intentional or mindful about her own (nearly) daily practice of mindfulness, especially during mindful movement. She became more curious about MBIs, both professionally and personally. Jarrett began to consider the possible underlying models, their applications, and how they might inform mechanistic psychological science. She integrated MBIs into her teaching with psychiatric residents and clinical psychology doctoral students. Similarly, she integrated MBIs into her clinical practice for patients with mood disorders and chronic pain.

Around 2014–15, Jarrett and Lumpkin began to consider how mindful practice could offer comfort to persons who grieve and then to formal and later informal caregivers to persons with life limiting illnesses. They developed a version of an interventional manual for Mindful Self-Care for Caregivers (Lumpkin & Jarrett, 2015) with that focus. The initial attempt to secure funding to test MSCC in the context of caregivers with life limiting illness failed.

Delayed but undeterred around 2017, Jarrett began to think further about how to extend MSCC to informal caregivers, particularly parents caring for youth with autism spectrum disorders. Jarrett collaborated with Katherine Bellone. PhD, a child psychologist specializing in autism spectrum disorders. Together they designed and implemented a small preliminary study funded by the Jerry M. Lewis, M.D. Mental Health Research Foundation, in Dallas, Texas. This open clinical trial of 13 parents showed that MSCC in person and virtually was safe, acceptable, and helpful to these parents (Bellone et al., 2023). Further, there was preliminary support for the MSCC

Mindful Self-Care for Clinicians and Caregivers. https://doi.org/10.1016/B978-0-443-29821-9.00002-9

model (described below) whereby stress reduction appeared to mediate improvement in mood and other depressive symptoms. These results nurtured and influenced the (refined) MSCC model.

Collins first became interested in mindfulness through her work with women as a personal trainer and wellness coach, as well as through her own personal practice of yoga. Observing the positive effects of connecting mind and body through movement—and recognizing the broader benefits of physical activity on mental health—inspired her interest in clinical health psychology and mindfulness-based practices. This ultimately motivated her to pursue a career as a psychologist. During her doctoral training, she deepened her understanding of mindfulness under the mentorship of faculty at the University of Texas Southwestern Medical Center (UT Southwestern) in Dallas. While there, she developed and facilitated mindfulness groups at a UT Southwestern community clinic. Her dissertation research examined the impact of a brief mindful-movement video intervention designed to help women manage anxiety and pain prior to pelvic examinations at a women's clinic.

In her postdoctoral fellowship at the Cleveland Clinic, Collins worked across various health clinics and medical settings, both inpatient and outpatient, using mindfulness interventions to address the complex and dynamic relationship between physical and mental health. Currently, as a consultation-liaison psychologist in the acute medical hospital setting at Cleveland Clinic, she continues to use mindfulness techniques to support patients experiencing acute health-related stress and other comorbid mental health concerns. Beyond her professional work, mindfulness and mindful self-care have become essential tools in her own life. These practices help her manage stress, reduce caregiver burden, and maintain well-being—particularly as a first-time mother balancing her roles as a psychologist and a supervisor for psychology fellows in training.

When the COVID-19 pandemic hit, in 2020, we authors began to consider how MSCC might benefit healthcare workers or formal caregivers. We were particularly interested in frontline clinicians and noted that mindful practices were being implemented for stress reduction among healthcare workers, but through which protocols or intervention plans? We noted that MSCC could be disseminated in a straightforward and practical manner, if tools and guidance were readily available to potential facilitators. Jarrett invited Lumpkin and Collins to collaborate in the venture that became this book, *Mindful Self-Care for Clinicians and Caregivers.* Until publication, we met consistently, debated, created, and revised. As our bonds deepened, we faced and shared the challenges that life brought each of us in caregiving, care receiving, and self-care. We were bound and connected as a small group … joined in similar ways that MSCC facilitators may observe in their own groups.

This book was nurtured by our curiosity about how these potentially effective and helpful strategies were being disseminated (or not). The curiosity was kept alive over more than 5 years by the potential of disseminating MSCC, as we extended and detailed our vision of and for MSCC. The spark kept burning through the joy we experienced in our collaboration and the unmet needs we observe. We aim to guide dissemination by providing detail, guidance, and tools to increase scale, uptake, and the public health potential such that the clinically significant effect sizes enjoyed in research settings are also found in community practice. Further, we hope to help facilitators study, contemplate, and then harness the power of the positive interactions as caregivers gather to support each other and share in the experience of self-care. We hope that this guide will ignite the passion and skills of active researchers and those in training to learn more about MBIs and MSCC, in particular.

The Model and the Evidence Base for Mindful Self Care for Clinicians and Caregivers

With the need for caregiver coping and resources for resilience established, the models and research base for mindfulness (in general) and MSCC (in particular) are described below. We overview the biopsychosocial framework as a foundation for the mechanistic model of MSCC, hypothesizing how MSCC may work. Research on mindfulness-based interventions (MBIs) with varied populations provides the initial evidence base for MSCC and underscores opportunities for expansion.

Mindful Self-Care During Caregiving: The Concept

Mindful self-care has the potential to reduce stress, burdens, and burnout that can be associated with caregiving. It allows the caregivers to use all their senses to experience fully "what is present." *Mindful Self-Care for Clinicians and Caregivers is a mindfulness-based intervention that aims to provide caregivers with skills to access the privileges and benefits of giving care, while also coping with the inherent challenges of consistently providing outstanding care, often and/or for long periods of time.*

The Biopsychosocial Model: Foundation for the Model Underlying Mindful Self-Care for Clinicians and Caregivers

In seeking to introduce and inspire a comprehensive understanding of self-care, the generic biopsychosocial model provides a foundational paradigm (and serves as an antecedent model) for MSCC. The biopsychosocial model (BPSM) is an integrated framework that highlights the important interactions of physical health, emotional health, and social structures, that impact human functioning, illness, health, and well-being (Engel, 1977). This framework is attributed to the work of George Engel who published the biopsychosocial model in 1977 (Engel, 1977) and has influenced the education of health professionals thereafter. This model was originally developed to promote a more comprehensive approach to health, emphasizing the need to balance **biological, psychological, and social factors**. It highlights the interconnected nature of:

- **Biological factors** (e.g., physiology, physical health conditions, and genetic history)
- **Psychological factors** (e.g., cognition, emotions, mental health, and stress)
- **Social factors** (e.g., support networks, social connections, and broader societal influences)

By integrating these elements, the model underscores the complexity of health and the importance of addressing multiple dimensions of well-being. The BPSM proposed a more complete and inclusive framework for understanding health, as contrast to the traditional medical model which postulated mind body dualism, and a reductionist view of biology as solely comprised of physics and chemistry (Bolton, 2023). The BPSM shifted focus within the medical field to include the impact of psychological and social factors on health conditions, illness, and medical outcomes (Engel, 1977). The BPSM, still utilized decades later, has been supported by research within interdisciplinary areas of medicine and related fields, as well as research on social determinates of health (Marmot, 2005). Empirical findings over the past decades lend support to the BPSM, and the role of utilizing this framework in discussions of health and creation of interventions that support well-being (Bolton, 2023).

This model is fundamental to understanding the concept of self-care and provides a heuristic for both the caregiver and care person, who exist within a dynamic relationship. Within the context of caregiving, caregivers themselves are influencing another individual's physical, emotional, and social functioning. Equally important is the caregiver's health and biopsychosocial domains can be influenced by the care person's physiology, emotions, and social factors. Caregivers' health and well-being can be reciprocally affected and can then these factors can feedback to affect the care person. (This dynamic and reciprocal influence is why we later will use the metaphor of the "dance" between the caregiver and care person to remind the reader of this dynamic). In this way, the BPSM underscores all the domains in which a caregiver may foster and support health while emphasizing the need for nourishing self-care to optimize caregiver welling. Specifically, the domains include the ***biological*** (physical health of both caregiver and care person), ***psychological*** (supporting and addressing the mental health needs, strengthening adaptive coping, and promoting emotional resilience for both persons), and ***social*** (fostering support for caregivers and care persons on the family, community, and larger systems levels) (Schulz & Sherwood, 2008).

Figure 1 applies the BPSM to the dynamic between caregiver and care person, illustrating the reciprocal and interacting nature of the domains and the people. This model can open conversations and advance research about the importance of intervening with mindful self-care across domains. In the process, the model can promote an understanding of how all and each of these domains interact to affect the health and well-being of both the care person and the caregiver.

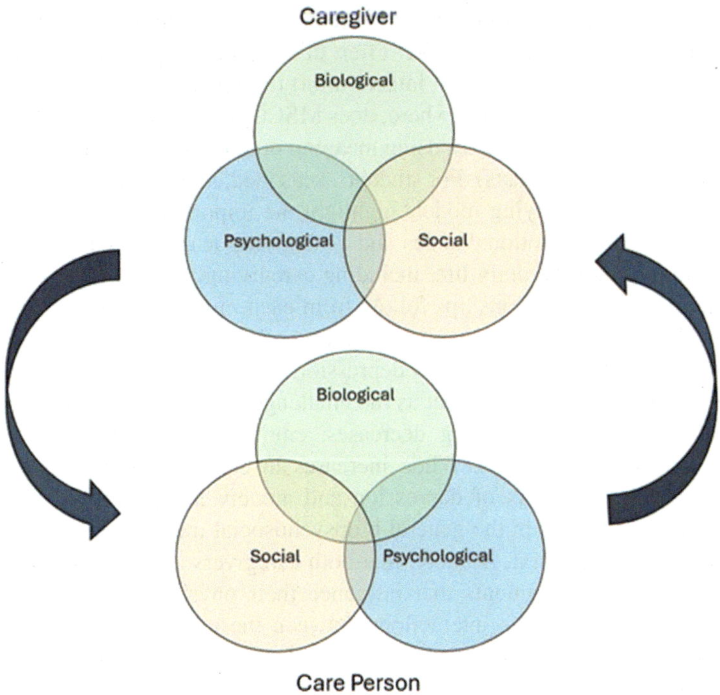

Figure 1 The biopsychosocial model and the dynamic between caregiver and care person.

In the context of Mindful Self-Care for Clinicians and Caregivers, the growth of mindfulness skills creates a pathway for caregivers to explore the strengths and limitations of their self-care as they begin to listen more closely to what their inner experiences convey. Without mindfulness, this inner sensing may be absent or rarely heard. With mindfulness, biopsychosocial needs become privileged avenues for insight and self-care actions.

Conceptual Models Underlying Mindful Self-Care for Clinicians and Caregivers: Models A and B (Jarrett, 2022)

Drawing from the biopsychosocial model as a foundation, we developed *A Guide Facilitator's to Mindful Self-Care for Clinicians and Caregivers* using the following two conceptual models (A and B) developed by Jarrett (Jarrett, 2022) that articulate potential relationships among challenges to caregivers, their emotional reactivity, their self-efficacy in caregiving, and learning the skills inherent in mindfulness. These models provide a paradigm for understanding emotional states and the potential for MSCC. Both models are founded in the generic biopsychosocial model described above. Model A predicts relationships between the process of caregiving and caregiver mental health and well-being. Model B posits possible putative mechanisms through which the intervention, MSCC, improves caregiver well-being. These conceptual models not only informed the development and delivery MSCC intervention we describe but also inform future research (e.g., aims, hypotheses, design, selection of measurement, and outcomes). We offer this *Guide* to researchers as a well-articulated independent variable (an intervention) to explore in terms: its indications (i.e., for which caregivers, located where, does MSCC work best), how to produce the largest and most robust effect sizes using meaning outcomes, and what mediators and mechanisms underlie its effects). For students, seasoned, and aspiring facilitators who deliver MSCC, the underlying models highlight the importance of and rationale for attending to caregiver emotional states and to fostering learning their learning skills to practice mindfulness in daily life, including caregiving.

Specific directional relationships follow from each model. Model A hypothesizes predicted relationships among caregiving and emotional states such as feeling well (i.e., well-being), stress, anxiety, and depression. Specifically, Model A (a specific biopsychosocial model) predicts that as the challenges and burdens of caregiving increase, self-efficacy in caregiving decreases, emotional reactivity increases, and caregiver well-being decreases. When increases in caregiver stress are prolonged and/or intense, then the risk of depression and anxiety in the caregiver increases. As Model A is embedded in the general biopsychosocial model it acknowledges the importance of social context. Namely, that both caregivers and care persons interact in complex social environments that influence their physiology, emotional states, and cognition, as well as the interactions between the people involved. While full consideration of these factors is beyond the scope of this book, the authors acknowledge the importance of environmental and social systems on the people who interact within them. Much has been written about the importance of social systems (e.g., how workflow is conducted in work and health systems) and these associations with burnout in clinician caregivers (e.g., NICE, 2022; Ussett et al., 2024). Further, informal caregivers frequently report feeling overwhelmed with their interactions within the bureaucracy of healthcare, ranging from how to park to making life altering and/or life and death decisions for their care persons (Figure 2).

Model A (Figure 2): Relations of Challenges of Informal and Formal Caregiving and Emotional States (Jarrett, 2022)

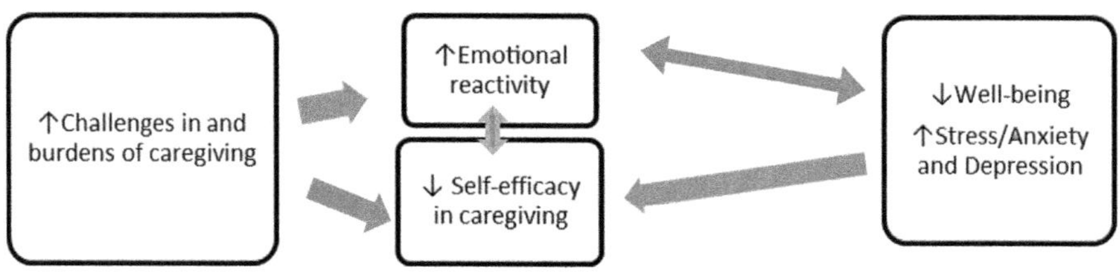

Figure 2 (Model A) Figure illustrates relationships among caregiving burdens, and challenges, emotion reactivity, self-efficacy, well-being, and mood states.

Model B (an interventional model) shows the predicted relationships in learning the skills of mindful self-care, self-efficacy in caregiving, emotional reactivity, and emotional states in the formal and informal caregiver. Specifically, Model B predicts that as a caregiver develops skill in mindful practice (including less attention to emotional reactivity), their self-efficacy in caregiving will also increase, followed by improves well-being, as well as lowered risk for stress, anxiety, and depression. A corollary of these hypotheses (as described above) is that we also predict bidirectional relationships within the dyad of caregiver and care persons. See Khoramirad et al. (2024), for an example of these bidirectional effects in mothers and infants in the neonatal intensive care unit). Specifically, we predict that as caregiver stress decreases and well-being increases, the probability of less stress and greater well-being in the care person will increase as well. Conversely, the corollary also predicts that as the well-being of the care person decreases, the risk to the well-being of caregivers with fewer coping skills will also decrease. It is that problem that MSCC is designed to address (Figure 3).

Model B (Figure 3): Relations of Mindful Self-Care for Clinicians and Caregivers, Their Skills, and Emotional States (Jarrett, 2022)

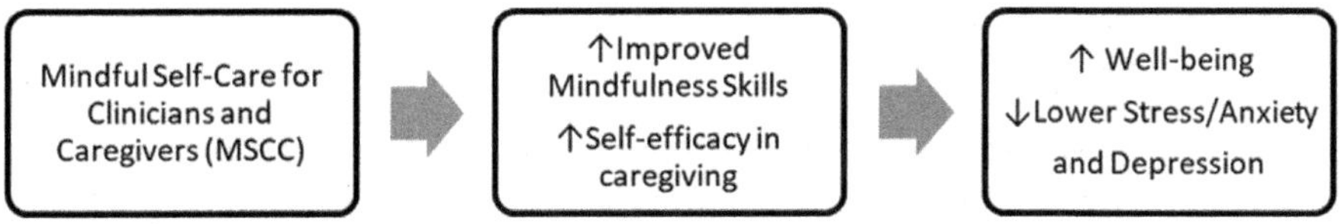

Figure 3 (Model B) Figure illustrates the mechanistic model underlying the psychosocial intervention, Mindful Self-Care for Clinicians and Caregivers (MSCC).

Mindful self-care for caregivers and the underlying models were evaluated by Bellone and associates (Bellone et al., 2023) using an earlier version of Mindful Self-Care for Caregivers developed by Lumpkin and Jarrett (2015). The sample, in this proof-of-concept study, consisted of parents (N = 13) of youth with autism spectrum disorders. While this small sample provides only an initial test, findings suggested the parents, group facilitator, and center administration found MSCC highly acceptable and feasible. Depressive symptoms and stress decreased over the 8-week course of MSCC. While the sample of parents was carefully screened by mental health professionals, participation in MSCC occurred without any adverse events. Further, MSCC was feasible if both in person and virtual delivery modes and the group facilitator was a master's prepared Licensed Professional Counselor who received minimal and basic training in MSCC. The parents requested that MSCC virtual groups continue after data collection ended and the health system approved continued delivery to support the parents. As this initial test was small, we encourage a controlled test of MSCC in a larger sample of caregivers, with a randomized design.

Secondary findings suggested that gains in mindfulness skill and increases in a sense of competence in parenting children with autism spectrum disorder reduced the stress the parents reported, supporting the interventional Model B of MSCC. We encourage attempts to replicate these findings in larger samples of both formal and informal caregivers across diverse settings.

Evidence Base Underlying Mindfulness-Based Interventions

The purpose of this section *of A Guide* is to connect facilitators of MSCC with its underlying evidence base. While not comprehensive, the review below will help facilitators sample and begin to access the exciting and growing literature establishing mindfulness-based interventions as effective for: a—the general population (including nonclinical samples) in managing stress and promoting well-being, b—formal and informal caregivers in promoting well-being and reducing the risk of burnout, and c—patients seeking relief of the symptoms of anxiety, depression, chronic pain, as well as other psychiatric disorders or related symptoms. In the final section (d), we only sample interesting parts of the developing literature on the putative mediators and potential mechanisms underlying the beneficial effects of mindfulness-based interventions and practices. We note that the literature on mindfulness-based interventions has progressed from "emerging to beginning to mature." We encourage facilitators to keep abreast of new findings that inform how to best offer MSCC to promote human growth (across the lifespan) and well-being across diverse settings. We encourage researchers to identify the gaps and advance understanding in both basic and applied branches of science.

Introduction to Active Hypotheses and Steps Forward in Research and Dissemination of MSCC

While our focus is on Mindful Self-Care for Clinicians and Caregivers (MSCC), the purpose of this section is to describe some of the key findings from the general research literature on mindfulness-based interventions (MBIs) that form its evidence base. While a comprehensive review of the literature on MBIs is available (Goldberg et al., 2022) and beyond the scope of this chapter, the sections below support the bold **hypothesis** that *MBIs are evidence-based-interventions that are available for broad dissemination and/or evaluation by qualified providers to diverse populations to reduce stress and increase well-being.* Specifically, the evidence we cite below propels the hypotheses that MBIs increase mental health and well-being, reduce symptoms of stress and distress for: average people, those seeking treatment for common psychiatric symptoms, and clinicians and caregivers. Further, MBIs may improve, and/or protect, physical, and brain health (Creswell et al., 2019; Hölzel et al., 2010). Mindfulness-based interventions appear to have the potential to boost immune functioning (Black & Slavich, 2016) and decrease inflammation perhaps slowing signs of an aging human brain (Rosenkranz et al., 2013); we assert that MBIs are particularly exciting due to their potential to boost mental health when learned and practiced frequently by the average person, at some yet to be determined dose and duration.

Mindfulness-based skills when learned can be used free of charge and without a provider, offering promise for promoting mental health with scalable methods that can increase access worldwide. By building on the contemplative traditions, that are "personalized" to secular and diverse settings and populations, we underscore the potential of MBIs to advance public health. Based on the available data, this advancement can be concurrent with rigorous and careful research of specific effects, indications, and processes of delivery and scalability.

More research is needed to determine how to best advance learning and continued practice of MBIs by the learners. For example, we note the number of digital applications that are developing for MBIs that require testing for safety, efficacy, and indications. At this writing (January 2025), there is no commercially available app for an MBI approved by the Food and Drug Administration (FDA). At least one company has raised capital and is attempting to earn this approval. It is yet to be discovered what, if any, effects on learning and outcomes digital apps have for which populations compared to type of MBIs learned: without an app compared to facilitator-assisted learning, compared to self-paced learning with or without a group. These are just some of the parameters awaiting evaluation. This area is ripe for research in the field of digital therapeutics, informed by contemplative neuroscience.

We assert further that clinicians and caregivers are not immune to the burdens and acute and accumulated stress or allostatic load (Guidi et al., 2021) associated with their challenging roles and healthcare systems. Clinicians and caregivers can benefit from MSCC to increase the likelihood that they: protect their mental health, reduce burnout, and sustain their commitment to their field and care persons. In fact, our motivation for writing this book on MSCC is to create a pathway for qualified professionals to provide mindfulness-based interventions to clinicians and caregivers, as well as to advance research in this area by providing a standard, yet flexible interventional protocol that is easily replicated across studies. We also assert that the benefits of MBIs are available to clinicians and caregivers based on the evidence available.

Illustrations of key findings below can aid the reader in accessing and understanding the expanding literature on MBIs and their effectiveness. We organize the large, emerging literature through the basic lens of: what are the outcome benefits of MBIs for whom compared to available experimental controls? We focus primarily on meta-analyses to simplify and to increase the accessibility of the research findings.

a. *Mindfulness-based interventions reduce stress, reduce risk, and promote well-being in the general population, including nonclinical samples.*

We begin our literature review with research on the effects of mindfulness-based interventions (MBIs) on people who are neither identified as caregivers nor as diagnosed with a psychiatric disorder. These are people who likely vary along a continuum of how they cope with chronic stress. They are not typically prescreened or diagnosed, and the MBI research tends to include such variation in symptoms, measured, and unmeasured. Heterogenous samples create predicted variation in individual outcomes, with the potential for those most distressed to improve more, while those less distressed have less room for change (i.e., there is a ceiling effect). Also, often studies tend to compare their MBI participants to controls who do not receive an active comparative intervention. These are important considerations in interpreting research results and for improving future research (Galante & Friedrich, 2023). Meta-analyses of MBIs from the general population offer consistent support for the effectiveness of mindfulness programs; some are described below.

Querstret et al. (2020) conducted a meta-analysis of 49 studies (including 25 randomized controlled trials) for a total of 4733 people. This meta-analysis focused only on studies using MBSR or MBCT on nonclinically diagnosed subjects. They found that these two MBIs: a—increased overall well-being and b—decreased psychological distress, tendencies to ruminate or worry, and depression. Earlier, Khoury et al. (2015) included normal samples totaling 2668 participants across 29 trials of both MBSR and other MBI variations. Findings supported increased quality of life and decreased stress, anxiety, and depression. These positive results were maintained for an average of 19 weeks of follow-up. Similarly, Galante and Friedrich (2023) in a rigorous Cochran meta-analysis evaluated 13 randomized controlled trails (2371 participants in all) of the effects of MBIs, primarily MBSR, on those from the general population. Findings suggested lower psychological distress (including anxiety and depression) from 1 to 6 months after the intervention.

Peering deeper into the data, the investigators (Galante & Friedrich, 2023) hypothesize that community dwelling adults who participate in mindfulness-based programs or groups led by teachers do report less psychological distress. They also noted that selective or targeted MBIs (for those like caregivers) were more effective than universal MBIs at preventing mental health problems. Both conclusions offer meaningful support and have implications for Mindful Self-Care for Clinicians and Caregivers.

On the research horizon are ways of looking at the impact of MBIs on not just self-assessed stress and well-being but physiological markers of stress and well-being. One example (Pascoe et al., 2017) is an analysis of 45 randomized controlled studies measuring the impact of mindfulness meditation on specific signs of stress reactivity. The investigators found that mindfulness meditation overall lowered the stress markers of cortisol, c-reactive protein, systolic blood pressure, and heart rate. We can expect more studies in the future which aim to evaluate such specific multisystem benefits as the MBI research evolves.

b. *Mindfulness-based interventions reduce burden, burnout and stress in informal and formal caregivers (clinicians) alike.*

Caregivers of all types appear to benefit from mindfulness-based interventions, much like the general population. We predict that both informal and formal caregivers' response to the MSCC will be similar to those described above, as the mindfulness-based interventions are based on related principles and processes. In fact, as mentioned previously a small open trial of the MSCC, yielded promising clinical effects and supported the underlying model of caregivers (parents) of youth with autistic spectrum disorder (Bellone et al., 2023). Additional findings supporting the benefit for caregivers, with the broad definition (e.g., from caregiving of children to the frail elderly) that we offer in the *Guide*, are illustrated below.

Mindfulness-based intervention produces positive outcomes in homogenous caregivers or in symptoms related to caregiving. Studies show that mindfulness-based intervention (usually based on MBSR) is effective in reducing the stress and depression levels of caregivers of patients with specific disorders like Alzheimer's (Brown et al., 2016), dementia (Paller et al., 2014; Whitebird et al., 2013), children with chronic illness (Minor et al., 2006), children with autism (Dykens et al., 2014), adults with developmental disabilities (Singh et al., 2016), and the frail elderly (Kovach et al., 2018).

I. *Informal caregivers*:

A growing number of studies lend positive support for the benefits of mindfulness practices on informal caregiver stress and well-being. Meta-analytic studies incorporating randomized controlled trials show decreases in stress, depression, anxiety, and caregiver burden. Mindfulness-based interventions (MBI's) varied. Many analyses used MBSR or MBCT. Others used formats with similar elements: developing mindfulness through practices based on breath, sitting meditation, movement, sensory engagement, and informal brief daily pauses to evoke mindfulness in relation to some pleasure or to coping with stress.

One meta-analysis of 12 randomized controlled trials claimed to be the first to comprehensively integrate studies of caregivers of those with various chronic diseases (Erdoğan Yüce et al., 2024). This analysis found that MBI's significantly improved stress, anxiety, depression, and caregiver burden for those caring for persons with cancer, dementia, neurodegenerative disease, as well as the elderly with chronic illness and frail older adults. The MBI's were either MBSR or MBCT. In another meta-analysis, MBIs were varied (3 used MBSR, one used MBCT, 10 used other MBI's). Subjects were caregivers for those with Alzheimer's, cancer, and chronic physical conditions. Results showed improvements in stress, depression, and anxiety (Li et al., 2016). With some variations in outcome, other meta-analyses and systematic reviews found similar results for caregivers of those with dementia (Saragih et al., 2024; Collins & Kishita, 2019; Shim et al., 2021; Cheung et al., 2020; Whitebird et al., 2013), for older adults (Fernández-Portero et al., 2021), for those receiving palliative care (Jaffray et al., 2016), and those with mental illness (Zhang et al., 2024).

Regarding single studies, mindfulness-based interventions showed promise in two RCTs of informal caregivers outside the US. In a study of 141 Chinese informal caregivers, post-treatment results showed that MBSR significantly reduced symptoms of anxiety and depression (Hou et al., 2014). At a 3-month follow-up, gains were maintained for depressive but not anxiety symptoms, and MBSR increased self-efficacy in controlling negative automatic thoughts and in mindfulness, significantly more than the control. The control group received an informational booklet on caregiving but did not participate in any structured intervention, highlighting the added value of the MBSR program beyond psychoeducation alone.

In Germany, Kögler et al. (2015) showed that compared to TAU, "Existential Behavioral Therapy (EBT)" (in which mindfulness was a primary element) significantly reduced stress in 130 informal caregivers of relatives receiving palliative care. It is noteworthy that 71% of the caregivers were bereaved when EBT began. While the similarity between EBT and MSCC (proposed here) is hard to assess, mindfulness significantly predicted improvement in stress, meaningfulness, and quality of life at a 3-month follow-up.

Qualitative studies have an advantage of probing more deeply into caregiver responses to MBI's through in-depth interviews. In one study (Stjernsward & Hanson, 2018) caregiver subjects were asked about their experience with a web-based MBI with similar features to MSCC. The intervention practices were brief and developed mindfulness skills through practices with the breath, body awareness, movement, and the senses. There were several interesting comments of interest to facilitators. Caregivers appreciated the program's flexibility, given their care person's illness fluctuations and the unpredictable nature of crises and changing life situations. All participants said they experienced positive effects regardless of their training and practice time, though those with more time experienced more positive effects. Training was valued as space to attend to their own needs for self-care. Positive experiences in training were significant motivators for commitment to the training. Also, the mindfulness program offered new ways to relate to others, especially the care person. The structure and style of MSCC play well to this emphasis on flexibility, brief practices for people with demanding schedules, self-care, and the fostering of positive experiences.

II. *Formal caregivers*

The potential efficacy of mindfulness-based interventions to mitigate stress and promote well-being has particular significance for professional caregivers, due to growing concern regarding stress and burnout in healthcare settings. While the prevalence of burnout varies among studies and within specialties, research suggest as many as 43% of physicians experience burnout (Medscape, 2020) and more than half of surveyed nurses (American Nurse Foundation, 2023). In a 2017 study surveying nurses who reported leaving their jobs, 31.5% reported burnout as a contributing factor (Shah et al., 2020). The mental health of healthcare workers overall appears to be worsening, with the incidence of burnout rising from 11.6% of health workers reporting feeling burnout "very often" in 2018 to 19.0% in 2022 (Nigam et al., 2023). This holds true for mental healthcare providers as well, with 40% of mental health workers report emotional exhaustion (O'Connor et al., 2018) and rates of burnout among psychiatrists ranging from 25.9% to 50.3% according to a systematic review and meta-analysis (Bykov et al., 2022).

The term "burnout," while now fairly commonplace, originated in the literature from a paper titled "The Staff Burn-Out Syndrome in Alternative Institutions" written by Herbert Freudenberger in 1975 (Freudenberger, 1975). Freudenberger describes burnout syndrome as occurring within the context of employment with symptoms including exhaustion, gastrointestinal distress, shortness of breath, anger, and depression. The definition of burnout, however, has continued to evolve, with Maslach and colleagues developing a widely utilized burnout measure called the Maslach Burnout Inventory (MBI) (Maslach & Jackson 1981). Maslach and colleagues define burnout as a syndrome with three dimensions: emotional exhaustion, depersonalization, and reduced personal accomplishment (Maslach et al., 2018).

There continues to be debate, however, among researchers regarding the differentiation of burnout among related psychiatric disorders including depression (Bianchi et al., 2017). With respect to depression, researchers have highlighted the overlap between burnout's dimension of emotional exhaustion and depressive symptomatology; some assert that suggest the concept of burnout may be a depressive subtype (Bianchi et al., 2021).

While burnout syndrome is included in the International Classification of Diseases (WHO, 2019) as one of the "factors influencing health status or contact with health services," it has not been designated to this date as a medical condition. It also is not considered a psychiatric disorder based on the most recent diagnostic manual of mental disorders: The Diagnostic and Statistical Manual of Mental Disorders, Fifth Edition, Text Revision (American Psychiatric Association, 2022). Some emphasize that the symptoms only in the workplace, thus distinguishing burnout from depression. Some prefer the term burnout to avoid the potential stigmatizing effect of a psychiatric diagnosis like depression.

Research on burnout with samples of healthcare professionals varies in the way burnout is measured (e.g., formal MBI, where others rely on caregiver self-report, measures of perceived stress, or well-being assessments). The variability in study methods creates nuances in the conclusions that are drawn regarding the effect of mindfulness on burnout. Nevertheless, the results suggest that mindfulness can have a positive influence on a wide array of work-related symptomatology.

In a like manner, a growing body of research underscores the potential benefits of mindfulness in mitigating emotional exhaustion, reducing perceived stress, and enhancing overall well-being of formal caregivers. A systematic review by Conversano and associated examined the impact of MBIs among healthcare professionals and, highlights benefits of mindfulness in reducing stress, improving emotional regulation, fostering resilience, preventing burnout, as well as positively impacting quality of life (Conversano et al., 2020). Another systematic review and meta-analysis found similar results regarding the effectiveness of MBIs in reducing stress related symptoms among healthcare professionals, including small to large effects on burnout, stress, anxiety, depression, and psychological distress (Ong et al., 2024).

Nurses, specifically, have been studied extensively in the literature related to these themes given the nature of their caregiving work, as well as the documented rates of burnout present in this population as noted above. Nurses who participated in mindfulness training reported had less psychological distress and improved resilience (Karo et al., 2024). Similarly, nursing students exposed to mindfulness reported reduced anxiety and stress (Heinrich & O-Connell 2024). A systematic review and meta-analysis exploring the impact of MBIs among registered nurses found that mindfulness reduced psychological distress, depression, and dimensions of burnout (Ramachandran et al., 2023), and additional research by Suleiman-Martos and colleagues found that MBIs specifically reduced the burnout dimension of emotional exhaustion (Suleiman-Martos et al., 2020). Similarly, a review evaluating interventions aimed at improving mental health and wellbeing among both nurses and physicians found that MBIs reduced symptoms of burnout, stress, and anxiety and improved emotion regulation and resilience (Melnyk et al., 2020).

In addition to nurses, a randomized controlled trial looking at caregivers of individuals with intellectual and developmental disabilities found that a tailored mindfulness intervention titled "Mindfulness-Based Positive Behavior Support (MBPBS)" significantly improved compassion satisfaction, decreased compassion fatigue (i.e., burnout), and decreased caregivers perceived stress (Singh et al., 2020).

In addition to various types of healthcare workers benefiting from mindfulness, various types of mindfulness interventions have been shown to be efficacious. The more formalized and structured MBSR has demonstrated efficacy in improving psychological functioning and reducing stress and burnout among healthcare professionals (Kraikous et al., 2021) as well as positively impacting overall well-being (Lomas et al., 2018). Additionally, brief mindfulness interventions have been shown to reduce stress and improve wellbeing among healthcare workers (Ameli et al., 2020; Mistretta et al., 2018) and decrease burnout and improve coping mechanisms in nurses (Green & Kinchen, 2021) including both in-person and smart phone app delivered mindfulness training.

Qualitative studies of professional caregivers suggest that mindfulness may foster empathy and compassion and contribute to improvements in patient–caregiver relationships (DiMauro et al., 2019).

The literature also emphasizes that mindfulness as an intervention, skill, or training opportunity can be included as part of larger organizational, systemic, and structural changes designed to advance and sustain improvements in healthcare professionals' well-being and mental health (Melnyk et al., 2020).

c. *Mindfulness-based interventions (MBIs) improve an array of psychiatric and psychological disorders and related symptoms, based on positive meta-analyses.*

Goldberg et al. (2018) conducted a meta-analysis of mindfulness-based interventions (MBIs) that included 12,005 participants with a variety of psychiatric disorders. The most frequent disorder studied was depression; also studied were anxiety disorders, pain, eating disorders and obesity, post-traumatic stress disorder, and alcohol and substance use. In the 171 studies retained for analysis, results showed: MBIs were found to be superior to no treatment (with an effect size of $d = 0.55$), minimal treatment conditions (effect size $d = 0.37$), nonspecific treatment conditions (effect size), and specific treatment conditions (effect size $d = 0.23$). Further, MBIs did not differ when compared to other evidence-based treatments. Mindfulness-based interventions demonstrated medium to large effect sizes on outcomes for anxiety, depression, pain, schizophrenia, and eating/weight-related disorders with Cohen's *d*s ranging from 0.45 to 0.89. They concluded that research has produced an empirical evidence base for the positive effects of MBIs on clinical psychiatric symptoms with therapeutic effects similar to other first-line psychological interventions and minimal variation across specific disorders.

The evidence base for MBIs is growing. Zhang et al. (2021) plotted the increase in the number of publications on MBIs from 2000 to 2020. In 2020 the number of publications on MBI was similar to that of CBT. Further, and similar to other reviews, they conclude that there is evidence to support using MBIs to help people suffering with depression, anxiety, pain, stress, addiction, psychosis, hypertension, weight control, and cancer-related symptoms and to promote prosocial behaviors. They note methodological issues yet to be solved to improve rigor and confidence across studies and populations.

In 2022, Goldberg and associates (Goldberg et al., 2022) extended their review further through an informative report on the "empirical states of mindfulness-based intervention" by systematically reviewing 44 meta-analyses restricted to only randomized controlled trials. The report used rigorous methods and included 336 randomized controlled trials with 30,483 participants. Like others, they note that the breadth of this literature on MBI is comparable to that of the other psychotherapies, including evidence-based psychotherapies, particularly cognitive behavioral therapy (CBT). Further, they conclude that the effectiveness of MBI is comparable to CBT for persons with depression. Importantly, they conclude that mindfulness meditation may potential across diagnostic categories, and that as a "family" MBIs are partially supported by the evidence depending on which population of disorders is evaluated. They also provide specific recommendations to increase rigor and fill gaps in the available findings.

Goldberg et al. (2022) note that treatment guidelines from the National Institute for Health Care Excellence (NICE, 2009) and American Psychological Association of Clinical Psychology (Goldberg & Segal) recommend mindfulness-based cognitive therapy for depression (MBCT; Segal et al., 2013) as an effective treatment. Further, mindfulness-based cognitive therapy has been shown to prevent depressive relapse based on meta-analyses from randomized controlled trials (Kuyken et al., 2016). Preliminary results show that mindfulness-based cognitive therapy may also be therapeutic for women suffering from perinatal depression (Dimidjian et al., 2016). Additionally, MBIs may help improve access for this important population (Tilden et al., 2022).

As mentioned above MBIs hold promise in improving symptoms of pain, schizophrenic spectrum disorders, eating disorders, as well as sleep disturbance with variable effect sizes reported, depending on methods. Illustrative and interesting details and nuances follow.

For a patient suffering with *acute* pain, there is some evidence that the MBIs have moderate effects on pain tolerance based on a meta-analysis by Shires et al. (2020). Note earlier, however, that McClintock and associates (McClintock et al., 2019) evaluated the evidence as inconclusive and provided constructive recommendations for improving methods in future studies. The benefits of MBIs for patients with *chronic lower back pain* include lowering short-term pain intensity based on a meta-analysis of 1005 patients within 12 studies (Schmidt & Pilat, 2023). For chronic pain, the promising effects of MBI reported vary by type of chronic pain sampled and which pain metrics are used.

Mindfulness-based interventions, as adjunctive treatments, have been shown to be safe and effective for persons with schizophrenic spectrum disorders according to a meta-analysis consisting of 22 randomized trials and 1500 people Specifically, they found that MBIs reduced negative symptoms and prevented relapse (Sabé et al., 2024). Qin et al. (2024) came to similar conclusions. Qin et al. (2024) concluded that MBI as an adjunctive therapy improved well-being of persons with schizophrenia based on their meta-analysis of 18 randomized controlled trials. Their measures of benefits included decreased symptoms, increased psychosocial functioning, increased insight, and increased mindfulness.

Kechter and Black (2020) reviewed the literature on MBI interventions for substance use disorders and binge-eating disorders and concluded that the promising effects were both "trans-therapeutic" and similar to those of CBT. Similarly, Korecki et al. (2020) also reviewed the literature and concluded that MBIs benefit persons with substance use disorder, and benefits may extend to reducing risk of relapse. However, after a meta-analysis of 17 randomized controlled trials with 1228 people, Demina et al. (2023) stated that while MBIs are promising due to methodologic limitations, they were unable to conclude that MBIs have medium to large therapeutic effects. They recommend more rigor in research on MBIs for individuals with substance use disorders. Promising but inconclusive statements have been made regarding problematic eating (e.g., binge and emotional eating) (Yu et al., 2020).

We note that the effects of MBIs are apparent not only in self-reported measures but also in biomarkers in psychiatric samples. Sanada et al. (2020) found that MBIs improved biomarkers associated with low-grade inflammation in patients with selected psychiatric disorders. Dunn and Dimolareva (2022) report similar findings, based on meta-analyses of 48 randomized controlled trials, albeit with heterogenous samples having no medical problems, medical problems, or psychiatric symptoms. They report that MBIs decrease inflammation (i.e., decrease C-reactive protein, and interleukin 6), improve infection control (i.e., increase $CD4^{+}$ cells), and decrease biologic aging (i.e., increase both telomere length and activity). They assert that these specific effects support the use of MBIs in somatic disorders.

d. *Putative mechanisms of effects of MBIs*

As the evidence base for MBIs develops, researchers ask: what is mindfulness really (i.e., how is it operationalized), under what conditions do the benefits of MBIs occur, for whom, and through what? (Note that we have partially applied the fundamental question attributed to Gordon Paul who asked: "*What* treatment, by *whom*, is most effective for *this* individual with *that* specific problem, and under which set of circumstances?" (Paul, 1967). In this section, we consider through what *mechanisms* does MSCC achieve its effects? For mechanistic hypotheses, we encourage our readers to read the pioneering work of Richard J. Davidson, PhD. and colleagues who have a broad interest in mindful meditation having studied it and the underlying neuroscience for decades. A short podcast available at: https://www.apa.org/topics/mindfulness/meditation introduces readers to pertinent issues. Facilitators can further advance their knowledge by reading *Altered Traits* (Goleman & Davidson, 2017) and the related literature in the emerging field of contemplative neuroscience.

An abstract of this fascinating work by Davidson and colleagues is that mindful meditation is a learned practice that can change the brain and increase brain health and human flourishing. Dr. Davidson asserts that since the brain is plastic, it is changed when people learn to self-regulate both their attention and emotions. He asserts that such human flourishing occurs through the "four pillars of well-being" consisting of: awareness, social connection, insight, and purpose. His team has developed a digital *Healthy Minds Program* that maps onto these four skills and the app is freely available at https://www.portal.hminnovations.org/launch.

Other related and interesting hypotheses regarding putative mechanisms of change underlying the benefits of MBIs include that of acceptance and expanding awareness of sensory experiences. For example, the attitude of acceptance of all one's experiences, whether positive or negative, is a core factor in mindfulness skills (Kabat-Zinn, 2013). It is opposite of judging or avoiding immediate sensations and feelings. Creswell et al. (2019) found that removing the instruction for acceptance in MBIs diminished the benefits of mindfulness training. Using dismantling trials, they concluded that identified acceptance is a key part of emotional regulation as well as a mechanism facilitating the effects of mindfulness-based intervention (Creswell et al., 2019). Additionally, a meta-analysis of 33 studies of mindfulness-based therapies for anxiety and depression suggested that acceptance (along with decentering and mindful attention) mediated improved symptoms (Johannsen et al., 2022). Further, Pan and colleagues examined two randomized controlled trials of MBIs with participants who reported anxiety and depression and found that distress tolerance was a key mediator in reducing symptoms (Pan et al., 2024). They defined distress tolerance as the willingness to tolerate unpleasant experiences, an attitude that appears close to that of acceptance.

Another interesting mechanistic hypothesis is that of expanded awareness of sensory experiences. This hypothesis focuses on how MBIs may influence the brain mechanisms and processes associated with the default mode network (DMN) and areas of the brain associated with the perception of sensation (Farb & Segal, 2024). The default mode network (DMN) is a network of brain regions that are primarily associated with "at rest activities" such as daydreaming, self-reflection, mind-wandering, and other introspective mental activities. The DMN includes areas like the medial prefrontal cortex, posterior cingulate cortex, and angular gyrus.

Over several studies of neuroimaging, Farb and Segal (2024) were surprised to find that the benefits of mindfulness were not associated with decreasing or dampening parts of the brain associated with self-focused thinking or self-referencing (the DMN). Instead, the benefits were most evident in those whose awareness of internal and external sensations widened or expanded beyond usual self-oriented preoccupations. "Rather than turning *off* the parts of the brain that support judging, people trained in [mindful] sensing had learned to turn *on* other brain regions dedicated to sensation … Stepping away from thinking and striving, stepping into our body's ability to sense the world … can … ease stress and clear the mind" (Farb & Segal, 2024). These investigators point to the power of sensory engagement found in MBIs as a core influence of the impact of skillful mindfulness.

Chapter 2—Setting up and Managing the Process of Mindful Self Care for Clinicians and Caregivers (MSCC)

Abstract

Chapter 2 discusses specific topics related to delivering an effective group intervention. Guidance is provided regarding the structure of each session and facilitating a positive group dynamic. Group adaptations are also highlighted, including a pathway for adjusting the length of the group from 6-8 sessions depending on need, and adapting the group for use in specific environments such as a hospital, nursing home, church/place of worship or classroom of trainees in the clinical/health professions. Special populations are also addressed including individuals who provide care to the elderly, chronically ill, individuals with cognitive impairment or children or others in palliative care settings. Cultural adaptations are discussed and strategies for integrating various forms of spirituality and other important cultural factors as relevant is highlighted. Virtual groups are also mentioned with information about providing this intervention via a HIPAA secure virtual platform. Finally, this chapter includes a list of the sessions that will be presented in subsequent chapters.

Keywords: Expectations; Informed consent; Managing group process; Risk/benefits; Roles; Safety

Mindful Self-Care for Clinicians and Caregivers. https://doi.org/10.1016/B978-0-443-29821-9.00003-0

"Path during Journey" - This photograph was taken while exploring Italy by Robin B. Jarrett. May your journey during mindful practice open a path to experiencing all your senses.

Author Reflections: The Anatomy of a Caregiver
By Robin B. Jarrett, PhD, ABPP

Caregivers are not born; instead, they are made. They are made by circumstances, models, and experience. For some, caregiving is a calling; they often prepare for it through formal education, training, and mentoring by more experienced caregivers. They often begin neither aware of the cumulative effect of their role, nor of the impact of their role across their lives and lives. For others, or at times, caregiving was unexpected … thrust upon them and unpredicted. They may feel unprepared and overwhelmed, cautious.

Nonetheless, most people will provide care of some type to another person during their lifetime. Caregivers include the young, the middle-aged, and the old. Caregivers are your partner, your daughter or son, your doctor or nurse, your friend and your neighbor. Care persons can include your partner, your parent, your daughter or son, your friend and your neighbor or your patient.

For some caregivers, it is not uncommon to hear syntax that suggests there are two groups: that of patients (care persons) and that of formal caregivers/clinicians. Often, these speakers have not yet experienced the role of being a patient and/or may not have witnessed a family member or friend catapulted into this role. At the same time, these speakers have observed suffering, illness, and death. They yearn to be exempt, and for a while, they consider that, somehow, they will escape "it" by staying safely and squarely in the caregiving role.

While reading A Guide you will note that we use the terms "caregiver" (for persons, both formal and informal providing care) and "care person" (for the person receiving care). Please know we use these terms to designate roles in particular settings and times. We use the terms as heuristics. Eventually, most caregivers, both formal and informal, will also need care. In life, there is only one category …. that of people, with needs. That of humanity, moving in and out of seemingly complex roles across the life span, approaching each with varying levels of confidence and doubt.

During our collaboration on A Guide, we were highly aware that each author served as a formal caregiver, an informal caregiver, and also a care person – one who received care and support from not only formal caregivers, but also from those who love us. We have held these multiple roles – all at once and/or in sequence and/or in separate times and spaces. We supported each other in these roles as we wrote, sharing our stress, our joy, and considering how mindful practice could help us grow. Like you, each of us has flowed in and out of giving care and receiving care. This interwoven thread is a powerful dynamic of human and interpersonal connection. In this dynamic, the care person is saying, "I will trust you because you are giving me something I cannot give myself." In the role of caregiver, you are saying, "I will give you my best to answer your need."

We wrote A Guide for Facilitators who plan to work with groups of caregivers, knowing that there is a special interpersonal dynamic and connection

Continued

available to people who gather and can share experiences in safety and comfort. Caregivers, who develop wrinkles not only from their frowns but also from their smiles, joined by the belief that there may be a more sustainable way forward. When joined together, they may share their laughter and also their tears. We offer A Guide to Facilitators to promote the special union of people who gather to cultivate self-care and mindful practice, as they move forward with the privilege and responsibility of caregiving.

The authors extend a heartfelt hope that the Mindful Self-Care for Clinicians and Caregivers (MSCC) Guide becomes a source of inspiration and transformation for facilitators and their caregivers and clinician participants during their journey as they learn the skills and experience the stages of mindful self-care. For facilitators, the Guide offers ways to deepen understanding of the challenged lives of caregivers and to uplift those who need what the experience of mindful self-care can offer. For participants, MSCC can be a way to bring care to the caregiver … to themselves. As the creators of this unique Guide, the authors have lived experience in all the relevant roles. In other words, the authors have been in the roles of: mindfulness group facilitators and committed caregivers, both professionally and personally, as well are people who have received care. As we wrote this Guide, we drew not only on our education, but also on our lived experiences at critical times and in each role. The authors take joy in imagining the powerful combination of facilitator and participant in your dynamic dance to the music of MSCC.

Facilitator Contemplation: What will you create in space between science and people?

Section 1—Setting Up Groups of MSCC

In this section, we use the framework of *informed consent* as a context to describe core conditions of participating in the MSCC process in a group setting. This gives facilitators and participants ways to describe and understand the MSCC structure and process, goals, roles, risks and benefits, and ways to promote psychological safety. Part A below extends the MSCC process to different formats (e.g., -person or virtual) and considers different possibilities and financial options (e.g., no cost, fees, insurance) to consider when developing an MSCC group.

Informed Consent: Preparing Caregivers for Group Participation

Written and verbal consents at the beginning of MSCC training are helpful in clarifying expectations, risks and benefits, and the primacy of self-care. Signing a written consent to participate in MSCC means a caregiver has been given the opportunity to understand what is described and consents to it. The content of a consent is best simply stated and concise. Below are possible parts of a consent:

- What is Mindful Self-Care for Caregivers? (structure, process, and aim)
- What Mindful Self-Care for Caregivers is not
- What are the possible benefits of MSCC? Risks?
- What is the role of a participant?
- What is the role of the facilitator?
- How are special circumstances handled?
- When might participation in MSCC be discontinued?
- Why and how to contact the MSCC facilitator?
- The role of self-care throughout training?
- What are some of the group norms during MSCC?
- How is confidentiality handled?
- Are there any financial considerations of participating in MSCC

What is Mindful Self-Care for Caregivers?

Mindful Self-Care for Clinicians and Caregivers (MSCC) is an 8-session group format for caregivers meeting to learn mindfulness and self-care skills to help them meet the special demands of caregiving. Each session is designed to be 90 minutes in length, in which participants explore various ways to practice and develop ways to savor nourishing moments in their lives and to unravel habitual stress reactions through calm, gentle attention. Learning is hands-on. MSCC was designed to actively engage all of the senses throughout the 8-week group format. The exercises herein attempt that. Mindful Self-Care for Clinicians and Caregivers involve structured exercises and meditations led by attitudes of curiosity and openness to experiment. Over time, participants select their most meaningful practices to integrate into their daily lives.

What Mindful Self-Care for the Caregiver is Not

A Guide does not present MSCC as a psychotherapy unless offered by licensed mental health clinicians. Facilitators need to know how to make referrals for group participants who require formal treatment with evidence-based psychotherapy and/or psychiatric medications provided by licensed practitioners. Facilitators need to recognize when participants will benefit from referral, particularly if or when a participant experiences distress or emotions that they are unable to self-regulate. While MSCC is not offered as a psychotherapy or medical treatment, in the hands of licensed providers, MSCC can be used as an adjunct to medical care, including evidence-based psychotherapy.

What Are the Possible Benefits of Mindful Self-Care for Clinicians and Caregivers?

Mindful self-care practices help caregivers refocus their attention on their physical, emotional, social, (and for some spiritual) spiritual needs to sustain self-renewal through the caregiving journey. To do this, mindfulness strengthens nonjudgmental, clear attention to the present moment, which then reveals choices to reduce stress, savor positive experiences, increase aliveness in one's senses, and heighten positive connection to oneself and others. Mindfulness counters old habits of living too much on autopilot, out of touch with the feelings and sensations that make life come alive. Experience in mindful practice can help participants learn emotional regulation.

What Are the Possible Risks of Mindful Self-Care for Clinicians and Caregivers?

There are some possible risks associated with Mindful Self-Care for Clinicians and Caregivers. One is misunderstanding this intervention as a type of psychotherapy or treatment for stress disorders. Mindful Self-Care for Clinicians and Caregivers is offered as psychosocial education flexible enough to be used by licensed clinicians as an adjunct to psychotherapy and/or medical care and also as mindfulness training in the hands of experienced facilitators who may work outside of traditional clinical settings (e.g., community settings). In the latter case, MCSS is not a formal treatment for disorders. Instead, MSCC draws from evidenced-based psychosocial intervention and promotes skill development. At the same time, mindfulness training is a paradoxical approach that loosens the tension of having to do something in the "right" way or to get somewhere specific. In this way, it opens the door for discovery-based and experiential learning. There is a risk of taking on the attitude of fixed expectations for certain predictable results and finding that very attitude blocks the positive results hoped for. As an example, someone may come to a mindfulness group expressing a need to find a way to eradicate their intense anxiety. This person would need to understand that mindfulness skills can potentially alleviate stress, but there is no guarantee that being in an MSCC group will alleviate specific symptoms of anxiety. Learning mindfulness skills benefits from an experimental attitude that is alert to its effects on one's own individual experience.

The MSCC group offers only a kind of laboratory to experiment and find out for oneself. If there is a fixed need for a more predictable outcome, other approaches like cognitive behavioral therapy can offer a first-line effective treatment for panic disorder (Papola et al., 2022). Facilitators who can offer such information and make such referrals can help participants find a match between what MSCC can offer and what the participant might be seeking. Additionally, participants undergoing current psychotherapy or medication treatment may benefit from MSCC, as long as they understand what to expect from these different interventions and their mental health provider agrees that MSCC might benefit them.

Engaging in MSCC may involve some possible discomfort for participants. In fact, transient frustration and distress are often seen as a part of the process of learning meditation (Aizik-Reebs et al., 2021). Knowing this, as part of the informed consent process, prepares participants in MSCC sessions to helpfully frame these experiences as part of the process for some and as possible concerns for others. It is not uncommon for those unaccustomed to carefully attending their inner experiences (a core aspect of mindfulness) to be surprised at the discomfort that may present, in the form of unfamiliar experiences or anxiety. For example, when one of the authors first attended a week-long silent mindfulness meditation retreat, he was taken aback by the profusion of scattered and often anxiety-arousing self-judging thoughts and emotions. This came up in the numerous sitting meditations during the day. What was happening was that he was becoming acutely aware of mental activity normally screened out by his usual habits of focusing attention on practical tasks and familiar activities. Although uncomfortable, this was a highly important discovery in meditation, allowing him to see clearly the origins of stress and to develop over time a mindful way of nonreactive observation of inner events. In a like way, during meditation, another author experienced transient pain in her right arm akin to the acute and severe pain she felt the morning after major surgery, when pain relievers were unavailable.

Some session participants may experience these insights as disconcerting and be tempted to think it is the mindful practice that is creating discomfort, rather than shining a light on something already there but unobserved. Facilitators can prepare participants to simply notice what occurs and to value it as part of the learning process. The facilitator's accepting, nonjudgmental manner in hearing these kinds of reports transmits a sense of normalcy that is often then absorbed by the participant.

Some people seeking mindfulness training may have histories of psychiatric and physical disorders, including trauma. While mindfulness meditation practices can help alleviate stress reactions, they can also trigger emotionally embodied experiences connected with disorders. This is more common with anxiety and trauma symptoms. Although not an issue with the majority of participants in mindfulness sessions, these issues can occur, so facilitators should be aware.

A useful perspective on meditation and mindfulness practice effects is given by a study of the negative impact of Mindfulness-Based Cognitive Therapy on subjects seeking help for anxiety and depression (Britton et al., 2021). Following guidelines from the World Health Organization, *side effects* of this treatment were defined as any effect (positive or negative) that was not the intended goal of an intervention. *Adverse effects* were more intense experiences of subjective unpleasantness that sometimes provoked some countermeasure to deal with them. *Lasting effects* were adverse effects (like hyperarousal or dissociation) lasting more than a day, more than a week, or more than a month. Negative consequences could show up in either one or several domains: emotional, cognitive, perceptual, sense of self, somatic, and social. The authors conclude that adverse effects from this and other studies are more common than generally acknowledged and often go unobserved by meditation facilitators because they are not actively monitored as opposed to passively monitored (dependent on the participant's spontaneous reporting). Most adverse effects came from intensive meditation retreats emphasizing practices of longer duration (more than 1 hour a day). Existing psychopathology accounted for another large segment of adverse effects. Mindful Self-Care for Clinicians and Caregivers is likely at the safer side of the risk continuum as it uses only brief meditation practices and encourages participants to choose and adopt practices they are attracted to and bring about positive experiences.

Given the potential of negative effects in the broad array of mindfulness and meditation practices, MSCC encourages active monitoring of side effects (positive or negative), adverse effects, and lasting effects. Facilitators can use the inquiry or Socratic questioning part of learning sessions (particularly during Session Check-Ins) to invite and elicit both positive and negative experiences from the previous mindfulness exercise. Aside from facilitating opportunistic learning through inquiry, this method of participant reporting can be noted for any potential concerns to be simply remembered to monitor an individual over time or to be used to follow up with a participant after the meeting.

In addition, facilitators might consider how to best encourage their participants to report on the effects of their mindfulness practices. The goal is for the participant to describe any positive or negative, or challenging experiences related to in-group or daily personal practices stemming from MSCC sessions. Such questions can be asked during group sharing as sessions start and/or privately with the facilitator who "hangs back" remaining present and available as sessions close, either virtually or in person.

Facilitators should offer participants the chance to ask questions as part of the informed consent process in the first session (more on this later). For more information, know there are books available on the use and impact of mindfulness practices on various conditions, including anxiety (Roemer & Orsillo, 2013), depression (Segal et al., 2013), and trauma (Treleaven, 2018), for example. One helpful resource is David A. Treleaven's *Trauma-Sensitive Mindfulness: Practices for Safe and Transformative Healing* (Treleaven, 2018). The following are some practical considerations for facilitators when hearing participant reports of emotional discomfort:

1. There is a difference between discomfort that can be tolerated and worked on within mindfulness practices and overwhelming discomfort that seems to spiral in intensity and/or duration. Facilitators can inquire about the distressing experience to help the person decide to stay with a practice or refocus attention to help deescalate the stress. Participant self-care is always primary. This may entail discontinuing a practice, focusing on breathing, or walking around. Facilitators can support the person in choosing a preferred way of coping as they extend a calming presence toward him or her.
2. In certain cases (e.g., when self-regulation is absent and seems unlikely), facilitators may need to have the person consider mental health resources as an alternative or adjunct to mindfulness training. Unless participant safety is a consideration, the decision is left up to the person in a supportive conversation.
3. If a particular practice triggers intense discomfort while other practices do not, the person can elect to avoid it and stick with friendlier ones.
4. Ultimately, it is the person who is empowered to decide the best way to understand and manage the distress effects of mindfulness practice with the support of the facilitator.
5. It is a helpful advantage to the facilitator to have a consultation resource with a mental health professional when needed. Such resources are best established as a routine practice rather than when the need or emergency arises.
6. If the facilitator is a licensed mental health professional and participants report that they are experiencing suicidal thoughts with intent, then the mental health professional may be required to help the participant seek treatment, including evaluation for hospitalization, voluntary or involuntary. The mental health professional may

consider the involvement of family members and/or significant others when there are imminent safety concerns. Licensed mental professionals who facilitate mindful self-care groups need to provide this type of disclosure (and additional ones, depending on state requirements, as part of the informed consent process provided prior to participation in MSCC). Licensed mental health professionals are encouraged to review the requirements of their state or province regarding mandated reporting and other requirements for participant safety.

Another risk for MSCC participants is the violation of confidentiality. When personal information shared in confidence to a facilitator or within a group session is given out without permission, damage to trust can occur in the group or facilitator. Broken confidence can lead to feeling psychologically unsafe and vulnerable. At that point, the potential effectiveness of the MSCC experience may be impaired. It is important to safeguard what is shared in group sessions by everyone even if the information shared seems innocuous and to have all participants indicate their understanding and agreement to protect confidentiality.

Breaches in confidentiality can be in person or online. A participant may be overheard discussing one's report of caregiving anxiety to another group member. Or the facilitator may inadvertently give an unnamed example of a meditation obstacle that came out of a group session in another session or group email. Often, leaks in confidentiality are innocent but harmful, nonetheless. If a facilitator, for example, wishes to share some aspect of a participant's experience or life, permission should be given to do so first by the person.

In a group setting, confidentiality is set as a norm but in the end, cannot be guaranteed. It is set up as an expectation based on the cooperation of group members. This should be explicitly stated in the first session. Further, if MSCC is offered virtually, then confidentiality can be breached if a participant fails to keep their commitment to keep their physical, including "ear," space private. Facilitators should emphasize the importance of maintaining confidentiality during informed consent, but participants should also be reminded that it is always their choice about what to share and what not to disclose. The facilitator emphasizes this freedom of choice in their tone and voice throughout the MSCC process.

Missed MSCC sessions may risk a negative impact on a participant's stages of learning mindfulness and self-care skills. MSCC sessions build on each other. Missed sessions will be a reality for some participants caught in unforeseen events of caregiving. If participants have consent to allow sessions to be videotaped or audiotaped, then a participant can access a taped session that was missed. In general, participants are invited to attend the sessions they can and use the last two summary sessions to help make up for a missed session or two. Although MSCC sessions are graduated and iterative, participants can still find learning benefits and group support in any session they attend. *No one can predict when even a single session will become a turning point for someone.*

What is the Role of a Participant?

Mindful Self-Care for Clinicians and Caregivers depend on participants being present as active learners who, through trial and experiment, develop their own mindful self-care skills, crafting their own set of preferred practices. Each MSCC session provides several exercises for participants to cultivate an "inner" sense of mindfulness and try out a variety of ways to evoke it. After each exercise, there is an opportunity to briefly share experiences with other group members. In this way, caregiver participants learn a great deal from each other. After each session, there is an invitation to take up some self-selected practices to try them on during the week. People who practice some set of skills consistently get the most out of MSCC.

Mindful Self-Care for Clinicians and Caregivers has been designed to apply to a wide range of caregivers. It is for both formal and informal caregivers who have diverse professions and/or life circumstances. To identify caregivers who may safely participate in group MSCC, facilitators can design recruitment materials that highlight the purpose and nature of the group. Depending on whether this group is being led through a medical center, mental health clinic, or community-based organization, the steps participants take to register and enrol in the group may be different and can be described in the recruitment materials.

What is the Role of the Facilitator?

The following Guide for MSCC is created for facilitators already prepared as mindfulness facilitators or those directly supervised by an educated, experienced mindfulness skills facilitator. Facilitators need to be trained and experienced in group process. Experience in and knowledge of group process, as has been described by Napier et al. (2025), is essential. This Guide complements the antecedent, supervised experience the reader has completed. Teaching mindful skills to diverse caregivers requires skills typically learned through systematic education and experience. To use this Guide safely and effectively, facilitators need these prerequisite skills in mindful practice and group facilitation. These prerequisites are the foundation for creative and safe application to the MSCC personalized to the concerns of a particular group of caregivers working in each context. The user (our reader) is responsible for implementing the MSCC group session process as an educated facilitator responsible for participant safety and effective curriculum use. In so doing, the facilitator promotes psychological safety while encouraging appropriate participant experiments involved in new learning. Facilitators who use the Guide without the necessary background, education and/or supervised experience do so at their own risk. Unwanted side effects or adverse effects are more likely to occur when facilitators are not formally and experientially prepared.

The MSCC Guide is designed to free the experienced facilitator from having to create a group structure and materials. The Guide offers the facilitator a structure that can be adapted to the facilitator's individualized sensitivities and style as well as to the context, setting and needs of the participants. Facilitators can view this guide as a set of prompts for caregivers to begin to experiment with mindful practice of self-care.

The facilitators of MSCC may come from a variety of backgrounds. What they have in common is training and experience in fostering mindfulness skills training in groups. This usually means they have formal education and competence in teaching mindfulness concepts (ideally including familiarity with the growing array of research on mindfulness neuroscience and the impact of mindfulness on stress and mental health). This preparation includes strong experiential development and, often, hands-on supervision or guidance, over and above what one typically receives in day or weekend workshops. Mindfulness skills and attitudes evolve with practice and close guidance and encouragement from experienced trainers. Once one's own skills and practices are developed, further training is pursued in using group processes to bring mindfulness skills to others.

This Guide to MSCC might also be used by those in mindfulness training under a seasoned mentor. Also, those wanting to glean ideas for their own mindfulness development as a caregiver or a future mindfulness facilitator, and/or MSCC facilitator, may find *A Guide* useful. Fortunately, there are many pathways that can prepare a person to be a mindfulness group facilitator. Training may be embedded in academic or professional programs in psychology, social work, psychiatry, pastoral counsel, medicine, nursing, or guidance counseling, for example. It may be offered in stand-alone mindfulness training programs, with or without a certificate. It may be, and often is, a combination of both. For example, the person may undergo workshops in such formats as Mindfulness-Based Stress Reduction. The result of mindfulness training is the cultivation of a mindful presence, comfort with a variety of practices, confidence, and skill in working with group processes, and an ongoing commitment to deepening one's own mindfulness growth.

Importantly, facilitators need to know what mindful self-care is not, and for whom mindful self-care practice might be associated with adverse effects. If the group is led through a mental health clinic or medical center and the facilitator is a mental health professional, the path to participation may include an individual completing a psychiatric and/or psychological evaluation prior to enrolling in the group to screen for appropriateness for the group. If participants are not completing a psychiatric and/or psychological evaluation prior to registering for the group, the expectation is that patients will "screen" themselves to discern potential benefit, based in part on the educational information the facilitator provides. (See below). The facilitator should be prepared to offer referrals to mental health services when participants ask or as needed. When comprehensive screening (i.e., psychiatric assessment) has not taken place prior to group registration, the facilitator will reinforce the need for participants to "self-screen" during the informed consent.

Facilitators help participants understand what self-screening involves. Facilitators help participants to understand that MSCC is not designed to treat any specific mental health diagnosis and is not designed to be a replacement for psychotherapy or other medical treatment.

By choosing to participate in the MSCC group, participants are consenting to the intervention and acknowledge that they understand the potential risks and benefits. Participants are encouraged to continue to assess over time whether they feel the MSCC group is meeting their needs and expectations. Participants are encouraged to talk with the facilitator at any time to request referrals or additional resources.

A descriptive brochure or handout could be used to highlight the process of MSCC, risks/benefits of participation, and self-selection guidelines. The nature of MSCC refers to its skills focus and the context of participating and sharing experiences in a group. Basic risks and benefits may be summarized.

A note on self-screening: To assess the appropriateness of MSCC for oneself can be challenging. On the one hand, it is expected that most participants are signing up to learn ways to better manage the stress involved in caregiving. On the other hand, those in acute emotional crisis needing more direct and immediate relief for their distress would find the developmental pace of MSCC and its invitation to experience (rather than avoid) inner feelings and sensations more of a hindrance than a help. These may be people with intense depression, suicidal ideation, and often intolerable anxiety. Psychotherapy and/or psychiatric medication would be more fitting for this type of acute crisis. When in doubt, people considering MSCC could be invited to consult with the facilitator and a health care professional (e.g., primary care doctor, psychologist) about the decision to participate.

A Note on Formal Screening: Facilitators who are licensed mental health professionals and plan to screen participants prior to enrolling them in the group should be aware of the potential contraindications to MSCC group participation. Contraindications include active suicidal ideation, psychosis, active substance use, or individuals currently in active crisis. Persons with cognitive impairment may or may not be appropriate for a group setting based on the level of impairment, and this should be assessed on a case-by-case basis. Similarly, people with a trauma history and/or diagnosis of posttraumatic stress disorder (PTSD) may be evaluated with an eye toward individual benefit versus risk and ability to adhere to established group norms. If contraindications are possible, a formal psychological assessment prior to enrolling an individual in the group can help address the benefits versus risks.

As noted above, however, screening with a comprehensive psychiatric and/or psychological assessment may or may not be feasible or appropriate given the facilitator's credentials. When screening is not a prerequisite to group participation, then the facilitator takes on the task of providing information regarding risks/benefits of MSCC participation, both in the recruitment materials, prior to the initial MSCC session, and periodically during the MSCC sessions offered. Many participants need help understanding and interpreting the various experiences that arise in learning the skill and the effects of mindfulness practices.

Although we try to ease and guide decisions on the use and appropriateness of MSCC, ultimately, facilitators must take full responsibility for the implementation of this rich resource and ensure that their educational and experiential background prepares them for these responsibilities. This MSCC Guide is meant to help the facilitator evaluate his or her preparedness for this venture.

How Are Special Circumstances Handled?

Participants not able to attend all MSCC sessions are given opportunities to continue. Caregiving is often unpredictable in its demands. Group members are asked to notify the MSCC facilitator to accommodate these challenges. Sessions 7 and 8 were created, in part, to expose participants to what they may have missed in earlier sessions. Those having distressful experiences from practicing an exercise or meditation are requested to discuss these with the facilitator. Some experiences may be usual; some may indicate a need to alter practices.

When Might Participation in MSCC Be Discontinued?

If a participant is interacting within the group setting in a way that is harmful to the group process or otherwise negatively impacts fellow participants, the facilitator should provide feedback about the behavior. If feedback fails to elicit change, the facilitator then directs the participant to leave the group. This might include behaviors that are disrespectful to others, not adhering to group norms (see section on group norms), or otherwise disruptive to the group and mindful learning. If a participant is deemed to no longer be appropriate for the group, a facilitator may suggest other referrals for individual counseling or psychotherapy.

Why and How to Contact the MSCC Facilitator?

The MSCC facilitator is there to guide and to consult with participants, if needed. If there is little time to do this in or after sessions, the facilitator may give participants a means to contact him or her after group (email, phone, etc.). Most concerns will be addressed during sessions with opportunities for participants to "check-in" with their experiences and questions.

The Role of Self-Care Throughout Training?

First and foremost, all participants are asked to prioritize self-care both during and after training. Self-care means staying attentive to one's needs and acting to meet them. This contrasts with ignoring needs and feelings in order to be compliant with whatever is being asked of one. The overarching message of MSCC is the prioritization of self-care and the ability to renew oneself and be healthy to care for another. In session, this could be as small as taking a needed bathroom break or as large as asking for a way to manage missed sessions. Mindful self-care involves both a clear acceptance of the challenges of learning something new and self-kindness in the way one meets those challenges.

What Are Some of the Group Norms During MSCC?

Group norms represent agreed-upon shared standards of behavior for participation in MSCC. They may be formal or informal, spoken explicitly or inferred through discussion of the overall values of the group. They represent rules that all group members are willing to agree to about how they will interact and engage during MSCC. It is typically most helpful for group norms to be discussed and decided on collaboratively during Session 1 of a group process to ensure these standards are determined at the outset of the group. As informed consent is reviewed and important aspects of group process are discussed, other group norms can be included. These may include expectations for how participants will show up and engage throughout the sessions, such as maintaining professional interactions with others, keeping confidentiality, dressing appropriately, avoiding behaviors that would be disruptive to other group members, and treating all group members with respect. Eliciting feedback from group members about the group norms that they feel are important for all MSCC participants to abide by can be a helpful way to engage the group in the process of determining norms.

How is Confidentiality Handled?

There is an inherent risk of a loss of confidentiality in the nature of participating in a group. Participants should be informed of this during the initial session. With that in mind, establishing group norms for confidentiality will be important to ensure that the environment feels safe for participants to share and discuss content. Facilitators should elicit agreement from all participants at the start of MSCC that content from the group will stay within the group to ensure that participants' confidentiality and privacy are maintained to the extent possible.

Are There Any Financial Considerations of Participating in MSCC?

Facilitators will need to consider whether MSCC is being offered free of charge, as part of a nonprofit group or community organization, or with a fee for participation and how this may impact access to the group for various individuals. If the facilitator is a licensed mental health professional, it is possible that insurance might be billed if appropriately based on the population and format of the group, whether psychological assessments have been completed, and/or diagnoses obtained to meet criteria for insurance billing. Specifics regarding billing and insurance are outside the scope of this book and will differ based on the setting of the group, state-by-state laws and policies and the ever-evolving landscape of mental health billing practices. If participants must pay a fee for each group session, all billing policies and fee information should be provided at the outset of the start of MSCC and this is part of the written informed consent.

Adapting MSCC for Specific Populations

Mindful Self-Care for Clinicians and Caregivers groups can be tailored to specific populations—for example, a group offered through a medical center for caregivers of patients with cancer, or one designed for Intensive Care Unit nurses. Alternatively, MSCC groups may be held in community settings, such as churches or community centers, and open to caregivers more broadly defined, resulting in a more heterogeneous group of participants.

If a group has a more defined and homogenous population, such as nurses, or caregivers of individuals with a medical condition (i.e., Alzheimer's Disease, cancer, clinicians with a shared specialty or mission, etc.), facilitators may choose to integrate specific content that is tailored directly to the needs and experiences of these unique participants. For example, it may be helpful to include psychoeducation for caregivers of individuals with memory challenges that highlights common experiences or identified themes, or helpful research-based suggestions for coping.

For instance, groups for nurses, other health care providers, or formal caregivers might include educational materials about the rates of burnout, or a mention of the literature regarding aspects of health care that may contribute to emotional exhaustion or compassion fatigue. Including this type of content can enrich the group experience, introduce valuable information that highlights themes related to the caregiving experience, and serve as a springboard for conversation and discussion. A facilitator may also inquire or highlight shared experiences between group members, which may foster group cohesion.

Considering the makeup of a group may also help guide decisions on group location, virtual/hybrid/in-person, frequency or adjusted length of session meetings, size of the group, and/or specific group content. Once the group has been established, thinking about the unique composition of group members will guide decisions the facilitator may make based on caregiver needs. For example, professional caregivers attending a group through their place of work may feel less open to sharing personal experiences or information about their private lives as opposed to a group of lay people in the community. Recognizing unique challenges or circumstances that are group-dependent and adapting in response will help each group best meet the needs of the participants. Virtual groups may be uniquely suited for reaching participants who are not closely colocated but may share other unifying characteristics. Virtual groups may also reduce barriers to caregivers attending by allowing participants to join from home while navigating other caregiving responsibilities.

Cultural components should be thoughtfully considered when leading an MSCC group. This includes being mindful of whether participants share certain cultural backgrounds or bring diverse and unique cultural perspectives. Exploring these elements can enrich group discussions and deepen understanding. An important part of the learning process is helping individuals identify how mindfulness fits into their lived experience. For some, incorporating mindful practices into daily life may align well with their cultural values; for others, especially those from more collectivist cultures, prioritizing self and "self-care" may feel unfamiliar, inappropriate, or even frowned upon. Part of the facilitator's role is to support participants in integrating mindfulness in ways that feel authentic, respectful of their cultural context, and realistically sustainable. Understanding that many daily tasks can be done mindfully—such as completing housework, eating a meal, or taking a pause during a daily routine—offers participants flexibility in how they choose to engage with mindfulness during the group.

Honoring participants' beliefs, including their religious and spiritual views (see below), as well as their culture and perspectives on life, self, and self-care, is a core component of MSCC. Mindfulness is most impactful when individuals can practice in ways that feel authentic and aligned with their lived experience and cultural background.

htegrating Spirituality

Another form of group adaptation related to culture is the integration of spirituality into an MSCC group. This might be particularly appropriate when the group is held in a church or place of worship, where participants share a common foundation in faith or spiritual practice. In contrast to secular groups—where the spiritual or religious roots of mindfulness may be minimized or intentionally separated, MSCC groups hosted through faith-based organizations may intentionally reference and incorporate spiritual elements.

As previously highlighted in this book, mindfulness has historical and philosophical roots in contemplative practices found across many cultures and religious traditions. For example, Lauren Artress (1995) provides a glimpse into the history of the labyrinth as a moving meditation that has been used across cultures and time, within spiritual practices.

Similarly, mindfulness practices such as meditation or mindful pauses can be included alongside prayer or spiritual reflection which may increase the level of meaning or purpose associated with the practice. Faith-based readings - such as scriptures, psalms, recited prayers, or hymns - can be woven into mindful breathing exercises, mindful listening practices, or mantras to include spirituality in mindfulness. This integration can enrich practice and make it feel more authentic and relevant to those for whom faith is a central part of daily life.

Participants who already have time set aside for religious reflection or prayer may be encouraged to incorporate brief mindfulness practices into those existing routines, supporting both consistency and spiritual alignment. At the same time, when the group involves caregivers who come from heterogeneous religious and spiritual cultures, including none, then the facilitator needs training and sensitivity in welcoming all diverse cultures present in the group. It is important that these differences do not become barriers to the social connection that might otherwise develop in the group.

Several authors have explored the compatibility of mindfulness with religious traditions. Thomas (2018) discusses how mindfulness can be viewed not as contradictory to Christian spirituality, but as a means of "making space for God" and deepening one's contemplative relationship with the divine (Thomas, 2018). Several scholars argue that addressing spirituality in MBIs is crucial for authenticity and acceptability. For example, Palitsky and Kaplan (2021) note that MBIs' historical associations with religion/spirituality influence how people perceive them, suggesting that clinicians should proactively respond to and integrate clients' spirituality as opposed to ignoring or minimizing spiritual components (Palitsky & Kaplan, 2021).

A qualitative study by Sapthiang and colleagues found that for some participants, when mindfulness is taught in isolation from its spiritual context, it may lose 'depth' and therefore the integration of spiritual principles could enhance the authenticity of the practice (Sapthiang et al., 2024). A 2023 review published in *Mindfulness* focused on adapting mindfulness-based interventions (MBIs) for Black Americans and suggested several culturally relevant adaptations to address conflicting perceptions of mindfulness. These included using familiar religious language, openly addressing spiritual concerns, offering mindfulness in church settings, and tailoring MBIs to fit faith-based contexts (Haidar et al., 2023).

Additional research has explored Islamic-based mindfulness, highlighting the integration of present-moment awareness and other mindfulness practices alongside religious observances within Islamic spirituality (Aldbyani, 2024). Overall, the literature supports the idea that when mindfulness programs honor participants' spiritual beliefs, they can enhance engagement, foster meaning-making, and, in some cases, improve psychological outcomes (Anderson et al., 2022). At its core, integrating spirituality into mindfulness reflects a commitment to a respectful, client-centered approach that values and incorporates the cultural and religious experiences of caregiver participants.

When navigating conversations about spirituality, faith, and religion in the context of mindfulness, there is rarely a one-size-fits-all approach—especially in a group setting. Some participants may hold strong religious or spiritual beliefs, others may view mindfulness as entirely secular, and many may fall somewhere in between. As a facilitator, it's important to acknowledge and speak to the diverse ways mindfulness can align with a range of cultural and religious identities. This flexibility not only broadens the applicability of the intervention but also empowers participants to shape their mindfulness practice in ways that feel authentic and personally meaningful.

Virtual or Hybrid Groups

The Facilitator's Guide to MSCC is written to give facilitators flexibility in deciding how to offer MSCC to caregivers: in person, virtually or a hybrid of the two. The goal in making this decision is to determine how to best allow caregiver participants to gather in an accessible space that is safe, both physically and psychologically. Depending on the needs, demands, and preferences of the caregivers, facilitators may invite participants to gather in person, or via virtual, remote connection, or in a hybrid format combining both in-person and virtual formats.

Ideally, all formats would allow caregivers to feel comfortable physically and emotionally in surroundings that are quiet and peaceful, free of distractions. In practice, facilitators will use the best resources they have available to promote shared learning of MSCC. If caregivers' organizations or institutions do not have physical space to offer, then virtual or remote access might be the only alternative. When virtual access connects caregivers and facilitators it is imperative for the facilitator to determine what technical platform produces the privacy required.

For example, licensed mental health professionals will be required to use HIPAA-compliant platform with a Business Associates Agreement and will need to be competent in the ethics of telehealth. All facilitators using virtual access need to know how to use the security measures within the platform they use for access.

Further, when virtual or remote access is the choice, the caregivers need a device (e.g., mobile phone, iPad, personal computer, or laptop) with the software or platform installed that allows access. Facilitators who select virtual formats will need to decide how to prepare participants for technological access prior to the first MSCC session. Below are additional considerations in weighing the advantages and disadvantages of each format.

In-person delivery of MSCC can be convenient for caregivers who are already physically gathered, perhaps due to shared employment or mission. For example, health care workers who are employed by the same organization (e.g., nurses, therapists, physicians, staff). They may choose to use the lunch hour as a time to hold MSCC sessions. Some participants state that they found in-person gatherings as one way to deepen their connection and shared experiences. Others state that the intensity of sharing private thoughts and feelings in person is best moderated, for them, through technology that increases their need for perceived control (e.g., I could arrange my camera and lighting to only show an outline of me rather than my full face). In-person groups are preferred by people who are not comfortable with learning or utilizing technology. Virtual or hybrid groups tend to be preferred by caregivers who find technology a more convenient, time-saving way to access MCSS. They may prefer technological access to spending time and energy driving to a different location.

Typically, group norms described during both verbal and written consent include the agreement to keep personal and private health information received in group. In all delivery formats, facilitators must consider their methods for obtaining informed written consent and for maintaining confidentiality and privacy. Prior to the first MSCC session, participants provide the facilitator with an emergency contact person and consent to contact this individual in case the participant has an emergency during a group session. During informed consent, participants are informed that the facilitator will contact emergency services as needed to maintain the health and well-being of the group and each participant. In virtual and hybrid groups, participants agree to keep their virtual space free of people and animals who are not part of the MSCC group. Such privacy includes keeping the audio and visual space private. Further, with virtual access, participants agree to keep their cameras on during the session and the microphones muted unless they are speaking. Further, they agree that they will not audiotape or videotape sessions.

Section 2—Managing the Process of Mindful Self-Care for Clinicians and Caregivers

Facilitating Group Sessions

In this section, elements of facilitating group sessions are covered. They are intended as considerations as opposed to strict directives. We respect the fact that facilitators are experienced in their way of teaching mindfulness and have evolved their own styles and preferences. We are sharing what we have likewise learned through experience, which is also ever evolving. We offer considerations to think about when making decisions about the structure, process, and norms involved in facilitating the process of MSCC. We expect facilitators will choose how best to use MSCC materials to fit their style, the makeup of their group, the setting, and time constraints. Structures in MSCC may be seen as canals shaping flow, rather than dams blocking ease and spontaneity.

Generic Group Session Structure

Although varied in themes, each MSCC session contains the same (or nearly the same) basic structure. The session structure has been designed to facilitate experiential learning, balancing conceptual explanations and imagery over a 90-minute session, with in-vivo practice. A special role is given to engaging the senses. There are several broad tasks for MSCC facilitators to: (1) teach usable skills, (2) develop group process to support and stimulate learning/experimentation, and (3) engage a variety of the senses in the experience of mindfulness. These tasks are woven into the texture of each session.

Sessions are 90 minutes in length. There are six sessions plus two supplemental sessions. Supplemental sessions are designed as optional sessions that can be included to provide opportunities for participants who may have missed sessions to review content and to reinforce prior learning, and provide a review for all participants. Ideally, participants are invited to attend all eight sessions; Sessions 1 through 6 provide the fundamental experiences. For facilitators, each MSCC session has an introduction, a detailed session guide, and a quick guide summary (good for quick reference time-keeping). For facilitators and participants, there are session summaries, handouts, in vivo exercises, and access to the session's meditations through audio or video formats. Photographs and music help set a mood.

Each session begins with a brief description of a learning aim that relates the theme to stages of mindfulness development in the context of caregiving. The text is structured to allow participants to follow the typical stages of learning whereby they: (a) begin to understand the rationale for skills, (b) acquire the skills, and (c) generalize the skills over situations, time, and in response to their own emotions, thoughts, and behaviors.

In addition to tying the skills of mindfulness to the development of full mindful practices, the sessions are also structured to connect mindful practice to the experience of caregiving. Within each session facilitators encourage participants to talk about how their skill development is influencing their experience of providing care to others.

Session 1 begins with introductions of group members and sets up the overall goals of learning, administrative structures, group norms, and group process. All sessions include weekly Check-In's where participants share experiences from the week prior and experiment with mindfulness practices. This gives participants a chance to learn by describing their experiences, hearing from others, and to learn from facilitator feedback. The length of time will depend on the size of the group.

Facilitators, with in-person groups, may find that sitting in a circle enhances group engagement and sense of inclusion. Setting the norm for virtual groups for cameras to be on during group and microphones turned off when the participant is not speaking fosters engagement and reduces distraction. Participants can be asked to share by simply opening the floor to volunteers, or can be asked to share by going around the group in order. The latter method has the advantage of efficiency and of lessening the pressure on participants when calling attention to themselves.

After the group starts, a Mindful Pause comes next. This is a brief, informal mindfulness exercise that moves participants into an experience of mindfulness in a way that is often more accessible than longer meditations. A Mindful Pause sets the stage for the session's experiential learning priority.

Each session also has a content theme, and a portion of the group dedicated to conveying information, denoted in the session guide as Highlighting Session Theme.

This section is designed to provide participants with brief sections of theoretical content about mindfulness to help them better conceptualize mindfulness and self-care. It is not meant to be a lecture per se, but rather a brief didactic section designed to encourage a higher level of understanding of mindfulness within the context of providing care.

A portal provides access to a photograph (for each Session) that can be used for groups that meet in person or virtually. Each session also includes two mindfulness meditation practices: Mindful Movement and Stationary Practices. These are introductions to formal (vs. brief informal) mindfulness practices that range from 10 to 15 minutes. All mindfulness meditation practices have audio or video recordings included, so everyone can access them via the portal. Alternatively, facilitators can use the transcripts as a guide and lead the meditations in their own voice and adapt as appropriate during the session to fit the setting or population of the group.

Meditations are followed by a Brief Inquiry and Sharing in which participants are asked about their experience of them. A few elicited comments are generally enough to capture aspects of the meditation experience. Each session ends with a Summary and Suggestions for Formal and Informal Practices During the Week. The session theme is summarized and related to the various parts of the session that support it. The suggestion is made for participants to select formal and informal (from the handout "Mindfulness in Daily Life" or the Mindful Pause) practices to try out on their own with the aid of audio/video recordings available to them. While facilitators encourage regular practice of MSCC exercises, participants are not given specific "homework" assignments for the week. Instead, facilitators encourage practice and engagement with the material as the caregivers choose. Caregivers are encouraged to craft their own personalized practice of MSCC. Prescribing all the practices presented is not given as an expectation. We expect the best and most engaged learning to come from choices participants make based on what attracts them and the time constraints in their often-busy lives. Participants usually gravitate toward a few practices they find personally useful.

Time Management of Sessions

Similar to facilitating other types of educational or experiential groups, time management of sessions is important. Each MSCC session includes numerous segments, and management of the time of each one can be a challenge. In the generic session structure give above, the following might give an idea about the timing of the segments: Check-In (10–15 minutes, depending on group size), Mindful Pause (5 minutes), Highlighting Session Theme (10–15 minutes), Mindful Practices (10–15 minutes each), Brief Inquiry following the practices (5 minutes), Summary and Suggestions (10 minutes). Total time comes close to 1 and ½ hours.

A mechanistic time structure, however, may not respond well to the organic nature of a group's living process and needs. A facilitator needs to be free to shape time to what she or he consider most impactful on learning. For example, the Check-In is a rich chance for reinforcing participant experiences and highlighting the significance of such experiences that the participant may not yet recognize. Lengthening the Check-In and shortening another segment may be a constructive decision. This is why facilitation experience in teaching mindfulness is so important. It tends to grow skills in conducting a session that are nimbler than rigid. By being familiar with a session's parts, a facilitator can more easily stay mindful of what is happening in the group and intuitively steer their time management. The key is participant intensity of engagement in the process of discovery, excitement of learning, and session flow. It is recommended that sessions keep to the 90-minute length, given the time pressures on caregivers and the time they feel they can spare away from caregiving. As facilitators become more familiar and experienced with the process and content of MSCC, they will learn how to move content around based on the needs, energy and momentum of their caregiver group.

How to Prepare for Sessions

Along with time management of sessions, what follows are considerations to think about as you prepare for your MSCC sessions.

1. Use your readings, personal experience, and empathic imagination to center your awareness in the world of the caregiver. Although the sessions can be used more generically, they were designed for the blessings and burdens of caregiving.
2. Become familiar with session materials. Expand from a surface acquaintance to a feel for each session's experience through the eyes and hearts of your participant caregivers. Said another way, develop an understanding a sessions external and internal logic. How (externally and internally) does the session flow from segment to segment, exercise to exercise? Does the generic session design, the way sessions relate to each other, and the flow of each session make sense? Did the content and process connect the participants to each other and to their own individual experiences?
3. Decide how you want to guide the meditations in each session. You can lead the practice yourself in your own words, inspired by the audios/videos/transcripts, or you can simply read the transcripts. You also have the option of relying on the audios or videos played directly in the sessions, or combinations of the above. You might find that you begin one way and transition to another as you gain experience with the MSCC protocol.
4. Decide on what aspects of a session to prioritize, depending on your assessment of the group and what they are drawn to and might profit from. If participants seem to be enlivened and learning from the Check-In experience, other session parts may be modified or shortened to make room for it, if more time is needed. In general, facilitator-centered talks may be shortened to accommodate time for the more experiential parts. Each group will differ in what best impacts them and motivates their week-to-week experiments with mindfulness and self-care skills. There is no strict agenda for which practices become important to a participant if inspiration to choose and adopt some mindful self-care practice as one's own.
5. Imagery, metaphors, pictures, poetry, and stories all have a place in learning and evoking mindfulness. Although we use prose descriptions in teaching, prose tends

to lack the vibrancy and embodiment of these other media. A good metaphor is often remembered longer and more vividly than a prose statement of the same idea. There can be too much of a good thing, however. Facilitators are encouraged to select but a few to use from these media to capture main points rather than overload the session with too many. The session content is designed with this in mind.

6. Remember, above all, that the MSCC material must come *through* the facilitator – you and your manner and presence and attunement are the real catalysts for the sessions' impact. Next to that, the building and fostering of group cohesion and the experience over time of practicing mindfulness, contribute to the efficacy of MSCC. Recall and harness the power of groups and of community.

Preparing Yourself as the Person Who Is a Facilitator

Formal education in mental health, mentored experience in facilitating groups and practice of mindfulness form the bedrock of facilitating MSCC. Next, there is the foundational review and understanding of the processes and protocol within *A Guide,* as described above and in the sections on how to use this book. Yet, we hypothesize that there is still more preparation needed.

We recommend that you create your own "ritual" or routine ahead of each group session. This routine involves preparing yourself - your presence and your mindset, and your attitudes. We wish to convey that this personal preparation may help you "show up" with a presence that facilitates social connection, psychological safety, acceptance, awareness, and curiosity. This "facilitator presence" is hard to convey and again the preparation for it will vary by facilitator.

We encourage you to figure out what works for you. Of use might be several **Facilitator's Contemplations** as one way to nurture "mediations of the heart" that inspire the "words" you need, in the moment, to foster this mindful process among you, the participants and the group as a whole.

Preparing the Space: A Word on Seating and Lighting

Just as the tone and presence of the facilitator shape the group experience, the physical environment in which a mindfulness group takes place also mirrors and reinforces that atmosphere. Chairs arranged in circles or curves communicate a different group connection than those arranged in rows. It is best when participants face and see each other. Lighting that is soft rather than glaring (like so many neon ceiling lights) communicates a more relaxed environment. Use of pictures or flowers brings a kind of liveliness and warmth that a room empty of anything, but furniture does not. Facilitators are intentional about selecting and including images or objects. Icons associated with a particular spiritual approach would only be included if those icons match the setting and participant backgrounds. The intent here is to create a room filled with presence and to offer safety and inclusiveness. On the portal and ahead of each session, we authors offer you a possible image to consider. Music is a subtle but powerful force in creating an atmosphere that calms and invites mindful openness to one's experiences. Facilitators might consider selections of soft meditative music at the beginning of sessions as participants enter the meeting space and settle in.

Protecting Participant Safety and Autonomy

A fundamental foundation of MSCC is the promotion of psychological safety to allow participants to take "risks" and try new things, even when some discomfort is present or could follow. The risks mainly involve exposing themselves to new experiences and being willing to share them. Safety comes from being in a supportive, nonjudgmental (accepting) environment in which one is always free to choose what one will do or share without coercive pressure. Facilitators set the tone for safety and autonomy by establishing and maintaining group norms at the beginning and leading through invitations to explore and experiment.

To keep its mission clear, MSCC distinguishes between training and education of participants in developing mindful skills via experience versus engaging in psychotherapy or counseling via treatment. A therapist or counselor may offer direct guidance or advice regarding a problem, whereas a MSCC facilitator stays in an invitational spirit, encouraging a "try and see" or experiential approach to learning MSCC. Participants are asked to be open and flexible toward expectations rather than searching for or expecting a particular outcome. Although mindfulness practices have been shown in the literature to offer many benefits to participants (see Section 1 above), MSCC facilitators encourage a focus on the process of learning and practice rather than a focus on outcomes or results. In this way, participants stay open and are encouraged to see themselves as resourceful, not deficient in deciding how to best care for themselves. In the same way, participants are asked not to advice each other, but, rather, to listen and accept what is shared in the group. Thus, the MSCC atmosphere is not oriented toward "fixing" the person; it is bent toward fostering freedom to learn in one's own way.

Clarifying boundaries and securing confidentiality are also pillars of safety and autonomy. Each of us cultivates a sense of personal boundary connected to our feeling of integrity. What we choose to share about ourselves publicly and what we choose to hold in private are central to feeling secure in our boundaries. Psychological violation is often felt when another judges or manipulates what is shared publicly and when the private space is invaded in some way uninvited. Again, MSCC facilitators set the norms for how boundaries are treated and respected. One important way this is done is to have group members agree not to judge, advise, or share what another shares in the group with others in or outside the group. Securing this norm from Session 1 onward creates an atmosphere of greater safety and, thus, an atmosphere that inspires curiosity and risk-taking. Participants are also reminded that confidentiality cannot be guaranteed in a group setting; therefore, facilitators encourage participants to consider thoughtfully what they wish to share.

One other way facilitators set a tone of safety and support is modelling empathic listening and responding. When a participant shares personal facts or experiences, facilitative listening means reflecting what was heard in a nonjudgmental way. This does not rule out the role of reflecting important aspects of a person's reported experience for emphasis and reinforcement. What is key is that great care be taken to avoid critical responses which presume a right and wrong statement or experience. Participants learn as the facilitator models these types of interactions and observes the effects of facilitative listening. The point is to support experiment and discovery, not to search for the "right" solution as defined by someone else.

It is important to hold to these norms outside of group sessions as well. Group members may seek out each other to offer mutual support in their practice. They may meet for coffee before or after the group, for example. Participants may seek out the facilitator for questions. These are all positive ways to reinforce one's practice. Nevertheless, it is helpful to remind the group that support and protection of boundaries goes on outside as well as inside group sessions. If groups are conducted virtually, participants might choose to exchange email addresses to stay in contact. These practices, however, are done at the discretion and initiative of the individual participant, and facilitators should intentionally strive to protect the privacy, autonomy, and boundaries of participants.

Principles of Facilitative Communication

A facilitator has several key roles in each MSCC session. In this section, we will underscore what most experienced facilitators already may know. Facilitators create a special atmosphere for learning mindfulness and self-care skills, using a form of inquiry as a way of guiding and reinforcing learning. The key is the fostering of curiosity to experiment.

Imagine taking a seat in a group room with a facilitator in front. As the group begins, you are quietly taking note of the atmosphere this facilitator is creating. Is the facilitator's tone open and friendly or closed and strict? Does the facilitator extend herself to the group or hold back as an expert to be followed? Does she respond to participants' responses in a manner that expects the right answer? Does learning seem centered in the authority of the facilitator or in the experiences of the participant? Do you feel safe to explore or pressured to get recognized for being correct?

The MSCC atmosphere is set up to inspire learning through participants' willingness to explore and experiment to learn by direct experience rather than typical didactics or lecturing. Experiential learning and experimentation require a special tone and presence of the facilitator. The tone is an expression of mindfulness attitudes, which include kindness, openness to all shared experiences, nonjudgment, and a patience that gives room for experiences to occur. This tone initiates a kind of holding environment that ensures psychological safety and the primacy of self-care for each participant.

The presence emitted by the facilitator models a way of mindful being and of approaching MSCC themes. A way of describing this presence is that it expresses comfort, trust, and openness to the facilitator's own current experiences as well as to what participants are experiencing. This presence is embodied. That is, it comes out of present awareness of not just one's thoughts, but one's sensations, feelings, and bodily states. Over time, this presence is the result of a congruence between what the facilitator does or says and what the facilitator is authentically feeling. Part of the openness of MSCC is the absence of the expectation that all group members will develop the same set of mindfulness practices. The facilitator invites not only the exploratory experiences of participants, but also the practices each participant chooses to adopt. The atmosphere promotes the message of "Try these experiments, play with these practices, and discover which ones best fit your self-care."

Facilitation of MSCC leans on the skill of inquiry to strengthen participant skills. Skills include being able to mindfully attend to one's present experience, to be able to sense the difference between direct embodied experience and "thinking about" ones' experience, and to have insight into how different ways of responding to one's experience produce different outcomes. Inquiry is expressed through a facilitator's presence as well as words. The primary inquiry question that may be used throughout MSCC sessions is "What did you notice?" This is asked in genuine curiosity and without expectation of a right answer. Yet, it is a question difficult for the beginner to answer specifically. There is a difference between "I noticed how nervous I felt at first in the meditation" and "I noticed I felt tense in my shoulders in the beginning of the meditation." The question is asking the person to separate a direct experience (tense in the shoulders) from general thoughts about the experience (nervous). This is the first step in learning mindfulness: to differentiate nonverbal sensations and feelings from verbal concepts and judgements about them.

The facilitator may shape feedback to show how sensations and judgments are separate experiences. To the person reporting feeling nervous, the facilitator might ask, "How could you tell you were feeling nervous?" This might prompt a more specific description of an experience ("My chest was tight, making it hard to breathe.") To the person giving a specific description, the facilitator might simply note that experience ("You found your shoulders were tight as you began the meditation.") Such feedback is like holding a mirror up to the participant's experience, making it stand out.

Feedback is what the facilitator selects to emphasize (for example, the difference between an experience and thoughts about the experience). By responding with genuine interest, a facilitator also validates experiences that the participant might minimize or take as unimportant. Too often, group members may judge their experiences as insignificant because they are beginners and not experts.

Inquiry or Socratic questioning with dialogue is a kind of opportunistic teaching. It includes invitations to "tell me more" or to ask for specifics to flesh out clear experiences reported. The more specific the descriptions, the more likely the person is to get close to his or her experiences in a mindful way. Other inquiry reflections or questions may try to evoke insight into how one's way of responding to an experience may determine differing outcomes. Participants might discover, for example, that uncharacteristically allowing, accepting, and breathing into a stress reaction keeps it from intensifying.

Facilitators listen for possible connections within a person's reported experience and may ask, "How might this experience be relevant to your daily life?" "How might this practice be used in your role as a caregiver." Such questions help participants to generalize their discoveries from the group to life. This type of question may be asked when it is clear that a person has discovered a mindful response through one of the meditations or exercises. Hearing a facilitator's response and feedback to one's answer to an inquiry has profound learning effects. We are clearer about our experiences when expressed out loud and when validated by another as important. Inquiry's invitation to share experiences ensures they are not simply left to one's private thoughts about the experience. For more exposure to the power of inquiry or Socratic dialogue, see the chapter on inquiry in *Mindfulness-Based Cognitive Therapy for Depression* by Segal, Williams, and Teasdale (2013) and *Dialogues for Discovery* by Padesky and Kennerley (2023).

Sensitivity to hdividual Participant Issues

Acknowledging Participant Differences

Group members show up with a variety of interpersonal styles, hopes, expectations, and possible mental health vulnerabilities. These are generally manageable if anticipated and monitored as part of a facilitator's mindful way of being present. We introduce some of the unique ways that participants are present in MSCC groups.

Interpersonal Styles

People differ in their comfort level in new, social settings and in their style of expression. The MSCC session structure and process help manage the flow of participant participation. For example, some individuals may tend to be highly dominant or quiet if left to their own preferences of interaction. The MSCC session structure intentionally builds opportunities for everyone in the group to have a chance to express their experience. The Check-In is such an example. In this session phase, the facilitator asks everyone to take a turn sharing, either by opening the floor or by going systematically around the group circle. Yet in other session parts (like inquiry following a mindful pause or meditation), a few responses are usually requested by the facilitator. A more socially dominant or talkative person may volunteer each time, whereas the quieter person may not volunteer. In this case, where there seem to be the same people taking the lead in responding, a facilitator might choose to gently ask a quieter person directly for their response. This works well when a person prefers to be asked for their input, feeling that volunteering is too presumptuous. Attending to a person's reaction to these invitations gives a clue as to their comfort level with speaking and sharing. Honoring the signals from their comfort level informs future decisions about such invitations to share responses. Handling participant responses with care, curiosity, and validation usually promotes group engagement. It can also be helpful after one individual shares to invite other group members to respond, and this can help facilitate conversation and engagement that feels more interactive. Other sections in this book will discuss strategies for managing group sessions completed virtually, but in general, interpersonal styles and comfort levels for participants on Zoom may be different from person. Additional prompting may be needed to facilitate conversation when groups are virtual, participants are on mute, and there are fewer opportunities for informal interactions or responding.

Hopes and Expectations

Ideally, people choose to come to MSCC sessions with an open attitude and broad hopes that the skills they learn will make a positive difference in their lives. This is a generally hopeful, try-and-see attitude. Openness ushers in an expectation that learning new skills comes gradually and with practice. Yet some will come to MSCC with strict expectations for specific outcomes, lacking the more ideal flexibility, or perhaps with some level of skepticism. These styles may be associated with less comfort in experimenting or "going with the flow" of learning experiences. The inflexible expectation may obstruct learning mindfulness, which is itself grounded in an attitude of openness to whatever experience brings.

Sessions in MSCC begin with the attempt to facilitate and encourage loosely held expectations and exploratory curiosity. The facilitator continually suggests, "let's see what happens. Let's note that what happens may differ by person, place, time, and other contexts or histories." As participants respond to various exercises and meditations, a facilitator may hear the struggle of overstriving or a quickness to be self-critical in the face of various obstacles. Using reflection and feedback, a facilitator may separately provide feedback on the person's reported experience as well as highlight specific self-critical judgment (as "judgment"). Later in the session, there will be opportunities to draw attention to the challenge of accepting one's experiences while noticing thoughts of judgment. In this way, participants are invited to see the difference between our usual judging mind and observing mind. In the Summary part at the session's end, another opportunity may exist to normalize the struggle to observe and not fuse with critical judgments.

Opportunistic teaching takes advantage of what is heard directly from participants in this way. The open and accepting attitude of the facilitator models a contrasting approach to a person's reactive self-judgment. Further, the facilitator is modeling a mindful manner that participants can take away into their lives.

Mental Health Issues

Some people come to MSCC with hopes or expectations that participating in this group may help alleviate various mental health problems or symptoms they currently or previously have experienced. Mindfulness instruction is getting broad exposure in the public media as a way to treat various mental disorders or simply to mitigate against experiences of anxiety and stress. Coming to MSCC with concerns over symptoms of mental disorders, some caregivers may overly focus on what mindfulness can do to alleviate troubling symptoms. For example, if an individual is struggling with panic attacks, there may be a temptation to focus on how mindfulness techniques can help prevent or reduce panic attacks specifically. While it may be true that certain aspects of mindfulness training, perhaps breathing exercises or grounding techniques, may help with panic attacks, MSCC is not designed to function as a specific treatment for any mental disorder. Facilitators should aim to clarify this in early sessions and encourage caregivers to differentiate this group from other specific mental health treatments for diagnosed disorders.

Given the possible mix of expectations and mental health backgrounds, facilitators may also be concerned about the possible adverse effects of mindful exercises. Specifically, facilitators may ask if mindfulness exercises and meditation practices can exacerbate a mental disorder rather than help with it. The answer is that adverse effects are only recently being evaluated in general psychotherapy literature, and more research is needed. In the absence of a randomized clinical trial of MSCC designed to evaluate adverse events, our best answer is yes, it is possible that MSCC, and other mindful interventions, could intensify preexisting physical, psychiatric and psychological conditions for certain individuals. This underscores the value of mental health assessments of suspected at-risk people and the attuned discernment of experienced facilitators. This is based on our own experience in clinical settings and the considerations below.

When Kabat-Zinn (2013) developed Mindfulness-Based Stress Reduction, he worked with people with both medical pain and psychological symptoms of depression and anxiety. For many individuals, mindfulness training has been therapeutic. There are those, however, who can experience a worsening of symptoms (Treleaven, 2018). Learning to turn toward and observe inner experiences that one usually tries to avoid often initially increases discomfort. It is easy to assume (falsely) that it is mindfulness practice that causes heightened distress. In fact, it is part of the learning process. As one directly faces previously avoided experiences such as stress or anxiety, this exposure lays the foundation to practice acceptance in a new way. Over time, mindful awareness and acceptance of uncomfortable experiences usually deescalates the experience of stress, allowing room for further calming practices like deep breathing. At the same time, for some, closing one's eyes and focusing on direct feelings can trigger rapidly escalating anxiety that may feel intolerable. The effort to force practice under these conditions creates a vicious circle of intensifying distress. If a facilitator sees a participant caught in this pattern, there is a kind of "first aid" that can help: opening the eyes, shifting the body, looking around the room, and slowing, deepening breathing are all ways to stop the exercise and shift attention away from threatening feelings. For individuals who have this experience, a different mindfulness practice may be more approachable, like moving meditation or informal mindful pauses in the day.

A history of trauma and/or a current diagnosis of a trauma disorder may predispose some individuals to the kind of symptom-triggering described above. Research has found that the prevalence of exposure to traumatic events is higher than previously assumed (van der Kolk, 2014) and experiencing trauma can have negative impacts on both physical and mental health. Traumatic memories and associated distress can emerge from not only focusing on stress aroused in a mindfulness practice, but from focusing on body areas that were a part of the trauma event. Sexual trauma memories can be elicited, for example, by a Body Scan focusing on one's pelvic region (Treleaven, 2018).

Although MSCC facilitators may not necessarily be mental health practitioners, it is important for facilitators to understand and be aware of the range of possible reactions participants may have to mindfulness exercises and meditations. There are several possible courses of action to mitigate the risks described earlier. People with mental health diagnoses can participate in MSCC training as long as they understand that MSCC is not a substitute for formal treatment of specific mental health disorder(s). Ideally, such participants would discuss the potential advantages and disadvantages of MSCC with their treating provider prior to participation. (Note that this assumes that such participants are engaged in adjunctive treatment with a licensed mental health provider). Overall, a facilitator is on firmer ground when promoting self-care as not only an outcome of training but as a practice to engage in throughout training. This is the message to pay mindful attention to one's comfort as well as distress tolerance and to act with gentle kindness toward oneself always.

Resources for Facilitators and Caregiver Participants

There are numerous learning and practice resources available to facilitators and participants in MSCC. Books, videos, and meditation supplies abound. This section will mention but a few that are particularly relevant to MSCC and may help facilitators deepen their understanding and practice. (Note that the reference section of MSCC is more comprehensive, but the listing below is provided to "launch" facilitation of MSCC).

Books

Mindful Caregiving

Abbit, L. (2019). *The conscious caregiver: A mindful approach to caring for your loved one without losing yourself.* New York: Simon and Shuster.

- A book that nicely parallels themes in MSCC around the use and purpose of mindfulness in caregiving.

Mindfulness Skills

Kabat-Zinn, J. (1990). *Full catastrophe living: Using the wisdom of your body and mind to face stress, pain, and illness.* New York: Bantom Books.

- This is perhaps the classic elaboration of Mindfulness-Based Stress Reduction and is full of colorful examples of issues people bring to mindfulness training programs. Its spirit informs much of MSCC.

Rosenbaum, E. (2015). *The heart of mindfulness-based stress reduction: A MBSR guide for clinicians and clients.* New York: Springer.

- A clear and systematic presentation of MBSR by one who was there at the beginning of this renowned format for teaching mindfulness.

Segal, Z. V., Williams, J. M. G., & Teasdale, J. D. (2013). *Mindfulness-based cognitive therapy for depression.* New York: Guilford Press.

- Modelled in large part on MBSR and combined with cognitive behavioral therapy for depression, this work presents clear descriptions of its 8-session format with transcripts, supporting research, and meditation practices. It has a particularly useful chapter on the art of inquiry for facilitators, and it is also tailored to participants who suffer from depression

Lumpkin, M. (2014). *Into the music of the world: Living life mindfully*. North Charlston: CreateSpace.

- In it, there is a rich description of the various ways informal, daily mindfulness can be experienced. It has a chapter on therapeutic mindfulness, which lays out the principles of how mindfulness positively alters one's handling of stress and suffering

Mindful Meditation as Part of a Christian Culture/Tradition

Artress, L. (1995). *Walking a sacred path. Rediscovering the labyrinth as a spiritual tool*. New York: The Berkley Publishing Group.

Brooke, A. (1978). *Hidden in plain sight. The practice of Christian meditation*. Nashville: The Upper Room.

Facilitating Mindfulness with Inquiry

Segal, Z. V., Williams, J. M. G., & Teasdale, J. D. (2013). *Mindfulness-based cognitive therapy for depression* (second ed.). New York: Guilford Press.

- See the chapter on inquiry.
- Note the special needs of participants who struggle with depression.

Padesky, C. A., & Kennerley, H. (2023). *Dialogues for discovery: Improving psychotherapy's effectiveness*. Oxford: Oxford University Press.

- This entire book explores the wide range of ways inquiry and Socratic questioning can be used to evoke insight into one's inner experiences.

Mindfulness and Trauma

van der Kolk, B. A. (2014). *The body keeps the score: Brain, mind, and body in the healing of trauma*. New York: Viking.

- This book provides a deep dive into the profound impact of trauma and ways (including mindfulness) to therapeutically help trauma survivors.

Treleaven, D. (2018). *Trauma-sensitive mindfulness: Practices for safe and transformative healing*. New York: W.W. Norton & Company.

- This is a book written to sensitize mindfulness facilitators to the possible impact of various mindfulness practices on those with trauma histories.

Meditation Supplies

Numerous online sites offer sales of meditation supplies. Dharma Crafts, Dharma Shop, and Gaia have online stores selling meditation cushions for those who want to sit in that fashion. Bells, gongs, and sound bowls are available for facilitators wishing to use them to mark beginnings and endings of exercises and meditations.

Transition to Part B: Intervention Sessions in Mindful Self-Care for Clinicians and Caregivers

We hope that facilitators now have a sense of the landscape of caregiving, the need for caregiver support, and the rationale for *Mindful Self-Care for Clinicians and Caregivers (MSCC)*, a mindfulness-based intervention to help caregivers access the positive aspects of caregiving, while mitigating its inherent risks. With this background, we proceed to Part B, the heart of the MSCC method and guide. We start with an Interlude to evoke the possible experience of an MSCC participant and facilitator.

> *Facilitator Contemplation: What will help you to be mindfully present, open and curious as your group forms?*

Part B

Intervention Sessions in Mindful Self-Care for Clinicians and Caregivers (MSCC)

Facilitator Note: An Interlude—The MSCC Journey

Below, we reflect on Robert Frost's famous poem, *Stopping by Woods on a Snowy Evening* (Frost, 1923). In it, the farmer-poet is heading home in winter on a horse-pulled sleigh after a day of getting things done. As he heads home, he ceases to think about his to-do list and quietly marvels at the sight of fresh falling snow. His horse, used to getting from here to there without pauses, shakes his harness bells impatiently. Then, for a moment, the farmer-poet stops, looking into the deep woods filling with snow, savoring the loveliness of it all. Just for a second—then he remembers his duties and yanks himself back with thoughts of obligations yet to keep and "miles to go before I sleep" and rest.

Stopping by Woods on a Snowy Evening
By Frost (1923)

Whose woods these are I think I know.
His house is in the village though;
He will not see me stopping here
To watch his woods fill up with snow.

My little horse must think it queer
To stop without a farmhouse near
Between the woods and frozen lake
The darkest evening of the year.

He gives his harness bells a shake
To ask if there is some mistake.
The only other sound's the sweep
Of easy wind and downy flake.

The woods are lovely, dark and deep,
But I have promises to keep,
And miles to go before I sleep,
And miles to go before I sleep.

The world of caregivers is full of obligations and the sense of being on-call for those under their care. For many, this is not a detached sense of duty but an impassioned responsibility to "take care of." Many with impassioned responsibility too

Mindful Self-Care for Clinicians and Caregivers. https://doi.org/10.1016/B978-0-443-29821-9.00004-2

often do. Living on call in automatic pilot can become the heavy trudge of so far to go "before I sleep" with little time to nourish oneself.

Like Frost, a part of us seeks pauses in life to stop, come into the fresh present, open, and touch what is inside and around us. This is the gift of mindfulness. It is a gift with a vision and various practices to refresh and rebalance caregiving lives under pressure. Its vision is a way of appreciating a life beyond lists of tasks and constant vigilance. It restores a kind of living connection to oneself and the surrounding world, often absent in the numbed existence of constant thinking and rushing. It offers a way, a set of skills, to reroute spiraling stress and to find vitalizing refreshment in taking in life's woods filling up with snow. It balances other-care with self-care. It fosters a kind of listening to ourselves to more lovingly hear what is needed under the usual mental-emotional noise. It sensitizes a kind of attention to others in our world, particularly the care-person, when a moment of listening leads to a renewal of connection.

Perhaps the best way to describe the path of mindfulness for caregivers is to allow a caregiver to take the microphone and speak from experiences before, in, and after going through a series of sessions on Mindful Self-Care for Clinicians and Caregivers. Here is Tobias in his own voice.

Tobias

I am an emergency department (ED) nurse (RN) and have been for the past 11 years of my career. On top of the usual variety of crises, COVID-19 knocked us all for a loop at work. But I am still here and have survived—still loving what I do. Not long ago, I was afraid that my compassion was collapsing under the strain of caring for so many patients who were so sick—and, I now know, not just the strain itself, but the way I was handling the strain.

The time of downward crashing strain was a gathering storm of long work weeks, overcrowded wards, and greater numbers of deaths. All of us in the ED no longer walked; we ran. COVID was the new predator, and its attacks left us feeling helpless many times. We watched and held the hands of dying patients isolated from their families. Heart-breaking. I remember going home after a long day and looking at loads of undone chores I was too tired to do. I would crash and wake up to rush off to work. I had no real life outside the hospital. Friends and family (parents and sister) were on hold. To make things worse, I was not able to say no to the coworkers who need coverage or supervisors pressing for overtime. I was in a race that had a life of its own. I was always tired or wired from coffee, energy drinks, and fast food. Looking back, I was living in a mix of being always on-edge while sinking into lower and lower morale.

Inside, I was tense. My edginess could spiral into irritability and, unfortunately, temper bursts. My head was always buzzing nonstop. I couldn't stop thinking about my longer and longer list of things to get done. I was not at my best, adding more pressure on myself.

One day, I noticed, as I was getting coffee, an announcement of a new opportunity on the staff bulletin board. It was a series of some sort of training meetings called

Mindful Self-Care for Clinicians and Caregivers. I thought, "Who has the time?" Then I noticed it was at the end of my shift for a little over an hour each time and once a week. It wasn't just a relaxation session. I already knew about those techniques. It seemed to teach skills to use during the day to better balance and even out. Okay, why not? Let's see what's behind this mindfulness thing I've been hearing about for a while. So I went.

Now that I have gone through all eight sessions, here's what stands out to me 6 months later. It's hard to capture all the phases I went through learning what I did. I can say that what I learned happened gradually and with a lot of encouragement from my facilitators and group members. Maybe it was because I had to unlearn the old familiar ways I thought about and reacted to things, emotions, and thoughts in my life.

The group of 10 people was a mix I didn't expect. My group members included an internist, several nurses, a rehabilitation therapist, three at-home caregivers of their chronically ill spouses or parents, and an elementary school teacher. Our different backgrounds soon blended into surprisingly common experiences—the heavy load of caregiving that seemed to swallow our daily lives. In each session, we began by talking about our experiences playing around with different aspects of mindfulness (as we understood it) and its practices. This, quite frankly, kept me inspired by hearing of other's discoveries and, sometimes, struggles.

From the first session on, we jumped into practicing and experiencing mindfulness. It was not at all academic as I half expected. The very first question blew me away, "How do you know you are being mindful?" I could say that I although mindfulness was about calming myself by not worrying so much. But I soon found out I just didn't know. I wanted its benefits (calmer) but did not know what being mindful felt like. Through some session exercises, I did recognize mindlessness! It was the state I'd been living in! It was a tense body, frantic emotions, and a hyperactive mind always thinking and always talking to or at myself, criticizing or complaining. Wow. Then over the next three sessions, we were given exercises and short guided meditations to step into the shallow end of mindful state and gradually go deeper. It was inspiring that this could be done, but not always easy. For example, I tried to focus only on body sensations in one of the meditations by fighting back my thoughts, trying to make my mind quiet. But I learned that fighting thoughts only made them bigger! I thought I'll never learn to do this. Our teachers understood this and said everyone goes through this, encouraging us to relax, not fight our minds, and just try "just noticing." That this noticing is the beginning of mindfulness—this stepping back to look at what's happening in and around us without the old jumping into mind talk.

In each session, we were learning how to stop and pause for a moment to tune into our breaths, our eyes and ears, our body's feelings and sensations. We were guided through sitting meditations and moving meditations. In between sessions, we were asked to explore and experiment with the exercises and practices that most attracted us, not being pressured to do more homework than we felt up to. Short practice times in the day were just as valuable as longer meditations. We were encouraged to practice to really learn mindfulness, but we were left free to choose what to work on. Group members often tried different practices from each other, yet we shared our experiments in group, learning about ones we may not have tried. I tried out the guided recordings they gave us, finding I really liked the Body Scan. I tried pausing a few times in my day to stop my usual rush and notice how my body felt and how I was breathing. I am a multitasker, so a few times a day I just focused my attention on only one thing at a time. I also liked taking little breaks at the hospital to just stop outside and see the sunshine on things. There were certainly days I forgot to do any of this, but I learned to feel good about times I did remember.

I have to admit that simply tuning into my body's stress sensations and pausing to breathe helped me calm down. At other times, just focusing on something pleasurable (like savoring my coffee or watching a kid play in the waiting room) dissolved much of my strain. I felt I was being given a special secret that is simple to see if you knew what to look for.

A big test of my beginning mindfulness skills was using it to directly deal with stress and anxiety in a new, and hopefully, better way. First, I had to see what I normally didn't see—my usual way of reacting to stress! Before I knew about mindfulness, I focused only on what was outside me pushing my buttons. So many things did. For instance, when too many patients demanded my attention while I had a list of other things to do, I thought, "Why now of all times?" or "Where's the help around here?" or "Why can't patient X for once just be more cooperative?" At the end of the day, I could be edgy, exhausted, or just nervously wired. The day was a blur, a jumble of so many things I seemed to carry around in one big lump inside. Yet, I was learning something in a mindfulness session that sort of surprised me. Most of my stress really came from the way I automatically stoked my own reactions rather than the actual stressor I was reacting to. It was my thoughts about patient X that was feeding my stress, making it bigger. Once I stepped back to notice what was happening, it was a bit embarrassing how obvious it was. I began to accept patient X as he/she was, as well as my reactions.

All the work, learning to pay more attention to more of the moments in my life began to pay off when I wanted to bring mindfulness to my stress. I started by noticing when I was feeling stressed. I usually ignored this before until the stress in me got too big. For me, my neck and shoulder muscles would tighten, my chest felt taut and small, and my breathing was more like gasping. I would then see my stressful thoughts tumbling around and how I was being pulled into them. And I could feel myself gradually going from irritated to pissed off. The way I talked to myself was critical and hard. I learned over time not to judge these reactions, only pause to see and feel them. Then the next step was to stop feeding the stress spirals by the angry way I talked to myself, slowing down, and being more patient with me. I would focus on my breathing, fully feeling the way, it loosened and filled more of my body. Then I would decide on the best next action to take—and move on. It became like putting a bit of space between my tense emotions and the response I really wanted to make to the situation. Rather than chewing someone out, I would wait, feel what was happening, breathe, and either say nothing or something kinder. Man, it took a while to remember to do this in the heat of the moment! And I still go back to my old ways at times, but that's okay. This is a practice for the long haul, and I like the refocused me. When being more mindfully attentive, I felt stress draining out of me more easily, and I felt a new kind of confidence. My path to burnout was taking a turn.

I want to mention a couple of other mindfulness learnings that were kind of bonuses to these sessions. One was on how to be more sensitive to others, taking moments to connect rather than move past. As I began to pay more attention to my own feelings, I was surprised to find I was not as good at attending to other people as I thought I was. Yes, I often heard information or facts, but I didn't stop to take in feelings and real concerns. No wonder some of my patients and co-workers had a sense that I had too little time or too much to do to really hear and connect with them. And honestly, I was getting less and less emotional income from my work as a caregiver. So, one of my practices was to reinvest a little time pausing again to feel myself and feel the other person I was with. This meant stopping some busy work for a moment and turning my focus to what a patient was saying and what feelings were around the saying. I found my patients didn't complain as much to get my attention when the real attention was already there. I would often feel a patient relax when she or he sensed I was hearing them. And my reward? I felt moved by the connection and reminded why I want to give care.

Another bonus was taking seriously my own self-care. In session, we looked at what a balanced life is like and what personal needs and interests (often buried under caregiving others) were crying out for recognition from me. Trench mentality had narrowed my life to work and little left over. When I stepped back to see this, I felt a kind of sadness. What had I done to myself? Then the question was where to start. It was helpful to think of self-care like a pie chart sectioned off into different zones or pieces. In the biological part, I knew I needed to eat better, sleep longer, and return to jogging in my neighborhood. And meeting friends for softball on Saturdays hit both the physical and the social pie parts. A small thing I started doing was sending friendly energy to baristas in my neighborhood coffee bar. It helped start the day in a good way. The psychological zone I chose was changing the way I talked to myself—with less criticism and a softer, kinder tone. This led me to take better care of my time, say no more often to pressure to work longer hours. The spiritual part of the pie I am still exploring. I am considering joining a monthly online group supported by a local bookstore. They select a range of spiritual outlooks and ways to walk a more soulful path in life. None of this was possible until I stopped my "mindless" rat race and listened quietly and patiently to myself. It took a while to feel myself below the noise in my head and numbed out body.

Today, I am calmer and more content in my life. I run less from the past and wait less on the future; the present is where I seek to live and pay attention. In the beginning, mindfulness was in bits and pieces, seen just as a collection of techniques for better coping. But over time, mindfulness has come to mean a whole way of looking at fuller living and ways of caring for this life I have been given. I began to connect the dots of all this overtime. I would practice different meditations and exercises in pausing in the day, often feeling their possibilities in session, but not noticing clear benefit on my own stressed life until the practice seemed to settle into me. It might take two or 3 weeks of experimenting before I would wake up one day and feel my mind clearer, my mood more positive, and my energy smoothing out. I can see why the facilitators warned us against expecting too much too soon rather just playing with the ideas and practices in a looser way.

I have had times I relapsed into my old mindless ways and suffered the consequences. But I just see that as part of this learning path as well. Because of these slips, I am more convinced I need the simple power of these practices. I just pick myself up without fuss and start again. I use reminders like sticky notes on mirrors and my computer. My coffee cup says, "Mindfulness Is Not What You Think!" Another cup says, "You Can't Stop The Waves But You Can Learn to Surf!". I still use the session audios and videos, and worksheets too.

I ran into one of my mindfulness group members the other day. Noreen, an at-home caregiver, was bringing her husband with advanced Parkinson's to the hospital after he fell and broke a wrist. We chatted about our lives since the session and how much we miss it at times. She has been meeting with another session-mate to practice meditation together every other week and to talk about their other practices. She said she does progressive relaxation at night after tough days, and she does the qigong movements to wake up and release tension knots during the day. She felt she's slowed down, particularly when with her husband. Rather than "doing, doing, doing" all the time, she teared up a little when she said she gets a lot out of taking time out to listen, sharing their feelings about their days, and to quietly take in music together. And she was letting friends take her out to lunch at least once a week! She said something interesting, "I take time to check in with my inside self, more often. When I feel sad, I let myself be sad without pushing it away. When I feel uplifted, I let it in like sunshine." We ended up laughing when I reminded her to remember to "savor" the coffee she was holding.

Thank you for letting me share my ongoing trip with mindfulness. I know your trip will have some similar things in it, yet it will be different as well. You, like me, will find certain things that resonate for you and stand out. You will reach for them and take them as your own. Stay inspired.

As Tobias lays out, mindfulness is a rich tapestry with many interwoven threads. It is a way of seeing yourself in your life situation. It is a set of attitudes toward yourself, like patience, kindness, nonjudgment, and willingness to explore rather than grasp at results. It is a way of listening to yourself and others. It is taking time to see and feel your self-care needs. It is meditation practices, taking longer times to strengthen awareness. It is an informal mindfulness practice, like the way you pause from the noise and speed within to breathe, to deeply sense and feel the sensations of yourself and the inviting world around you. It is a way of responding to stress in a more liberating way.

Tobias also reminds us that mindfulness takes hold, deepens, and becomes a part of you *over time.* Learning takes practice and a willingness to just go with the flow and see what happens. You learn to listen to your own preferences about which mindfulness practices fit best for you. For, as the saying goes, all roads lead to Rome.

So, take heart from Tobias, not as a particular model, but as an illustration of how mindfulness can grow into and change your own individual path. For taking care of yourself can be even more challenging than bringing care to another.

A Facilitator's Perspective

Before you encounter the MSCC session guides, you might enjoy a taste of one facilitator's experience as she shaped her work with caregivers in a group she created and ran.

Jan's Journey as a Facilitator of Mindful Self-Care for Clinicians and Caregivers (MSCC)

I remember well Tobias' group– as this was my first time as a MSCC facilitator! Although there is a glow around the experience now, it began with a beginner's anxiety as well as excitement.

I am a nurse working in the same large hospital as Tobias, although we did not know each other at the time. Inspired by my exposure to mindfulness in such workshops, I was curious, would professional caregivers find the same benefits of mindfulness as others? Often formal caregivers recall the increased demands of COVID that grew to a crescendo, yet remain as we have to do more with less. I also wondered, would mixing professionals and informal caregivers work? They have such diverse backgrounds. I know that informal caregivers do not get a respite or a vacation, holiday or not. I wondered if the clinicians would find their similarities with the informal caregivers or focus on their differences? How will caregivers respond? Am I up to what they need

I thought back to my training in mindful practice. Training began with a psychologist experienced in mindfulness, who encouraged my growth in mindfulness. I then went on a couple of weeklong meditation workshops. Then the psychologist who encouraged me let me collaborate with him as a student co-facilitator in a couple of his mindfulness training groups. He also encouraged me to experience a weeklong silent meditation at a center called Spirit Rock. Then he supported my leading my own mindfulness group. From this came my commitment to deepen mindfulness through practices like brief sitting meditation, walking meditation, yoga, and small moments of taking a mindful breath and opening my senses to what is around me. I happily discovered the resource, Mindful Self-Care for Clinicians and Caregivers, as a guide to tailoring the mindfulness group to each diverse caregiver's world. Seeing some of my colleagues go through burnout and watching family members of patients overcome the stress of caring for a loved one, I was and still am moved by their responsibilities. I noticed how caring for themselves disappeared under such enormous pressure. I came close to this situation myself several times. Mindfulness skills opened a large door for me to find both solace and refreshment within the sheer demands of living and caring.

I was given a conference room space at my hospital to hold an early evening group. This was done at a change of shift time to catch people coming off work. I wanted community involvement, so I opened the group to all caregivers, limiting the group size to

Mindful Self-Care for Clinicians and Caregivers. https://doi.org/10.1016/B978-0-443-29821-9.00005-4

twelve. Using the MSCC Guide, I created a handout describing the group, its purpose, and emphasizing the self-selection criteria. I must admit that reading over the risks to group members unnerved me a bit. I had assumed that learning mindfulness was benign. I had forgotten my own initial struggles and discomforts in the initial stages of my own learning. I also remembered a member in the Spirit Rock retreat needing special attention around a reactivated rape memory during a prolonged Body Scan meditation. The psychologist who first introduced me to mindfulness helped me to draft a list of licensed mental health professionals to have on hand, if or when referrals were needed or requested. Overall, due to my training, I felt confident in knowing what to look for in separating out expected side effects from potentially more serious adverse effects ... in just being alerted to them. As it turned out, I was able to screen out and refer a young social worker who called me after reading the brochure. She wondered if mindfulness could be used to treat her depression. I was able to steer her toward a mindfulness-based cognitive-behavioral therapist that was happily covered by her health insurance.

What stands out about my first facilitator experience with MSCC? I will highlight several things:

- *I learned to guide the group through each session with greater ease after the first couple of sessions. I felt good about choosing what I wanted to emphasize and shaping the sessions with the help of the guide. For example, I really liked giving a little more time to the Check In because this group gelled, and the sharing was so rich! I enjoyed the flexibility within fluid guidance.*
- *I loved the sense that my mindful presence was crucial as a way of meeting people, helping them feel safe to express themselves and explore various exercises, and of modeling rather than explaining the experience of being centered in mindful awareness. Facilitation was just another form of mindfulness practice for me ... so seamless–and ready for me when I call on it.*
- *I did choose to show moving meditation videos while leading with my own voice, the sitting meditations based on what I took away from the audios and transcripts. This allowed me to be a participant with participants with the video.*
- *I remember one participant, Carl, who had worked in a COVID ward during 2020. When the group of fellow caregivers listened to Carl mindfully, he teared up. As the tears came, he remarked that not only did he feel the relief of being heard, but also, he was surprised at what he was able to hear in himself. For the first time, he talked aloud and acknowledged and felt the grief that he was tucking behind his busy sense of doing so many tasks.*
- *There is an inner smile that comes to me when I recall Tobias' reaction to the first Mindful Pause, introducing the experience of mindfulness through the senses. He lit up in the discussion afterward. "So that's mindfulness! I although it was about having a blank mind. Instead, it is about stopping to feel, hear, and see, experience all my senses, – which I rarely do. Wow!"*
- *Strange to say, but I loved the time before the group gathered as I felt the room in silence and quietly shaped the chairs in a circle and lowered the lighting. There was an atmosphere that invited and relaxed people.*

- *I realize that I have a mosaic of memories. I reflect on noticing what individuals chose as their preferred formal and informal practice. One chose to pause and mindfully breathe during the day. Another used the qigong slow-moving exercise on the video. One did mindful breathing meditation for 5 minutes in the morning and evening. Several chose to pause and practice mindful listening and responding to their co-workers and care people. In the group Check Ins, people spoke about their experiments with practices, often inspiring another group member to try out something new. The sessions were like intersecting inputs to learning, all interacting with such interesting and unpredictable effects, all as individual as each of the caregivers.*

Although Jan's experience was uniquely her own, we hope that, like her, you find yourself touched by the experience of touching caregivers through both the session structures and your own mindful approach of guiding them. Like a musical performance, you can use the musical score or session structure in your own interpretive style. Being a facilitator is a mindfulness practice in itself.

Facilitator Note: A Brief Overview of MSCC Sessions

Facilitator Note: Brief Overview of the MSCC Intervention Sessions which includes the Overview and A Word to Those Readers Seeking Self-Study and Mindful Growth.

Each of the following eight sessions will contain these sections:

- **A <u>Quick Guide</u> gives the facilitator a summary of the session for a brief reference and overview.**
- **An <u>Introduction</u> provides the facilitator with the rationale for the session's format and useful notes for the facilitator.**
- **The <u>Session Guide</u> describes the session's aim, content, and suggested instructions, used during facilitation**
- **The <u>Participant Summary</u>, often handed out to participants at the beginning of each session, provides a brief session summary and space to take personal notes.**
- **<u>Handouts</u> are handy references for aspects of the session that participants can refer to during the week, to keep the session fresh in mind.**

It is recommended that the facilitator become familiar with the Session Guide or Quick Guide before reading the Introduction. Each Session Guide is typically organized into these sections:

- **Check-In**
- **Mindful Pause**
- **Highlighting the Session Theme**
- **Moving Meditation**
- **Stationary Meditation**
- **Session Summary and Suggestions for Practice During the Week**

A Word to Those Readers Seeking Self-Study and Mindful Growth

Mindful Self-Care for Clinicians and Caregivers (MSCC) was written for interested and prepared facilitators or/and researchers, as well as their trainees. Yet, it is likely that some readers simply want some ideas and practices about how to grow their mindful practice without attending an MSCC group. We authors believe that such help might be found in reading over the intervention materials and selectively sampling various practices and perspectives. Audios, videos, and handouts offer a library of possible experiments. The MSCC Intervention Session can offer insights into the skillful means of responding to stress and to nourishing various kinds of mindful practices. The vignettes in the introductions to these sessions normalize and bring to life the ways mindful self-care play out in daily life. It can take, for some, just one or two basic practices to initiate the benefits of self-care. For self-study, consider reading through one session content each week, selecting mindfulness practices to try, and print the handouts for helpful reminders of how you can integrate mindful self-care into your daily routine.

Session 1—What Is Mindfulness?

Session 1 introduces participants to mindfulness, both through direct experience and conceptual understanding. The session begins with an opportunity for participants to get to know one another, fostering group cohesion, and includes guidance on how to engage effectively in the learning process. The structure of Mindfulness Self-Care for Clinicians and Caregivers (MSCC) is explained, covering its goals, roles, and group norms and dynamics. Caregivers will also have their first experience with mindfulness practice, giving them a direct taste of its benefits.

Mindful Self-Care for Clinicians and Caregivers. https://doi.org/10.1016/B978-0-443-29821-9.00006-6

"Sunburst Flower"—A picture taken by Martin speaks visually to him of the experience of waking up, senses alert in the present moment.

Session 1 Facilitator Quick Guide: What Is Mindfulness?

Session Theme: Clarifying the Meaning and Experience of Mindfulness as a Resource for Caregivers

Introductions, Welcome, and Goals for the Sessions

- Facilitator introduces self with background and passion for mindfulness
- Facilitator reviews the structure, process, and aims of the group and informed consent
- Facilitator describes possible goals for session, participant role, and exploratory attitude
- Participants introduce selves and caregiver context and desires for the session
- Administrative, session structure and process information

Mindful Pause: Shifting Attention to the Present

- "For the next few minutes, let us get a taste of what it is like to shift into mindfulness."
- Facilitator then guides participants through a three-phase mindfulness focus: locating the sensation of breathing, next adding the synchronized opening and closing of thumb and forefinger with the breath, and finally adding the sense of sight as one simply explores one's hand while being aware of breathing and moving.
- Inquiry: "What did you notice about this shift toward mindfulness?"

Highlighting Session Theme:

Part A: Monkey Mind and Mindful Mind: "The Radio and the Open Window"

- **Guiding Question: "How do you know you are being mindful?"**
- Image highlights the difference between the wandering or self-talking mind and the mindful mind: *The Radio and the Open Window*
- Review the difference between being carried away by the Monkey Mind and resisting it. Emphasize the role of acceptance, maintain attention on present-moment experience, and intentionally choosing a mindful focus.
- Asking, "What comes through to you as the difference between these two minds?"

Part B: Practices to Develop the Muscle of Mindfulness: Contacting the Present through Body, Breath, and Senses

- **The three pillars of mindfulness practice: the present moment, heightened awareness of body/breath/senses, and nonjudgment of what is experienced**
- Why Practice? Body, breath, and senses as anchors to the present moment and away from Monkey Mind, often our automatic habit
- A small experiment in mindful looking using the sense of sight

Moving Meditation: Qigong or Gentle Stretching

- **Using movement to focus and settle our minds through the internal sense of breath and the feeling of slow, relaxed movement.**
- Starting with standing with mindful alignment and grounding, and sensitively launching into upper body circular movements on a rooted lower body base
- Inquiring: "What stood out for you in this experience?"

Body Scan Meditation

- Another formal practice: Brief body scan meditation.
- Systematically bringing mindful attention to parts of the body usually left out of awareness
- Inquiring: "What did you notice during this exercise?"

Summary and Suggestions for Exploring Formal and Informal Practices During the Week

- Summarizing what was covered today: What is Mindfulness?
- Encourage participants to consider integrating formal and informal practices into daily life, emphasizing self-selections

Handouts:

- "The Radio and the Open Window"
- Session 1 Participant Summary
- Bringing Mindfulness into Daily Life
- Session 1 Qigong Video access
- Session 1 Body Scan Audio access.

Session 1 Introduction: What Is Mindfulness?

In this first session, after the facilitator describes group norms and the logistics, participants are introduced to three key themes.

The first is the recognition of the special challenge of the caregiver role. MSCC was created from heartfelt experiences with caregivers who often struggled with the weight of care decisions, the loss of their own prior life (particularly with the person receiving care), difficult emotions from the one cared for, and internal conflict over the need to balance their own needs with the pressure to meet needs/demands of the care-receiver. This challenge of the caregiver role evokes compassion and awe from those of us who witness it. Each person brings their own unique perspective on how to meet it. There are some who carry out the role with a meaningful sense of mission and gratitude, experiencing stress but not with internal conflicts about it. There are others who churn in inner turmoil along with the outer pressures and uncertainties. MSCC is particularly relevant for those whose stress levels are high and whose internal resources are diminishing, as well as those who want to lower the risk of developing diagnosable psychiatric disorders, like depression. Caregivers may feel guilty for not doing enough or having the right attitude, depression, which can take the form of exhaustion due to the wear and tear of long-term stress. Some may resent the loss of having their own life, or anxiety over not feeling in control, and/or despair and hopelessness about lack of future relief. Some may feel little permission to focus on their own feelings and needs.

The second theme is self-care. The word "care" wonderfully captures the dual aspect of tending to oneself: care as a form of love and compassion and care as the practice of healing and balancing one's life. Caregivers who thrive and flourish, turn a caring eye toward themselves and direct part of their energy to bringing rest, emotional nourishment, social connections that uplift, and add a sense of meaning to their life. Caregivers who languish tend to neglect self-care. From the start, MSCC sessions ignite attention to one's own needs and spotlight mindfulness skills and practices as a means to this end. Hope is based on developing internal resources one already has.

The third theme is mindfulness as a state, a skill, and a perspective. MSCC sensitizing the caregiver participants to the variety of ways one can access mindfulness and pivot away from mental habits that create stress, suffering, and loss of pleasure. Being able to shift from overthinking and ruminating to awareness of present experiences is a radical act. In lives consumed by the weight of the past and future, the discovery of aliveness in simply attending to what is happening now creates an occasion of freedom right under one's nose. From the point of view of mindfulness, this sounds easy to see but quite challenging to do. Session 1 begins by looking at the difference between mindfulness and our default or habitual preoccupations. Rather than relying primarily on conceptual learning, sessions use brief guided experiences and evocative metaphors or images to advance experiential learning. To avoid the traps of strain and effort in mastering something new, the facilitator invites participants to explore, experiment, and play with various exercises.

Session 1 begins the process of group sharing, called "Check-Ins," through participant introductions. Sharing can include caregivers' hopes and concerns for the sessions as well as their own caregiver context. Commonalities begin to meld a collection of individuals into a group. The facilitator may briefly share her or his background first, including the passion for and interest in mindfulness.

Session 1 offers the first exposure to mindfulness practice. A Mindful Pause is followed by the Highlighting Session Theme, which develops mindfulness perspectives and skills in stages from session to session. The informal practice of Mindful Pause is brief and simple, like many informal mindful practices, yet contains the basic aspects of mindfulness practices: body, breath, and one of the senses, in this instance sight. The Highlighting Session Theme repeats this with body, breath, and senses serving as anchors for present-moment attention. Session 1's Highlighting Session Theme is captured under the Guiding Question: *How do I know I am being mindful?* Part of this question contrasts our usual mental preoccupations, called Monkey Mind, and mindfulness. Images in "The Radio and the Open Window" at the end of the session sharpen this contrast, focusing on what it means to navigate between these different minds. The "how" of shifting attention toward mindfulness is rooted in the various zones used to bring the mind into the present utilizing body, breath, and senses. The facilitator invites curiosity about the nature of the mindful experience, what it offers as a contrast to Monkey Mind, and how to access mindfulness.

For participants who may want a more concrete definition, mindfulness can be described in terms of three dimensions or pillars: (1) focusing on present experiences, (2) integrating body/sensory sensations in self-awareness, and (3) bringing nonjudgment to one's perceptions.

The next two practices of Qigong, a moving meditation, and a stationary meditation, Body Scan, sharpen the point of the theme and make it more memorable. (In this *Guide*, Moving and stationary meditations have audios or videos—both with transcripts—that can be used as facilitator guides. These can be utilized as facilitator models or used directly in sessions to guide meditations, depending on the preference of the facilitator.) Apart from the advantage of variety, these two meditations reinforce each other with movement making the stationary practice easier to perform. Participants may find sitting meditation quite challenging, given the usual activity of our thinking process and Monkey Mind. This makes it tempting to see meditation as too difficult, with a walkaway judgment, "I'm not cut out to be a meditator." Having a more successful experience with movement usually softens the overly hasty judgment.

A few words about Mindful Movement

Formal mindfulness practices include various types of meditation, which is an umbrella term describing techniques for focused attention. Meditation can include mindful observation, mantra meditation, body scan or body-centered

A few words about Mindful Movement—cont'd

mediation, contemplative practices, visual or affect-centered meditation, meditation with sound, or meditation with movement (Matko & Sedlmeier, 2019). Meditation can be classified based on the object of attention, attentional mode used, or the practice context such as seated or moving. Practitioners may find one or another type of meditation to be more beneficial or effective. Some individuals may find certain types of meditation to be more challenging or less helpful as a technique to attain focused attention. In MSCC, different forms of meditation are introduced, including both seated and movement meditation types, to allow participants to try different techniques and find a practice that works best for them. Mindful movement, in particular, may have specific benefits for individuals who struggle with mind wandering, based on cognitive models related to working memories and the location of movement and attention centers in the brain. For practitioners, incorporating movement with mindfulness may assist with focused attention by reducing the cognitive resources available for mind-wandering (Russell & Arcuri, 2015). It has been hypothesized that mind-wandering and movement control utilize the same finite central executive resources, and therefore, motor control utilized during mindful movement practices may take up cognitive resources needed for mind-wandering and subsequently assist with focused attention (Russell & Arcuri, 2015).

Various forms of movement have been classified as "mindful movement" in the literature, including yoga, Tai Chi, Qigong, Pilates, and others. These types of movement share components including present-centered awareness, controlled movement, movement paired with breathing and body awareness but differ in modality characteristics, format, and origins. Mindful movement practices have been studied in conjunction with other mindfulness programs, as well as individually as stand-alone interventions. Qigong is an ancient Chinese system of various gentle, flowing movements that can be practiced mindfully to enhance well-being and calmness. It has been used as a moving meditation and gentle stimulator of healing (Cohen, 1997). It can be an alternative to the use of yoga in mindfulness-based interventions, offering similar slow embodied experiences with less risk of injury. Wang et al. (2014) used a meta-analytic research design comparing several Qigong studies and found qigong effective in reducing stress and anxiety in otherwise healthy adults.

The session then allows a pause for a brief inquiry, asking people to verbalize new experiences and for the facilitator to validate their experience.

The end of session 1 summarizes the session theme and activities. Resources are provided for participants to use and "play with." Participants leave Session 1 with a sharpened perspective on what, how, and why of mindfulness, backed by the informal practice of Mindful Pause and a formal movement practice of Qigong and Body Scan as ways to access this special state of mind.

Participants will vary in their understanding of mindfulness and how it might apply to their caregiver context. Listen closely to what people say about their understanding and their hopes for what it might do for them. Hope can be stimulated for the benefits of developing mindfulness and, yet, propose having flexible expectations ("Wait and see what comes out of your experience as you open to exploring this new ground.") The facilitator encourages curiosity. Session 1 plants mindfulness in the caregiver situation by drawing upon compassionate descriptions of caregiver challenges both offered and heard from the caregivers themselves. Make clear that mindfulness is understood and learned best in actual practice. Keep conceptual descriptions brief and concrete. A mindful manner, empathy, and invitation to practice self-care throughout the session supports an important sense of safety for participants. They will glean much from being in the atmosphere of care and calm provided by the facilitator. How else do we learn mindfulness than, in part, being in the presence of a mindful person?

Some Takeaway Points

In this section, we will shine the spotlight on some of the major points covered in Session 1. A couple of participants, Tobias and Belinda, will help us by sharing their experiences of this first session. How did they respond to the several themes of recognizing the special challenges of caregiving, the need for intentional self-care, and the introduction to mindfulness as a particular state? The skill in evoking that state can mean the difference between flourishing or languishing in one's caregiver role. As we will see over the sessions, participants will consider their perspectives on caregiving and self-care as they begin to consider integrating mindful practices, including meditation, into their daily lives. Let us introduce Tobias and Belinda, both caregivers. Each comes to the first session with unique uplifts and struggles of caregiving in different contexts.

Tobias is a 31-year-old, single, full-time RN in an emergency setting. He signed up for MSCC sessions after seeing a brochure on a nursing station bulletin board. He described himself as being always "in a state of overwhelm." The COVID epidemic seemed to put that extra strain on an already exhausting workload, driven by increased emergency care cases and absent or burned-out team members. He watched patients survive and, too often, die. Life became "robotic": going home, collapsing, then getting up again to drag himself to work, then "repeat." In the group introduction, Tobias said he wanted to find some way to restore his nearly depleted reserves. Tobias had heard of mindfulness from the popular media, although he was not sure what it was beyond a vague sense it involved meditation.

Tobias' response to Session 1: *"After listening to the others, I guess I didn't fully get how not just my workload was burying me, but also how the emotional toll from caring for patients I could not save was depressing me. I thought I was just feeling sorry for myself."* Here we can see how easy it is for caregivers to lose themselves in a role they do not see beyond. The need for intentional self-care may not make sense at first to those who do not grasp what their role is doing both for and to them. They may not see the eventual commitment to self-care will lift the caregiver beyond "just coping." Tobias comments on his takeaway after Session 1:

I felt compassion, hope, and doubt after this session. I felt compassion listening to the other group members. I was sorry for their struggle but also felt less alone and this led to some hopefulness. I was glad to have a chance to be heard. Being listened to was helpful. The hope that being more mindful might be a way through this hectic, overactive and reactive mind of mine was inspiring. At the same time, I doubted that I could be good enough at it to make any difference. There were moments in the first brief exercise and in the body scan where I lapsed into a more relaxed place and I was a little more able to stay focused. Man, I really did not realize how tense I am most the time. Again, there were times I fell back into worries, lists of undone things, or just tumbleweed thoughts. Can I do this? Jan, the group facilitator, was encouraging and heard me as although this was normal. She said we all deal with "reactive mind," so that is why mindfulness requires patient practice and is a skill. Jan suggested I approach this learning in a spirit of curiosity and play rather than pressuring myself. She seemed to get me and that spurred me on. If mindfulness can give me some of Jan's gentleness and calm, then let us see.

Tobias' response will have similarities to other participants. Compassion, hope, skepticism, and self-doubt are all possible and quite normal initial responses to this kind of learning. Responses to the session exercises and meditations may also be mixed. In Session 1, the facilitator focuses on creating a strong sense of rapport and safety. This is why it is helpful to elicit these reactions so the facilitator can normalize them as part of the learning process. It is possible that most participants wonder if they can be successful in acquiring mindfulness as a skill. As you can see with Tobias, the facilitator's own mindful presence and ways of encouraging less strain and more playful experimenting can go far in supporting fledgling attempts to risk oneself in this new way of learning while being supported by fellow participants.

Belinda is a 65-year-old, divorced, retired administrative assistant. Belinda signed up for MSCC sessions after her primary care physician mentioned the group as something that might help with stress. She described feeling lonely as well as physically and emotionally drained. Belinda has three adult children, who she raised as a single mother, and now has five grandchildren. She currently lives with her mother, who moved in with her a few years ago after having a stroke. Belinda is a full-time caregiver for her mother and helps watch her new one-year-old grandson so her daughter can return to work. Belinda is aware of her own aging and mortality. She is struggling with her own medical problems and is having difficulty balancing her role as a daughter, a mother, and a grandmother while trying to care for herself along the way. She was interested in the idea of mindfulness and open to giving the group a try, although worried about finding time for the virtual group each week.

Belinda's response to Session 1: *"Signing up for this group, I felt desperate for anything that might help me manage stress. Most days I feel so overwhelmed, I don't know where to turn. My few friends are not able to understand what I am going through, trying to care for my mother, my grandson and myself all at the same time. I felt support from my fellow group members. I identified with their struggles. I don't want to burden my children or mother by talking with them about my worries, so sometimes I just feel lost and invisible. After session 1, I felt encouraged to hear from other group members who were struggling with similar challenges and emotions. The brief mindful pause and the body scan exercise felt so relaxing, and I realized it was the first time all day I had paused to focus on myself. I did feel apprehensive about finding time to practice the exercises we learned during my busy days, but Jan encouraged us to start small with brief mindful moments, and that felt more attainable. Often, I have difficulty finding time to care for myself, even finding time to attend my own doctor's appointments can feel impossible. Sometimes it feels selfish to take time for me when my family has so many other needs. It was helpful to know that mindfulness can be done in small moments, minutes or pauses so at least I have a place to start."*

Belinda's response highlights the varied emotions that participants may bring with them as they enter the group. Giving time and space for the group members to support one another is important in Session 1 and continues throughout. Normalizing emotions that are often universal within the caregiving experience can be powerful, while also acknowledging that everyone has a unique experience that may feel similar and different. As you can see with Belinda, participants may struggle to imagine taking time for themselves to practice mindfulness or the thought of doing so may bring up feelings of guilt. As the facilitator, making sure to highlight small steps and offering brief practices and techniques that feel attainable can help keep the session from feeling overwhelming.

Key Concepts

- Key themes from this session will thread throughout the course, including the unique challenges of the caregiving role, the concept of self-care, and the role of mindfulness as a state, skill, and perspective.
- Building group cohesion, setting group norms, and facilitating a safe, confidential space where participants feel able to share openly is essential.
- Participants may come to group with preconceived notions about mindfulness, varying levels of experience or exposure to mindfulness skills, and different levels of motivation. Meet participants where they are with no judgment, curiosity, and compassion to facilitate openness and learning.

Session 1 Guide: What Is Mindfulness?

Aim of Session 1:

- To review the structure, process, and aims of the group and informed consent
- To introduce the concept and experience of mindfulness as a skill developed through practices, and the benefits of mindfulness in the contexts of caregiving.
- To begin to build group cohesion through a safe atmosphere and community.
- To establish group norms.

Introductions, Welcome and Goals for the Sessions
Aim:

- To ease participants into the structure and process of the group and begin to build a feeling of community and cohesion.
- To give caregivers a vision of the session goals and structure.
- To introduce mindfulness and self-care in the context of caregiving.

Suggestions: Begin with self-introduction of the facilitator which might describe their background and/or roles in caregiving, mindfulness, and inspiration for facilitating Mindful Self-Care for Clinicians and Caregivers. Briefly describe the rationale behind MSCC and its overall goals of facilitating mindfulness skills and self-care for caregivers both formal and informal. Picture the caregiving role as a possible mixture of the passion to offer care and the stress of its burdens that risk depletion and potential for burnout. Burdens might include self-doubt and guilt over not doing or knowing enough, lack of resources to support care, resentment over sacrificing one's own needs, time management challenges, and sadness and fatigue from overextending one's energy. Mindfulness and self-care are about ways to renew one's inner resources, energy, and balance in living.

Take time to go over some of the issues clarified in Part A Chapter 2 (Setting Up and Managing the Process of MSCC). These issues include what MSCC is and is not, risks and benefits, and the roles of the facilitator and participants.

Transition to group introductions: Ask each participant, as the facilitator goes around the group, to introduce themselves, their caregiver context including its ups and downs, and desired outcome of the sessions for them. The facilitator briefly summarizes the context, feelings, and desired goals for each person before moving on to the next section. This allows participants to feel heard and validated without any sense of judgment. Thank each participant for sharing.

Briefly describe the following: Sessions are built like a staircase, each building on each other. Yet even if a session is missed, participants are encouraged to keep attending whatever sessions they can. Participant roles include showing up (even if coming late), experimenting with each session's mindfulness practices, talking about experiences with these practices, and sharing what was tried during the week. Given the demands on caregiver time, there will be no homework other than to for the participant to select exercises for experimentation. The facilitator will hand out Participant

Summaries to help participants begin to integrate mindful practice into daily life. To make participant sharing safe, everything shared will be kept confidential among group members. Emphasis will be on learning through doing, since that is the only way mindfulness can be understood and learned.

Go over the following housekeeping items: Review session schedule, session length, and how to contact you the facilitator for resources and questions. Underscore confidentiality and attention to self-care through this training.

Mindful Pause: Shifting Attention to the Present

Aim: To provide a brief experience of shifting into mindful attention before providing verbal descriptions of it. This experience then becomes a concrete reference for introducing the concept of mindfulness.

Suggestions: This brief exercise of 3–4 minutes can begin with, "Let's explore an experience of mindfulness to begin to understand what it is like. What does shifting your attention to what is happening in the present feel like? Let's use the sensations of breath, body movement, and sight to find out."

Then offer the following guidelines: "Sit in a comfortable position with hands resting on your lap." The goal in this is to notice sensations without going off into your thoughts. Keep it simple. Begin with noticing the sensation of breathing: "What sensations tell you that you are breathing?" You might notice the area of your nostrils or chest or lower. Just follow the breath as it is. Note thoughts if they come up but don't let them take you away. What does breathing in and out feel like?

"Now let us add a hand movement. On the in-breath close one hand into a light fist; on the out-breath, open the hand. Let the breath guide the movement. Notice the feeling of the hand along with the breath. If thoughts are there, let them be in the background as you keep a focus on breathing and hand closing and opening.

"Now add another sense—sight—as you look closely at the hand and its movements with the breath. Just explore with curiosity what comes up with an open mind, just here in the present."

Continue the exercise for between 3 and 4 minutes. Then end with a deep breath in and out.

Discussion/Sharing

"What does mindfulness feel like? So often we are barely aware of what is going on in and around us in our busy lives. We live lost in thoughts while planning, being preoccupied, ruminating over something in the past, obsessing about some future worry … on and on. When we paused to feel our breath, the movement of our hand, and the looking at our hand, we might have felt a shift in our attention to what is happening in the present. We perhaps became more 'mindful' of sensations and feelings outside our thoughts and usual judgments.

"What was this brief invitation to be mindfully attentive like for you? What did you notice?"

Open the floor for responses and try to simply feedback what you, as facilitator, hear without interpretation. Simply validate the person's reported experience. See if there are opportunities at the end of the sharing to underscore experiences highlighting mindfulness or obstacles to accessing it, normalizing all responses.

Highlighting Session Theme: Mindfulness, Monkey Mind, and Accessing the Present Moment

- **Guiding Question: How do you know you are being mindful?**
- **Guiding Image: "The Radio and the Open Window"**
- **Part A: Monkey Mind and Mindful Mind**
  - Being mindful renews us by giving experiences of calm, clarity, and aliveness. It can be an alternative to minds that are restless and overburdened by reactive emotions and thought tumbling after thought. We refer to this scattered, restless mind as Monkey Mind, after jungle monkey screeching and leaping to tree limb after limb. Sound familiar? Monkey Mind is so captivating we often get trapped in it. Practicing mindfulness offers a way out.
  - Let us use an image of "The Radio and the Open Window" to illustrate these two minds. In the image, the radio represents our often noisy, Monkey Mind while the open window pictures the open, mindful mind. Read or cover the handout on "The Radio and the Open Window" as participants close their eyes to simply listen and take in the imagined scene. At the end, invite participants to use the handout to explore the image during the week as they try on various mindfulness practices presented later in this session.
- **Part B: Accessing the Present Moment**
  - Mindfulness is a state of mind and a skill. Participants are invited to try out and experiment with various kinds of practices to find what best suits each of them. There are both formal practices, either stationary or moving, that take more time, and there are informal practices that are brief. As examples, sitting meditation is a formal practice; pausing to find and feel your breath is an informal one. This will become familiar as we go along.
  - Mindfulness practices begin by using three areas of focus: body, breath, and senses. All three were used in the mindful pause we did earlier when we explored the breath sensation, the moving sensation in the hand, and the sense of sight when looking at the hand. Body, breath, and the five senses are what can be called anchors in the mindful present. They are areas to tune into when moving beyond Monkey Mind. These will become familiar as you practice various mindfulness exercises.
  - Now, a couple of mindfulness meditation practices will help these aspects of mindfulness come alive.

Mindfulness Practice Movement: Qigong, Blending of Breath and Body

Aim: This is the first introduction to a formal meditation practice. Qigong movements are selected because of their low risk of injury and their invitingly pleasant effects. Movement is placed at this point in the group because participants usually find it easier and less challenging than other formal practices like sitting meditation. It has a good chance of giving participants an early success experience. Seated or stationary meditation can involve trying to still or silence the restless mind, creating a spiral of frustration before one learns to relax one's focus and simply allow present experiences to simply be there. Moving can downregulate tension and restlessness, making the stationary meditation which follows easier. The goal is to experience a mindful awareness of the inner feel of synchronized breath and movements. This practice can translate into informal, daily mindfulness of relaxed attention to walking and other natural movements.

Suggestions: Qigong has several stages. It begins as standing and aligning, bringing in a sense of stabilizing oneself physically as a precursor to being grounded mentally and emotionally. Then, movements are met mindfully with attention to the inner experience of moving, not the outward checking as to how one looks or if one is doing it "right." The movements are done slowly with a sense of flow. Breathing is full and harmonized with the forms. There is a video (Session 1: Qigong) of this practice as well as a transcript (Moving Meditation: Session 1), which can be used to guide the meditation or to teach facilitators how to lead the practice.

Brief Inquiry and Sharing

What are a few words you might use to describe this experience for you? What might Qigong show us as a way to meet challenges in caregiving?

Mindfulness Practice Stationary: Body Scan Meditation

Aim: Body scan is the first introduction to a stationary formal meditation practice. It teaches systematic attention, letting go of absorption in the chattering, Monkey Mind, and the art of "just noticing" without commentary or judgment. It highlights embodied awareness, combining focus on breath and body sensations. Participants are learning to separate Monkey Mind from the mindful mind through the skill of gently directing attention to present sensations.

Suggestions: Facilitators can familiarize themselves with this body scan practice through reading the body scan description (in handout section for Session 1) and practicing with the body scan audio (see body scan in audio section). Once introduced and set up for participants, the audio can be used as a group guide or the facilitator may choose to lead. Body scan is presented as a formal meditation with the aim of directing attention to present-moment body sensations in a step-by-step way. A benefit of body scan is restoring a feeling of aliveness in a body which participants may have numbed or tuned out. While practicing "just noticing" without judgment, usual thoughts are acknowledged, accepted, and allowed to be in the background. A warm, gentle attention is encouraged rather than a tense effort to control one's mind. Two possible side effects of this practice are drifting into sleep or drowsiness and finding sensations in some parts of the body triggering pain or anxiety. Going to sleep is not judged as a failure but as a challenge over time to combine relaxation and alertness. If discomfort is triggered, a participant might choose to notice and practice acceptance of it. Or the participant is given support and permission to shift attention to breathing if the discomfort is too disturbing. It is important to encourage a group member with this experience to view it not as a failure or a deficit in learning mindfulness, but as a new learning.

Brief Inquiry and Sharing

What did you notice in this exercise of moving attention into sensations of the body? What was the after effect of this meditation on the state of your body? Your mind? Your mood?

Summary and Suggestions for Formal and Informal Practices During the Week

Aim:

- To underscore the session question: What is mindfulness?
- To clarify how each section of this session shed light on the question.
- To inspire participants to reflect on and process their insights from the session and to begin to experiment with mindfulness formal and informal practices during the week.
- To reflect on how mindfulness might be part of caregiver self-care.

Suggestions: Briefly summarize this session: Together we are beginning a journey to bring the gifts of mindfulness and self-care to our lives in caregiving we each shared with each other. We explored a brief shift into mindful attention through feeling our breath, our hand movement, and the sight of our hand. So different from being lost in thoughts and judgments is this manner of simple, present, direct awareness. We considered how mindfulness is different from our Monkey Mind which is restless, distracted, often scattered or preoccupied. The Radio and Open Window gave us an image of this difference and how we might take advantage of our power to shift attention toward the open window of the present. We practiced two types of meditation to explore further how to enter the mindful state and sharpen the skill of mindfulness over time. I am passing out "Bringing Mindfulness to Daily Life" for a list of possible ways to dip into mindful pauses during your day. I hope you will use this and the audio and video resources to pick and choose the practices you are drawn to and come back and tell us about your experience. See you next session!"

Then share resources of "Session 1 Participant Summary," "Mindful Daily Practices," "The Radio and the Open Window," and discuss ways to access the Qigong video and the Body Scan audio.

Handouts

- Session 1 Participant Summary
- Bringing Mindfulness to Daily Life
- The Radio and the Open Window
- Session 1 Video: Qigong Mindful Movement
- Session 1 Body Scan Audio

Session-Facilitator's Contemplation: What do you find in the stillness?

Session 1 Participant Summary: What Is Mindfulness?*

Guiding Question: *How do you know you are being mindful?*

Aim of Session:

- To review the purpose of group, its norms, and confidentiality requirements.
- To introduce the concept of mindfulness and mindfulness skills and practices as they relate to caregiver stress, burdens, and privileges.
- To begin to build group cohesion through shared experiences.

What did you notice in the **Brief Mindful Pause: Tasting Mindfulness?**

What did you notice in the **Mindful Movement (Qigong)?**

* Lumpkin, M., Collins, M.H., & Jarrett, R.B. (2026). Mindful self-care for clinicians and caregivers: A group facilitator's guide. Academic Press.

What stood out for you in **Body Scan Meditation?**

Monkey Mind and Mindful Mind: "The Radio and the Open Window": This illustration highlights the contrast between resisting one's experience and embracing openness and acceptance of one's feelings, thoughts, and sensations.

Practices to Develop the Muscle of Mindfulness: Contacting the present moment using Body, Breath, and Senses. Given the desirability of the mindful mind, how do we best access it and make it more available in our daily lives? To tame our unruly "Monkey Mind," it is helpful to give the mind something to focus on in the present moment. Focusing on the body, the breath, or sensory experiences in our environment can anchor us in the here and now. The body offers constant feedback—whether it is the sensation of your feet on the ground or your posture. The breath, always present, is another grounding tool. Additionally, paying attention to your sense and the things you can see, hear, smell, or touch brings you back to the present. These simple practices can be done anytime, anywhere—at work, home, during caregiving tasks, or while taking a moment for yourself. By practicing mindfulness, even for just a few minutes each day, we gradually build the mindfulness "muscle" and are able to return to the present moment more easily, especially when distractions or stress arise.

5-4-3-2-1 Grounding Exercise: A Simple Way to Stay Present

The 5-4-3-2-1 grounding exercise helps you focus on the present moment by engaging your five senses. This technique is useful for building the muscle of mindfulness.

Instructions:

- **5 Things You Can See**

Look around and identify five things in your environment. You can also select a color and identify five objects that are a certain color.

- **4 Things You Can Touch**

Notice four things in your environment that you can physically touch. This could be the texture of your clothes, the ground beneath your feet, or an object in your hand.

- **3 Things You Can Hear**

Listen and identify three distinct sounds in your environment that you can hear. They could be sounds nearby or subtle sounds in the distance.

- **2 Things You Can Smell**

Notice two scents that you can smell—you can also use essential oils, smell hand lotion you have nearby, or light a candle and notice the fragrance.

- **1 Thing You Can Taste**

Focus on one thing you can taste. This could be taking a sip of water or tea, placing a mint in your mouth and focusing on the flavor, or noticing the taste in your mouth.

Guiding Image of "The Radio and the Open Window": Close your eyes and vividly imagine this scenario. Does the radio's static resemble the typical chatter of your mind? If the open window represents a mindful state, pay attention to what happens when you either surrender to or struggle against the radio's noise. What occurs if you simply allow the radio to be as it is, accepting its presence, while gently shifting your attention to the view outside the open window?

Mindfulness practices can be formal, such as meditation or Qigong, or informal such as taking a mindful pause while on a walk and noticing the sun shining through the trees. Focus on working to include mindfulness in your life through daily practices that feel accessible and a part of your routine. Mindfulness is a lived experience, different from our default mode of mind-LESS-ness. To start living more mindfully, consider bringing into your everyday life mindful attitudes such as acceptance, non-judging, and flexible exploring, as opposed to controlling or striving.

Suggestions: Please experiment with mindfulness practices this week, either formally or informally. This week I plan to try:

List mindfulness practices you would like to try this week:	☑

Lumpkin, M., Collins, M.H., & Jarrett, R.B. (2026). Mindful self-care for clinicians and caregivers: A group facilitator's guide. Academic Press.

Bringing Mindfulness to Daily Life

1. Did you intentionally set aside time to slow down and savor some experience?

2. Did you have several times of intentionally pausing to enjoy an unexpected experience?

3. Did you have times when you intentionally took a pause to be mindful of breathing?

4. Did you give yourself times to quietly open to take in what was around you?

5. Did you pause to notice a spiraling stress reaction and choose a less stressful response?

6. Did you have times of tuning into your body's sensations to just notice and be aware of what was happening?

7. Did you choose to more quietly focus on a task rather than pressure yourself to get through it?

8. Did you listen to another person with full awareness rather than be caught up in your own thoughts?

9. Were you able to "be with" a difficult feeling or sensation rather than ignore or struggle to escape it?

10. Did you do any "formal" meditation such as Body Scan, Slow Walking, Yoga, Qigong?

11. Did you at times purposely treat yourself with greater kindness?

12. Did you let yourself feel times of simple gratitude?

Lumpkin, M., Collins, M.H., & Jarrett, R.B. (2026). Mindful self-care for clinicians and caregivers: A group facilitator's guide. Academic Press.

The Radio and the Open Window

Let's say our minds are like an upstairs
room you are sitting in.
In this room is a radio playing in the background
and you cannot turn it on or off.
and there's a large window.
Often you get entranced by the radio's constant
talk, talk, talk shows.
It is wearying yet somehow irresistible.
Getting so stirred up by
debates, arguments, and righteous shoulds.
you find yourself tense, wired or just tired.
Rest seems impossible.
You try shutting off the radio.
It refuses.
You try ignoring it, forcing it out of your mind.
It just pops back up.
You even yell at it. But it
is unmoved.
Then the window occurs to you.
You open it wide.
Immediately you smell the fresh grass,
feeling a wind across your face, and
oh the way things shine in the sun.
You breathe in breath after breath.
The radio still plays
but it is just background to this
Wonder.
This fresh now-ness
unthought, just
Sensed.

Mindlessness: Hooked into the constant chatter of the radio mind, either succumbing to it passively or fighting to resist it. Both ways get us even more stuck.

***Mindfulness*:** Allowing the Monkey Mind to settle into the background, neither falling into it nor struggling against it. Then, opening to present moment simple experiences of body feelings, breath, sights, sounds, and tastes. Letting yourself go into these experiences with curiosity and acceptance of the way things are. Always noticing, noticing without judgment or agenda.

Qigong Practices: An Introduction

Qigong and Tai Chi moving meditations have deep roots in Chinese history, well over 2000 years ago. They are gentle yet inwardly powerful practices designed for health and well-being. For our purposes, Qigong movements offer formal moving meditations that require and strengthen mindfulness. Like body scan, the more one can sensitively feel various body sensations the better one is grounded and embodied. Savoring inner sensations and feelings during movements is akin to mindfully savoring food textures and flavors. The result is a pleasurable centeredness amidst the bustle of life.

Standing: Grounding and Alignment

Before movement, there is aligned standing as a base for grounding ourselves physically and psychologically. Begin with feet pointed straight ahead, weight equally distributed on them, with a relaxed upright posture. Immediately, awareness infiltrates the body field, just sensing and noticing what is there. The knees are unlocked slightly, allowing the pelvic region and lower back to shift as although beginning to sit down. From the waist down, there is a sense of energy flowing through the legs and into the earth like roots. From the waist up, the spine is released to flow upward and lengthen. Shoulders are released of any tension and may shoulder blades may move down by the force of gravity. The center of gravity in the body is moved from the head and upper chest to a region slightly below the navel, called "*dan tien*" in Chinese. See if you can get a feel for this way of aligning and recentering. Take a quiet moment. When a movement occurs, see if it is possible to refer occasionally and mindfully to this dynamic alignment.

Movements: General Principles

We will play with the beginning level Qigong and Tai Chi movements. Keep in mind a few principles. Movements are to be inwardly experienced rather than doing an outer performance. They are done slowly and with a flow often compared to moving in water. The Chinese idea of "*wu wei*" means "effortless effort," movements that seem to do themselves without strain or force or too much will. Easier said than done, of course, but that is a guiding standard. In mindfulness terms, this means nonstriving and letting go of any unnecessary tension we tend to add to our actions. We trust our bodies to support us.

In Qigong, the bottom part of the body remains rooted with feet, knees, and hips facing forward and generally unmoving. Turns and rotations are done from the waist. The center of gravity is in the *dan tien,* just below the navel, and not in the chest or head. When arms move, shoulders stay dropped and not lifted. Joints in the elbows and wrists are kept open and relaxed. There is a sense of rising energy or unforced uplift in the spine. Breath deepens into the lower belly or *dan tien.* Movements are attached to the in-breath and the out-breath.

The overall sense is one of lightness, relaxation, flow, and gentle energy arousal. Movement sequences end by continuing to breathe slowly and deeply while placing one hand over the other on the navel for a moment or two.

References: Various Qigong exercises are available on YouTube. Watching them will give you a sense of the slow flowing movements, style, and attitudes of Qigong. You can then bring them into your exercises.

Session 1: Moving Meditation Transcript

Hello and welcome to mindfulness meditation using movement. We are going to be using a form called Qigong. If that is not familiar to you I bet that the cousin of Qigong called Tai Chi is. That graceful set of movements you see people doing in parks … circular, dance-like forms … almost hypnotic to watch. We are going to be using this as a way to attend to present moment experience … like sensations … quite aware of the difference between that and mental commentary and talking to ourselves about what we are doing … and making judgments. So, the movements, body, and breath are continuous anchors into this moment's experience … a place to go … if the head talk … overthinking … begin to get dominant again … we shift to the breath and body and movement sensations … over and over again.

So, Qigong begins by having our feet about hip-length apart … We are going to begin with just alignment … adding a stable base to movement … I would like for you to feel the bottom of your feet for a moment … being sure there is balance as weight is spread through the entire foot … and rising up through the legs … if knees are locked, unlocking them … feeling for a moment the waist, the small of the back (letting it go so it is free to move) … feeling the spine support the upper part of the body without muscles trying to hold us up … the spine allowing body to hang as if on a coat hanger … and allowing the shoulders to drop ….allowing the center of gravity (often caught up in the head or upper chest) to move downward … to just below the navel … our true center of gravity … now rooting us … From this we'll begin to coordinate breath, hand, and arm movements.

We will begin by having the hands move up … toward the chest … palms up … on the in-breath. On the out-breath, hands simply move down as though gently pushing energy through the legs, feet … into the floor. In-breath … and out-breath … in-breath … feeling the movements as though you were slowly moving in water … out-breath … allowing the breath to fall deep into the body … feeling sensations of the body in movement ….noticing, perhaps, places of some tightness or tension … letting that go … noticing how slow movements allow you to feel so much more … unlike the quick, darting movements of our usual life … to get somewhere in the future ….

Let us try another movement … very similar … Palms come up to just below chest level … facing each other … on the in-breath … making a big ball filling out with air … then … squeezing the air out … in … out … releasing shoulders … arms … giving up excessive tension … feeling the flow. Qigong and Tai Chi love circular movements … rounded ways of moving the body … so different from our angular ways of moving … Seeing what it is like to feel this … if the head wants to come in and talk to us, we simply notice it … coming back to breath … and movement

And we will try one more moving meditation. As the breath comes in … palms are facing down … as the breath leaves … palms simply turn up … arms, elbows feeling the pull of gravity … air comes in … without moving shoulders up … making a kind of circular arc over the head … air moves out … arms, palms come down again … moving air, energy through legs into … the floor … air comes in ….air goes out … air comes in … air goes out … staying with your sensations … staying here and now ….savoring the movements … once more ….now, just placing the hands for a moment … just under the navel … checking in with yourself … noticing the quiet body after moving … noticing the differences … and then ending the meditation … quietly … gently … as we move into our very next moment

Qigong Movement 1

Qigong Movement 2

Qigong Movement 3

Session 1: Body Scan Transcript

Body scan is a formal meditation that can last anywhere from 10 to 45 minutes. It can be done lying down or sitting, although lying down usually ensures greater relaxation as one gives into the force of gravity more fully. Evoking mindful embodiment, body scan is intimate, gently focused attention to various parts of the body, moving through the body systematically from head to feet or feet to head. The challenge is to bring mindful attention to areas of the body without comment or judgment or goal beyond just noticing and letting go of any tension or effort. It is like progressive relaxation outwardly, but it is primarily an awareness exercise and only secondarily might it lead to greater relaxation. Particularly when lying down, people find it easy to favor the relaxation aspect over the wakefulness aspect—and go to sleep. So, it is important to balance these two factors equally. Over time, body scan leads to enhanced body sensitivity and sense of aliveness.

Sometimes, focusing on a particular part of the body evokes uncomfortable memories like a traumatic event or painful experience connected with the past. If discomfort becomes anxiety provoking, it is usually best to shift attention to slow, deep breathing until the next body area is brought into focus.

This body scan will begin with the head and work down, ending with the feet. You can try the opposite direction to see which one you prefer. Body scan begins with bringing attention to one's body instead of a primary focus on thoughts. Thoughts are accepted but allowed to be in the background more than foreground. If thoughts or judgments arise and you momentarily get lost in them, simply take a step back, notice them, and return to the suggested focus in the body. Sometimes it helps to breathe into the particular body zone. Once awareness of the body expands, allow a letting go that encourages relaxation. Relaxed wakefulness is a skill.

Since this is a relatively brief body scan, the following areas will be explored by simply placing attention on them to see what is there, if anything, to experience in the facial parts of forehead/eyes. Muscles around the mouth/jaw muscles are brought into focus. Then throat and back neck muscles; shoulders and shoulder blades. Now the lengths of the arms, palms, and fingers. Next, down the torso by focusing on the chest and stomach and waist. Then the lower body focuses on thighs, calves, ankles, and ending with the bottom of the feet between heels and toes. Finally, the body as a whole is held for a moment in awareness.

The guiding instructions include naming the body area ("Now bring a focus to ____") and the invitation to "Pause and feel what sensation is there." Variations of the invitation might be "What do you notice?" or "What is there?" or "You might feel a definite, clear sensation or, perhaps, none at all … just see." Occasionally, a reminder, "If thoughts arise, notice that, and let them be as you bring your focus back to the body."

Body scan is a challenge to do without guidance, so using the audio recording is recommended until the process is quite familiar. Come out of the meditation gently and without haste or strain. Let its effects linger.

Session 2—Mindful Observing

Session 2 focuses on mindful observation of one's body, mind, and emotions and holding a stance of acceptance and non-judgment. The chapter also includes a written description of experiential practices for the session. The aim of Session 2 is to introduce the concept of mindful observing and practice cultivating a nonjudgmental and curious stance in regards to thoughts and emotions. It also introduces the connection between thoughts, emotions, and body sensations, and the value of increasing insight and awareness.

Mindful Self-Care for Clinicians and Caregivers. https://doi.org/10.1016/B978-0-443-29821-9.00007-8

"Perched watchful owl" — Martin caught this rare visit of an owl in his backyard. Those quiet wide eyes capture an image of mindful watchfulness and observing.

Session 2 Facilitator Quick Guide: Mindful Observing

Session Theme: Introducing the Experience and Practice of Mindful Observing as a Foundation Skill

Check-In:
- Participants share their mindfulness explorations and experiences since the last session.
- Focus on separating actual concrete experiences of mindfulness from thoughts *about* the experiences, as one learns to do in mindfulness practices.
- Caregivers are encouraged to share mindful experiences in the context of caregiving.

Brief Mindful Pause: A Journey Through the Senses
- Introduce mindful sensing as a way to access the present moment and highlight the difference between direct sensing and mental commentary and labeling about sensed experiences.
- Any of our senses is possible to open to connect to the present moment.

Discussion/Sharing
- What did you notice on this trip through various senses?
- Were you able to see the difference between direct sensing and thinking?

Highlighting Session Theme:
- **Guiding Question:** What difference might observing and connecting with our inner experiences make in our daily life versus our usual tendency towards inattention/preoccupations?
- **Guiding Image:** "The Radio and the Open Window" from the first session.
- **Part A: Mind-Body Connection**: Mental and physical health depend on staying aware of our inner body experiences and tuning into the information our body wants to tell us.
- **Part B: Mindful Observing**: Tuning in to our inner sensations and feelings allows us to step back and separate from the choppy waves of our mind chatter and find a place of calm and clarity in the present moment.

Mindfulness Practice Movement: Qigong/Gentle Stretching
- Building upon the last session's introduction to Qigong, mindful observing follows gentle, flowing movements.
- The attitudes of nonstriving and following the flow of movement are joined with sensing the breath and using movement as a way of physical and emotional grounding.

Brief Inquiry:

- What stood out to you in this experience?

Mindfulness Practice Stationary: Mindfulness Meditation with Breath

- Mindful observing is intensified as a relaxed but alert focus is brought to the body and the breath.
- The task of this meditation is to observe thoughts that enter and distract us from the breath and to patiently refocus this skill of attending and strengthen it over time.
- A poem at the end of the meditation, "Another Little Greek Tale," uses vivid language and images to illustrate how mindful breathing may liberate us from mental complications.

Brief Inquiry:

- What did you notice in your experience of this meditation?

Summary and Suggestions for Formal and Informal Practices during the Week:

- Summarize the session theme and the way the practices relate to the topic.
- Encourage continued exploration based on personal interests in mindfulness practices.

Handouts:

- Session 2 Participant Summary
- Session 2 Qigong Video or Gentle Stretching
- Session 2 Mindfulness of Breath Audio
- Poem: "Another Little Greek Tale."

Session 2 Introduction: Mindful Observing

Session 2 brings forward the first mindfulness skill: *intentional, mindful attending* or *observing*. What is observed? Look for experiences in the form of sensations, feelings, and thoughts as they are here in this moment. Why is this important? To free us from being lost in the spinning "Monkey Mind," the unsettled, restless, and uncontrolled mind that swings from thought to thought to thought, which leaves us scattered, wired, and tired. Mindful attending settles us in the clarity and grounding of present sensations, to directly reconnect us to our own inner states and read ourselves more accurately.

Guiding Question to Caregivers: "What difference might observing and connecting with our inner experiences make in our daily life, versus our usual tendency towards inattention?" This question is posed without pressing for discussion because that will follow in the section on Session Theme. It sets a tone for this session like a bell rung and contemplated.

Relevance to Caregiving: Caregivers are frequently focused on attuning to others and may suppress, ignore, or discount their own internal experiences or needs. Session 2 on mindful observing serves to encourage caregivers to connect and observe their own internal thoughts, including self-statements and images, emotions, and body sensations.

Mindful observing supports skills in the next two sessions because the skill of observing allows us to release old emotional stress, which then supports an increased awareness of one's own self-care needs. In this way, mindfulness transitions from being a practice or a skill to a style of living and responding. A more resilient response may become a lived reality.

The themes of Session 2 can be introduced and highlighted as the participants share their experiences with mindfulness over the past week. In the Check-In, they portray their tenuous ventures toward mindfulness and the first witnessing of their effects. They listen to others' accounts and often find inspiration in what others are discovering. They become emboldened to try more formal meditation or informal moments of mindfulness in daily life as ways of exploring mindfulness on their own. Some participants share experiences that directly touch on the session's theme or future themes. In these moments, the facilitator may momentarily catch and hold up these bubbles of experience to the common light for the group. The Brief Mindful Pause described below continues to cultivate moments of entering the present mindfully by using our senses to anchor us outside the usual dominance of mental commentary and judgments. Mindful Pausing is an accessible practice in and of itself. Consider the three pillars of mindfulness of present moment awareness, mind-body connection, and nonjudgment. These are threads woven into this simple, intentional shift into the present, entering body and senses nonjudgmentally. Inquiries follow mindfulness exercises, encouraging participants to engage by putting their experiences into words. The very act of describing these experiences gives them greater weight and clarity.

The two Guiding Questions in the section Highlighting Session Theme of "Why mindfully observe our inner experiences?" and "What makes this important to the caregiver's situation?" both encourage a moment of reflection. A few responses are helpful to encourage engagement from the group around this topic. Mindfulness is a general benefit, but this reflection regrounds it in the caregiver's life. As described in Session 1 with "The Radio and the Open Window," participants are guided to intentionally tune into their inner room intentionally, perhaps noticing the noisy thoughts and inner tension, and find their way towards the open window of listening to sounds, seeing the colors and shapes, or noticing breathing.

Mindful observing, moving out of our thoughts and into present sensations without mental commentary, is a foundation for physical and emotional health. When we lose contact with our inner bodily experience, we lose the sense of how we feel and how we are doing until the body lets us know in big ways like illness, depression, or burnout. Mindful observing takes the inner temperature and allows us to reset if our stress has gotten out of hand. If I look and find my shoulders and chest are tight and breathing is shallow, I know without analyzing that I am stressed or anxious. I might take a Mindful Pause to let go and follow my breath rather than ignore stress signals and tightly push through the day. Participants might be asked, "How do you know from the way your body feels that you are stressed or frustrated?"

Reconnecting with bodily sensations and feelings is one way mindful observing is helpful. Another is the way attending and noticing allows us to step back from the choppy waves of thoughts and emotions, not getting so lost and entangled in them. The observing part of me separates from the drama of emotions and whirlpool of thoughts, giving me a gap of freedom. This gap of simply noticing acts as a salve on the rash of runaway stress or tension. It's as if our body and deeper self yearn for our attention, increasing the noise of its signals until we finally turn to look. And when we do look, this body and deeper self relax and open.

The following Mindfulness Practices of Movement and Stationary meditation now gently intensify the experience of mindful observing. Qigong moves are often felt as relaxing and pleasurable. Emphasis is on being *inside* the movements, feeling so directly their flow and sensing alignment as both physically and emotionally grounding. Mindful Breathing Meditation is a classic mindfulness practice. It challenges participants to relax while keeping alert, noticing the pull into thoughts and then resetting one's focus on the breath, and mindfully following the breath sensation as a way of being present. Now all the ingredients of mindful observing are brought together.

The Summary and Suggestions can now gather the session's core lessons and experiences with an invitation to take various mindfulness practices out of the room into daily life. Audios and videos make the formal movement and stationary practices accessible to try at home. Informal ways of shifting into mindfulness, like Mindful Pauses and the list in the handout of Mindful Daily Practices, are spread out like cafeteria options. You might ask, "Which exercises are you most drawn to and want to try out?" After fielding questions and comments, the session ends. Handouts are distributed.

Some Take-Away Points

The nature of caregiving is *other-focused*, and for this reason, *self-care* often suffers. Little attention is returned to oneself unless it is exhaustion or stress symptoms too loud to ignore. In Session 2, the value of mindful observing is presented as a skill and tied to the need to connect more often with our inner experiences.

This does two things. First, it begins to sharpen the skill of noticing present moment sensations, feelings, and thoughts clearly, without getting so lost in one's usual reactions and judgments. It is a kind of noticing that values pausing to see what is occurring both inside and outside of us. Second, this encourages more frequent tapping into inner experiences and allows one to get to know one's bodily feelings. Sensing feelings directly and nonjudgmentally allows one to pause, ponder, and, perhaps, discover ways to reset ourselves. The poem "A Little Greek Tale" (Lumpkin, 2014) illustrates how a simple gesture of mindfully noticing one's breath can gently lead one out of being lost in our thoughts and reactions. The use of "The Radio and The Open Window" highlights the challenge and the advantage of stepping back to notice one's experience and reset attention to the window of present sensations, freed from mental noise. *The profound simplicity of mindfulness belies its power until participants play with its practices over time.*

Tobias, in the Check-In, spoke of being surprised at how unaware he was most of the day. He noted how rushing and multitasking had taken over his patient care. He thought he was providing the technical things patients needed; however, he realized how little he knew them.

Tobias' response to Session 2: *I am beginning to see how little I know about what is going on inside me during the day. Yet I can see that if I do not know what is happening in me, I pay a price, spending more energy than I have, keeping myself in a tiring spin until the fuses in my mind and body are simply blown. I wonder if I'll be able to turn this around. Mindful observing sounds simple, but it is hard to stay in. It seems I am always talking to myself or creating long to-do lists. I found the Qigong movements a little easier this time, particularly when I stopped trying to do it right rather than just went with the flow of it. The breathing meditation was mixed. It had moments of clear focus, along with several times of wondering if I'm doing it correctly, or restless thoughts of what I need to do tomorrow. Jan, our facilitator, said this was on par for the course! Without her counsel, I'm afraid I would just say this is too hard and stop. I have to say I really like the Check-In. Others in the group tried out different practices and inspired me to try some of them. Joyce, for example, said she did little Qigong breaks at her desk when she felt she was getting wound up. I may try that, since I like movements. I am realizing how alone I have been feeling in my patient ED work. Everybody there at the hospital rushes as I do.*

Tobias represents someone in the early phases of developing appreciation, understanding, and practice experiences in mindfulness. Like many, his observations are captured by how big the problems of living in an automatic pilot are in contrast to the more immediate gifts of mindfulness practice. This is where the group process and the facilitator come in to normalize this experience and to encourage staying with mindfulness learnings. It is tempting for some to be quite self-critical at this stage. Here, the facilitator extends a helpful hand by reflecting discoveries, like Tobias' reactions to the patient with dementia, as discoveries and instances of effective mindful observing, not prods to feel guilt or shame.

Belinda, in the Check-In, brought up challenges from her week related to finding time to practice mindfulness. She noted that every moment of every day seems taken up by doing something for someone else, and it feels impossible to take even 5 minutes for herself. She expressed that over the past week, the only time she was able to practice mindfulness was in the evening after her mother had gone to bed. She lay awake for a few minutes and practiced breathing mindfully and recited her prayers. She noticed that this did seem to calm her body and her mind, and she had not thought before to include a mindful pause with her nighttime prayers. Overall, Belinda shared feeling discouraged about her week, frustrated that she had not been able to practice the mindful moments or complete the meditation she had planned to do. Most of her statements were negative and self-critical, and she primarily focused on the practices she had not been able to complete.

Belinda's response to Session 2: *After learning more about the skill of mindful observing, I am realizing more that mindfulness is not always about the specific practices like "5 minutes of Qigong" or a meditation, but I could try to focus on connecting more mindfully with my body and myself. I am always so focused on my mother and my grandson, listening to their needs, and paying attention to any shift or change I observe in them. I rarely focus on myself or take the time to check in with how I am thinking, feeling, or what I am experiencing. I think I might be able to try doing a mindful check-in a few times throughout the day, although I practice mindful observing for a few moments. This could be a helpful way to bring this skill into my daily routine, and it feels simple to do.*

Belinda, in her Check-In, highlights a common tendency to focus on discouragement about what was not accomplished and discount the small, yet meaningful, positive steps taken. Group facilitators can assist by listening carefully and shining a light on the positive steps an individual shares, shifting the focus away from judgment, to be curious, accepting, and validating. If you notice several group members share in a similar way by criticizing themselves, stating that they "failed" because they were not able to practice mindfulness adequately in the week, you might comment on this trend for the group. Highlighting how easy it is for all of us to be critical and judgmental and slip out of a mindful space can be a powerful intervention. The Check-In itself can be an opportunity to practice mindful, nonjudgmental awareness and be a helpful teaching moment.

Key Concepts

- The skill of mindfully observing thoughts, emotions, and physical sensations can help connect to the present moment instead of being lost in "Monkey Mind."
- Caregivers may be more used to observing others and less accustomed to connecting to their own internal experiences.
- Increased awareness of one's own thoughts/emotions/physical sensations supports an increased awareness of self-care needs.

Session 2 Guide: Mindful Observing

Aim of Session 2:

- To introduce the concept of mindful observing and cultivating a nonjudgmental stance regarding thoughts and emotions.
- To describe the connection between thoughts, emotions, and body sensations, and promote the value of increasing insight through awareness of body sensations.
- Sessions 2 through 4 can be seen as three aspects of mindfulness that grow out of each other. Participants can be encouraged to see mindful observing as a fundamental skill that will extend to all subsequent sessions.

Check-In

Aim:

- To check in with participants about mindfulness practices they engaged in throughout the week and allow caregivers to connect, share, and learn from other group members. Are caregivers beginning to sense the value of inward, mindful focusing?
- To share experiences of caregiving that relate to the role of mindfulness.

Suggestions: In many ways, the facilitator's goal is to model a mindful approach through these sessions. For instance, if individuals mention self-critical or judgmental thoughts as they self-reflect on the week, this would be an opportunity for the facilitator to model a stance of self-compassion, acceptance, and curiosity. Or, when participants express a mindful experiment as a positive experience, they seek to validate it by noting its mindfulness aspect. Lift it out so the person is not as tempted to minimize it as something small and unimportant.

Check-In: Individuals are encouraged to share mindfulness practices they engaged in over the past week and discuss any thoughts or related observations. This also provides an opportunity to discuss barriers caregivers experienced and what might have gotten in the way of practicing mindfulness. Participants are invited to reflect on the past week from a place of curiosity and nonjudgmental awareness and cultivate a stance of self-compassion. This can also be a helpful time to share suggestions, strategies, and techniques that caregivers found helpful, which can be valuable to other group members. Facilitators lead these Check-Ins and encourage individuals to share as they are comfortable while monitoring the space to ensure all participants are allowed equal time to participate. Another approach is to simply go around the group in turn, with each person asked to share. Often, people respond better to being called upon than deciding whether to volunteer.

Check-ins are a vital part of the learning process. Often, participants make discoveries about mindfulness early on. To capture and reinforce these, facilitators can offer feedback after a person shares an experience. There can be three phases to this process, depending on what is offered by the participant. The first phase is simply validating the experience by reflecting and paraphrasing, or using the person's own words. The second phase is asking questions that help fill out the experience and its aspects ("and what happened after that?"). The third phase has the facilitator making connections among the aspects of the experience ("when (fill in the blank) occurred, you noticed that ______seemed to follow it"). The first phase is always used. Phases two and three depend on what is expressed and the indirect teaching opportunities it presents.

Brief Mindful Pause: A Journey Through the Senses

Aim: To introduce the concept of mindful observing by guiding participants to nonjudgmentally observe body sensations, thoughts, and emotions and shifting attention to the present moment. Participants will be guided through a mindful check-in with various senses.

Suggestions: Guide participants by highlighting the ways our senses evoke clear present experiences separate from the commenting, labeling mind. To simply observe without judgment or internal self-talk. To see the difference between direct sensations and thoughts. Participants can be guided to observe sounds, then the feeling of temperature, then the clothes on the skin, and then touch the fabric on their clothes. Give each sense a moment for simple mindful noticing. Remind participants to go slowly and to observe any thoughts arising without being taken away by them. This exercise allows individuals to begin to understand the concept of mindful observing and noticing without judgment.

Discussion/Sharing

After completing the mindful observing exercise, ask for brief comments. "What did you notice in this trip through some of your senses?" "Did anything surprise you?" It can be helpful to highlight the challenge of tuning into our sensations without immediately commenting and judging. Be careful to stay focused on the person's expressed experience by reflecting it and avoiding interpreting or praising.

Highlighting Session Theme: Mindful Observing

- Guiding Question: What difference does observing and connecting with our inner experiences make as opposed to inattention and "business as usual" as it relates to the caregiver experience?

  Aim: To amplify the effects one experiences when in the mode of mindful observing as opposed to usual modes of thin and scattered attention. To situate these effects in the context of caregiving.

Guiding Image: "The Radio and the Open Window"

Aim: To reintroduce this image after discussing it last session, and further extend the skill and practice of mindful observing. You cannot shift to the open window until you take note of the feel of the room and the radio's voices absorbing one's attention.

- **Part A: Mind-Body Connection**
  - Focus on body sensations to build a foundation for discussing mindful observing. When we are living mindlessly, we often become disconnected from our body, ignoring body sensations as well as our own physical needs,

etc. There is so much to learn from our body, and often emotions and stress become stored in the body when we avoid or ignore them. Introduce mindful observing by discussing observing the body to notice the information we can learn when connected to the body in the present moment.
    - Example: Noticing that our shoulders are tight or our chest is heavy can provide helpful insight about our stress, anxiety, and mood.
  - Body sensations also often help us identify emotions by asking questions, "How do you know you are angry? What do you notice in the body?" "How do you know when you are anxious. What do you notice in the body?"
- **Part B: Mindful Observing**
  - Mindful observing allows us to step back from the whirlpool of thoughts and emotions pulling us in, like standing on the shore watching choppy waves.
  - Noticing how body sensations underlie emotions gives us a new handle in self-awareness. Putting aside thoughts and judgments opens a direct and undistorted view of what is happening inside us. Mindful observation creates a space from which to choose.

Mindfulness Practice Movement: Qigong or Gentle Stretching

Aim: To focus on the practice of staying in the observing mode and accepting experiences as they come, whatever they are.

Suggestions: This movement practice also highlights the way breath can be synchronized with movement and builds on the concept of the mind-body connection. Nonstriving and going with the flow pave the way for expanding moments of enrichment in daily life. Another key principle experienced in moving is that of physical and emotional grounding. Body sensations and the senses provide a base outside of focusing on thoughts that we can always turn toward.

Brief Inquiry and Sharing:

"What stood out for you with this experience?"

Mindfulness Practice Stationary: Mindful Breathing Meditation

Aim: To provide a formal meditation practice that highlights the principles of mindful observing and awareness.

Suggestions: Mindful breathing meditation encourages individuals to focus attention on the breath, notice thoughts as they come into the mind and pass, and allow emotions to emerge while creating space and avoiding overattachment. Typically, with mindful breathing meditations, individuals are encouraged to start by noticing their breath without changing it. This can be followed by allowing the breath to open and deepen as it may want. Often, a helpful visualization is observing thoughts, placing them on a leaf, and watching them float out of sight down a stream. This helps solidify the concept of mindful observing and provides a formal meditation for practice.

Share the poem "A Little Greek Tale" to highlight principles of how breath awareness liberates us from lost-ness in thought loops. After reading the poem, lead participants through the Mindful Breathing Meditation using the script or recording provided.

Brief Inquiry and Sharing

"What did you notice during this exercise?"

Summary and Suggestions for Formal and Informal Practices during the Week

Aim: To review and reinforce the concepts discussed in the group, particularly the tool of mindful observing and how this anchors all other mindfulness practices.

Suggestions: Highlight the importance of observing without judging and observing internal thoughts, emotions, and body sensations, as well as externally with our environment through the senses. We usually do not separate parts of our experience and leave them in a hazy mixture. So, the patient and gradual practice of seeing sensations, emotions, and thoughts separately is a new and valuable foundation skill. Suggest patience and playfully exploring as helpful learning attitudes. This time serves to continually support participants' own experimentation with a range of possible formal and informal practices. Encourage participants to work to mindfully connect with body sensations and breath during the day. Resources might include the session summary, poem, video, and audio guidance.

Handouts:

- Session 2 Participant Summary
- Session 2 Qigong Video or Gentle Stretching
- Session 2 Mindfulness of Breath Audio
- Poem: "Another Little Greek Tale."

Session 2-Facilitator's Contemplation: What happens when you see?

Session 2 Participant Summary: Mindful Observing*

Guiding Question: What difference might observing and connecting with our **inner** experiences make in daily life, in contrast to our usual tendency towards inattention and preoccupations?

Aim of Session: To introduce the experience of intentional attention to inner experiences through different senses, through movement, and through body/breath sensations in meditation.

What did you notice in the **Mindful Pause: A Journey Through the Senses?**

What did you notice in the **Mindful Movement (Qigong)?**

* Lumpkin, M., Collins, M.H., & Jarrett, R.B. (2026). Mindful self-care for clinicians and caregivers: A group facilitator's guide. Academic Press.

What stood out for you in **Mindful Meditation with Breath?**

Mind-Body Connection: Mental and physical health depend upon tuning into body sensations in order to directly know what these experiences are telling us. The body is the first to signal states of tension, stress, well-being, as well as our emotional reactions and moods.

Mindful Observing: Tuning into our inner sensations and feelings allows us to step back and separate from the choppy waves of our mind chatter to create a place of calm and clarity in the present moment.

Guiding Image of "The Radio and the Open Window" from Session 1: If the room represents your mind space, the radio is the often-constant chatter and self-talk that pulls us out of the moment as it dominates attention. It is important, in this session, to take note of the room and radio or your thoughts and emotions before you shift to the window or some present moment sensation like the breath or noticing sights and sounds around you. Body sensations often offer a strong clue to when and how we are caught in Monkey Mind.

In this session, you may have experienced mindful observing as a relaxed, yet alert focus brought to what is happening now without judgment. Learning this skill takes practice. Old habits of getting lost in thoughts are strong, requiring patience and the willingness to notice when you are distracted and then to refocus attention to what you now feel and sense. It is a simple and powerful skill in reclaiming life in the present.

Suggestions: Please continue your own exploration and experimenting with your chosen meditations and options from the list of Informal Daily Practices that are brief entries into mindfulness. Feel free to use Audio and Video resources.

Lumpkin, M., Collins, M.H., & Jarrett, R.B. (2026). Mindful self-care for clinicians and caregivers: A group facilitator's guide. Academic Press.

List mindfulness practices you would like to try this week:	☑

Lumpkin, M., Collins, M.H., & Jarrett, R.B. (2026). Mindful self-care for clinicians and caregivers: A group facilitator's guide. Academic Press.

Another Little Greek Tale

(Lumpkin, 2014, p. 32)

She told the story of Theseus and the Labyrinth.

How a simple thread traced lostness back to freedom.

Then she said, You, too, can go inside your own

labyrinth, get lost, and come out alive.

She said the breath is a golden thread.

It is always tied to the door of your freedom.

I went inside the dark and into the maze of my mind.

I got lost in hallways and mirrors.

I remembered the golden thread.

I breathed my way back home.

Session 2: Moving Meditation Transcript

Hello and welcome back to moving meditation using Qigong a second time. Like what we did before … adding some movements … and, hopefully, in the mix of all those movements … you'll find some that will become favorites of yours … in their way of pulling you in to the present moment …

So, we're going to … like last time … focus on the interior sensations of the exercises … and not so much worry over whether you're doing the movements the right way or the wrong way … or concern how we look on the outside … or think about the steps ….We're going to feel our way into it.

So I'd like you to start with your feet about hip-width apart … letting those feet root … root … root … into the floor … as you give your weight up … into what's supporting you … underneath … feeling the feet spread … holding the body … in a very relaxed way … the feet are not tensed … just simply allowed … to be themselves … holding you up … without effort … and with much flexibility … bringing a little bit of spring to your feet … And I'd like you to bring that sensitive, mindful attention now … up through the legs … feeling ankles, calves … whether the knees are locked or unlocked (and if locked, unlocking them) … noticing what this is like … noticing unlocking knees releases the small of the back … to align itself a little more securely … and noticing as we bring attention up … through the waist … letting go … letting go … letting go … of any kind of holding, tensing, grasping … We're going to let breath, for a moment, breathe through the spine, letting the spine release its way … upward … so that there's a sense that the top of the head is gently pulled toward the sky … eyes and chin slightly dropped, released forward … shoulders allowed to widen … allowing the center of gravity to shift from the head or upper part of the chest … to the very important center a little below the navel … finding this with your breathing … and breath breathed into this spacious body allows stomach and chest to expand … making room for the breath … and feeling breath drop below into this new center of gravity … In Qigong, the alignment is a principle exercise in itself … a practice … in which we are ever more invited to … release unneeded tension …

So, let's begin a movement. We'll hold a ball in front of us. We're going to get more waist action this time … so that where we move and turn … we'll not be using the knees and legs … we'll be only using the waist as a pivot … without using the shoulders to turn … the waist will turn the upper body. So, as I turn with the ball … waist only is doing the turning … breathing in … now breathing out … breathing in … breathing out … breathing in … breathing out … feeling the waist action now … as it starts to "wake up" … we immobilize the waist so much in our lives … this may feel a little strange at first … as we bring the waist back "on line" … feeling for any kind of tension or effort in the arms and shoulders … and releasing it … simply … let go … feeling … feeling … feeling … from the inside out. And now, coming to a rest … feeling for a moment what's been happening … checking in … thoughts may arise or judgments … we just let them fly by … like birds across the sky …

This next movement we'll work with circles … and waist … a little more. I'll start with my left hand on my left hip … but you can start with your right hand on your right hip … so we'll mirror each other. We're going to do circles … I'll turn again from the waist … arms up, breath out all the way … turn … breath in … breath out … keeping joints spacious and open. Let's change sides for a moment … breathing in … breathing out … breathing in … breathing out … feeling how the waist is all that is needed to pull arms, hands … all that's needed to turn head, shoulders … what's it like to feel the waist in action again … feeling the graceful, floating circles … coordinated with your breath …

Coming to a rest … This is a movement found in both Qigong and Tai Chi. Feeling now the inside energy state of your body … the fullness of breath … the intent now … to take mindfulness into your next moment … when you cease the exercise … and move again in your own way … even with a little of this Qigong sensitivity added … So until next time …

Qigong Movement 4

Qigong Movement 5

Breath Meditation Script

Introduction and Overview

There are three phases to this brief meditation, which uses the breath as an attention anchor. The first phase sets the stage by bringing attention to body sensations. This allows reconnection with one's body as distinct from the usual privileging of preoccupation with thinking or wandering thoughts. This shift is made easier by attending to the sensation of aligned posture, followed by a selective Body Scan. The second phase involves the intent to let go and allow deepening relaxation while maintaining alert wakefulness. Relaxation makes focusing easier since body tension reinforces striving effort and an overly active thought process. The third and final phase is fostering a relaxed yet sustained focus on the sensations of breathing. Focusing with ever-sharpening clarity is encouraged. Thoughts, self-talk, and distracting images will arise and are to be treated as quite normal. The way to deal with them is to acknowledge them without fusing with them. One learns to see this dynamic more clearly with practice and to learn to patiently and gently return to the focus on breath sensations as nothing to be concerned about. If people find it a struggle to step back from thoughts, an image might be useful. One can imagine putting thoughts on leaves floating downstream as one way of meeting strong distractions.

Guidance of Breath Meditation

Phase 1

"Now let's shift attention to a meditation that fosters relaxation, wakefulness, and clarity of focus. We will move through three phases: attuning attention to body sensations, settling into relaxation while maintaining alertness, and focusing on the breath as a primary anchor for attention while letting go of our usual preoccupation with thoughts. This meditation is best done with attitudes of patience, gentleness toward oneself, and releasing any effort to get some outcome. As you explore your ability to shift attention to the chosen object of the breath, consider allowing a wider background awareness to quietly hold other experiences that come and go. The wider awareness is like your internal sky that contains birds, weather, and landscapes that arise and disappear. The narrower focus of attention is given more weight as you work with releasing thoughts and clarifying the chosen zone of sensation."

The facilitator now invites attention to one's upright, supportive posture, followed by a very brief scan of body parts. These parts can be chosen by the facilitator but might include: the bottom of one's feet, thighs, waist, and small of the back, shoulders, neck, and palms of the hands. Attention is gently placed on the area with the simple invitation to simply notice what is there without comment or judgment. Phase 1 might take around three or 4 minutes.

Phase 2

"Now, returning to a sense of the body, simply notice the body's state of tension or relaxation. If an area feels tight or tense, simply allow the body to let go in its own time. You might breathe into that area for a moment. Continue to allow the body to settle, to open, to let go."

This phase might take a couple of minutes. The emphasis is on moving into greater relaxation rather than sustaining a focus on the meditation object of the breath.

Phase 3

"Now, for our final phase, you might gently find your breath. Where do you sense your breathing occurring as opposed to thinking about breathing? [Pause] The point is to just notice your breathing sensations up close, intimately. No judgment or commentary is needed. If you get distracted or pulled away by thoughts, which will happen as a rule, just notice this has happened and gently walk your attention back to the breath. Try not to make this a problem; it is part of training our attention, like teaching our internal puppy to stay rather than leap after anything that grabs its attention. Now, let's explore the ways the breath moves in our bodies."

The facilitator can begin with the sensitive nostrils and the feeling of breath entering and leaving them. This can be followed by the rising and falling of the chest and the expanding and contracting of the rib cage. Finally, the sense of the breath falling like a gentle waterfall into the bowl of the belly can be explored. The meditation can now continue until the end by following the breath wave by wave in any place the participant chooses as easiest. The final invitation is simply to continue to sense the breath while feeling the body as a whole for a moment.

Session 3—Mindful Responding

Session 3 focuses on mindful responding to self and others, with helpful strategies for managing distressing emotions. The Guide also includes a written description of experiential practices for the session. The aim of Session 3 is to highlight a contrast between reacting versus *mindful responding, demonstrating how mindfulness can serve as a tool to regulate and navigate difficult emotions.*

Mindful Self-Care for Clinicians and Caregivers. https://doi.org/10.1016/B978-0-443-29821-9.00008-X

"Light amid the Storm" - This photograph was taken in New Mexico (2023) by Robin B. Jarrett. Where does your eye take you? What happens when you refocus your gaze?

Session 3 Facilitator Quick Guide: Mindful Responding

Session 3 Theme: The Difference Between Reactivity and Mindful Responding to Stress

Check-In

- Invite each participant's response to what was experienced when experimenting with mindfulness this week. There are no wrong responses here.
- Listen for early experiences with mindful responding to stress and the savoring of caregiver privilege and the "see-saw" between the two; the dynamic between the roles of care person and caregiver; then connect these experiences to the session theme.
- Shared experiences of mindfulness can be separated into what was tried and what concrete experiences came out of what was tried.

Mindful Pause: Noting and Letting Go of Stress Reactions

- Begin with mindful attention to current body sensations, followed by sensing the breath.
- Clear a space inside to allow a recent moderately stressful experience to come forward.
- See what it is like to simply notice the memory and any reactions arising in the mind and body, such as tension or tightened breathing *without* adding any thoughts to it.
- Then find out what happens when attention is moved to mindful breathing as the focus of the memory, so that reactions that automatically arise can be released.

Brief Discussion/Sharing

- Note the two aspects of the above mindful pause: Seeing impartially one's concrete, specific automatic reactions to the memory and the experience of allowing the memory experience to fade away as one turns to mindfulness of breathing.
- This is a challenging exercise because we are not accustomed to sensing a memory and automatic reactions to it without becoming absorbed in them and feeding them with more reactive thoughts and emotions.

Highlight the Session Theme: Mindful Responding

- Guiding question: What difference do you notice between emotionally reacting to a stress experience and mindfully responding to it? What difference does mindfulness savoring of positive experiences make on overall stress levels?
- Guiding image: Chinese handcuffs
- Part A: Seeing the vicious circle of reactive struggle and resistance to stressors

  - Using the playful image of Chinese handcuffs, notice how vicious circles are created by getting lost in our reactions to stress and how using this kind of coping to escape makes the stress experience worse and prolonged.
  - Caregivers might reflect on how this shows up in their lives in the caregiver role.
- Part B: Mindful responding to stress and pleasant experience
  - What is the parallel to releasing trapped fingers from the Chinese handcuffs and responding mindfully to a stressor? Might it be pausing to become aware of immediate experience instead of getting lost in reactivity? Can the caregiver "catch" their response? Then can they step back to slow down, breathe, and release the struggle–the "release" phase? Are they then able to find a response that better fits the situation–the "choose" phase?
  - Would caregiver participants be willing to experiment in their daily lives with this Catch-Release-Choose way of responding? Are there questions or concerns?
  - What might it mean to savor and attend more fully to positive feelings when they arise? Do we value these experiences or minimize them next to our inner pressures and negative self-talk?

Mindfulness Practice Movement

- Pairing breath and movement while seated or standing, mindful attention is brought to the sensations of such slow, rhythmic, breath-infused ways of moving.
- The three parts of this practice: The flower, mindful head rolls, and sunrise.

Brief Inquiry and Sharing

- What was noticed during movement meditation? Sensations? Effect on tension levels?
- Was staying focused on movements and breath challenging?

Mindfulness Practice Stationary: Mindful Emotional Processing

- This is a three-phase meditation related to the earlier Mindful Pause exercise. It begins with bringing a sense of care and kindness to oneself. After a moment of clearing, awareness is opened to receive any spontaneous memory of a recent stressful event. After meeting that experience with simple mindful attention as opposed to just thinking about it, letting it go and clearing a space for the next memory that arises. All that is required in emotional processing is to see and acknowledge the experience without adding reactions to it. After a while, the meditation ends with bringing warm attention to one's heart.
- This meditation ends with the poem "Patience".

Brief Inquiry/Sharing

- What was it like to remember stressful experiences in this way? Did you notice any pull to obsess or ruminate over a memory? How did you try to handle these? Could you simply allow them without judgement or commentary?
- What was your experience holding yourself in warm, caring attention at the beginning and end of the meditation?

Summary and Suggestions for Formal and Informal Practices during the Week

- Briefly summarize the session theme on mindful responding to stress.
- Suggest the Chinese handcuffs as a useful image to remind oneself to slow down and Catch-Release-Choose.
- Offer an invitation to continue to choose brief mindful pauses during one's day as well as to try out meditations one is drawn to.
- Reminder: Bring a small food item for the next session's mindful eating exercise.

Handouts/Resources:

- Session 3 Participant Summary
- The poem "The Space in Patience"
- Mindful movement video
- Three simple mindful movements

Session 3 Introduction: Mindful Responding

Caregiver's worlds are filled with challenges and pressures that are ongoing. They must make critical assessments and decisions based on their care person's often fluctuating medical and emotional states. They may struggle with knowing some, but not all the factors involved in such decisions. They must meet and deal with the pain, anxiety, and irritability of the one for whom they care. They must find a way to take on the stress of being the brunt of the patient's complaints and frustration. And they must find a way to have a life that keeps them in some balance and sense of significance. At the same time, caregivers often also find gratitude in the privilege of caregiving and feel special in that they can provide care and were chosen for the role. They often find glimmers of who their care person was prior to the illness or disability and feel grateful that their care person is still present. They relish the thank you's and again are reminded of the special and unique role of caregiving, considering the dynamic of trust again.

In Session 3, participants build on prior mindfulness skills in order to respond to stress in a healthier way. As it turns out, many caregivers are unaware that it is the way one responds to stress and not the stressor itself that results in the impact of stress growing large and chronic or being met in a way that allows it to be digested and released. Mindfulness encourages awareness and choices, taking note of vicious circles of stress spirals and electing to respond to the situation with greater equanimity. Mindfully observing reactive emotions and the thoughts that feed them creates a space between an automatic inner reaction and the response one chooses to make. Without this space, people may fall into a current of emotions, thoughts, and behaviors and are carried on impulse and habit. And given constant stressful challenges, unmindful reactions collect and accumulate into states that may overwhelm, coming up as chronic resentment, anxiety, and depression. Session 3 introduces this mindful perspective on stress and fosters the hope and possibility of meeting stress in the moment without fueling it into the future. This is an exciting stage in the promise of mindfulness. The mindful perspective on relating to stress takes one beyond coping techniques and into the realm of insight and responses based on present moment insights.

After briefly stating the theme of this session, turn to the growing momentum of the Check-In. Warmly invite participants to share their experiments with mindfulness, creating a safe space to express one's experiences without feeling judged or graded. Brief empathic summaries and the validation these bring help to give significance to these experiments. Don't be surprised by participants who anticipate the theme of this session, which is the impact of mindful observing and choosing one's response to caregiver stress and privilege. If stress happens, observe it as impartially as possible, gently refuse to feed it, and refocus on a more helpful response. Caregivers can positively impact their stress levels in a couple of basic ways: to mindfully respond to stress experiences or to invest time and attention in mindful moments that evoke positive emotions like relief, joy, and pleasure. Rather than lecture, try staying close to participants' discoveries as they arise in the sharing of their thoughts and feelings along the continuum of the caregiving experience.

The Mindful Pause gives participants an experience of mindful responding. Note that it starts with bringing attention to one's body as the primary base for observing inner states.

Bringing in breathing awareness repeats a familiar way to anchor one's attention in present moment experience, a place outside the Monkey Mind's usual dominance. The memory of a stressful experience should be of moderate intensity rather than extreme. Moderate intensity increases the chance that this initial skill will be more manageable. Since stressful memories tend to be fed with thoughts and self-talk, the experience of simply observing the bodily response, such as the effect on breathing, is new in its simplicity. This phase of the exercise allows a chance to feel one's reactivity directly and concretely, without the usual fog of mental elaborations. It relies upon the principle of acceptance rather than struggle to escape. The last move in the exercise is the return to breath focus. The power of gently redirecting one's attention to the breath is in the release of the stress experience by electing not to obsess or ruminate. This small practice will be elaborated in the later Stationary Meditation. Caregivers are often beleaguered by numerous or ongoing stressors that accumulate into a congestion of unprocessed emotional experiences. They might wonder if such a simple mindful approach could be all that effective. See if you might honor such doubts, if they come up, while inviting caregivers to see mindful responding as a possibility needing to be validated through their own experiments.

The next section, Highlighting the Session Theme, takes a little time to conceptually map out the experience of mindful responding to stress. It should play off the Mindful Pause and any related stress experiences shared in the Check-In. The Guiding Question asks the caregiver to begin to discriminate between mindful responding and our often default mode of reactivity. You might suggest an image to keep in mind the difference between the two modes of relating to stress: the Chinese Handcuffs. Metaphors tend to be held in mind and memory more than discursive, abstract descriptions. Have a little fun with the image, as we all need to smile at ourselves for the way we can struggle in the briar patch of our thoughts. One gift of mindfulness is its light touch. Chinese Handcuffs can be simply described and gestured by bringing index fingers toward each other as they enter the straw tube, pressing toward the center. Then, with some force, the fingers are pulled back and out only to feel the straw tube tighten around them. At that point, the fingers are stuck and trapped. The greater the effort to pull out, the more the tube tightens. If you prefer, these handcuff toys are also cheaply available for sale online. See if it is possible to move through this section simply, without overexplaining.

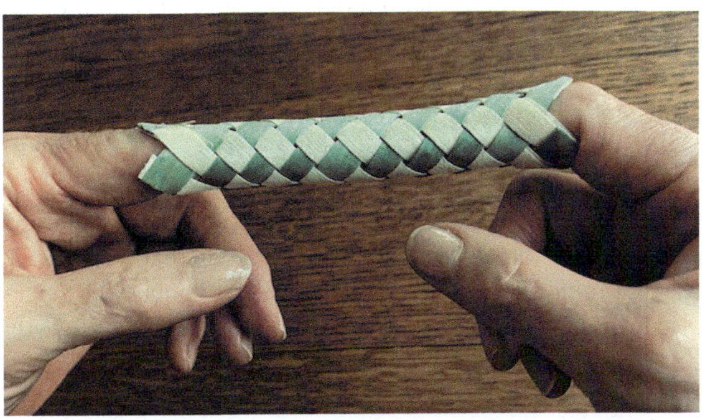

"Chinese Handcuffs" - Martin thought this intriguing toy was such an apt image of how we trap ourselves by force and effort to escape a tense situation inside ourselves. The opposite of mindful awareness and acceptance that lets one respond more freely.

Parts A and B knit together in a natural sequence. They end with an invitation to caregiver participants to experiment with the principles of Catch (the stress experience), Release (the effort to resist and feed it), and Choose (a response which may be both internal, like focusing on the breath, and external, like calmly communicating). One way of mindfully defusing tension from stress reactions is through mindful movement. This Mindfulness Practice brings everyone back into body awareness after a period of conceptual focusing. It demonstrates one way of anchoring in both breath and bodily movement to realign attention outside the head mode. These movements done with mindfulness often allow the body to release stress knots and allow the breath to become unstuck in restricted shallowness. The result is often a rise in quiet, calm energy.

The Mindfulness Practice done sitting or stationary reconnects with the Mindful Pause earlier. It might be called Mindful Emotional Processing. It begins with encouraging an inner atmosphere of holding one's current experiences with care and kindness. This is the heartfelt side of mindful attending and is added to the more neutral mindful observing. The mindful attitudes of gentleness, self-kindness, and self-compassion are evoked. They stand in contrast to self-judgments and self-criticality, which can come in the wake of automatic emotional reactions.

During this meditation, participants are reminded to simply see what arises rather than try to fix, control, or ruminate. Recent memories of frustrations or stress are internally invited to arise on their own. These are simply and heartfully held for a moment, then allowed to be released as the next memory arises. The processing principle is this: What has not been acknowledged often presses for attention in us. If obsessing, ruminating, or avoidance occur, these emotional experiences remain unprocessed. When given mindful attention without judgment or reactions added, these pressing experiences begin to lose their pressure. This is an organic rather than a willed dynamic. Returning to the breath as an anchor, along with palm over heart, provides an experience of fluid attention unstuck by fixation on any experience. The poem "The Space in Patience" reinforces the attitudes within the meditation. The inquiry will allow you to hear various responses to this way of meeting internal stress. It may help you assess the level of challenge that mindful responding offers caregiver participants. Keep in mind that people grow their mindfulness skills at different rates, and all need a kind of permission to be where they are with the process.

The last section, Summary and Suggestions, gives you a moment to connect the various phases of this session to the theme of mindful versus mindless responding. It is also a good time to honor the courage to risk new experiences in the process of discovering what mindfulness is all about. The last request of a small food item is for an exercise in mindful eating in Session 4. In Session 4, mindful awareness skills will be brought to self-care.

Some Takeaway Points

Caregivers are often on-the-spot responders to ongoing needs and crises involving their care person or persons. This makes it easy to go into high alert stress mode and stay there, running on emotional reactions with little time to reflect on the most adaptive response to a situation. It is tempting to think that one's stress reactions are driven by external pressures and obstacles. From a mindfulness perspective, the way one responds to stress is the main driver of stress spirals. As the image of Chinese Handcuffs reveals, efforts to fight or frantically escape only tighten the grip of stress. Mindfully stepping back, observing one's experiences, and anchoring in the breath creates a clearer inner space from which to decide one's best response. This is a skill set based on Session 1's recognition of the state of mindfulness and Session 2's skill of mindful observing. Pausing to mindfully savor positive experiences in our lives also helps reset the mind, body, and emotions to avoid staying caught in the trenches of stress preoccupation.

Here is Belinda's response to the Check-In: *This past week was difficult for me. My grandson started kindergarten, so my routine changed since I'll be picking him up in the afternoon before my daughter gets off work, while also caring for my mom. I had a moment this week when I just lost it and snapped at my grandson, which is not like me. I think I was just stressed with all the changes. I felt awful because he doesn't deserve that, and I do not want to take my stress out on a five-year-old. After I noticed that I was getting frustrated I stepped away for a moment and I went into the bathroom to take a few of those mindful breaths. I checked in with myself to observe what I was experiencing in that moment and was able to identify that I was feeling overwhelmed. I think it helped because when I went back into the room, I was calmer. I still feel guilty, although, that I snapped at my grandson who is only five. Sometimes it makes me feel like I can't be a good grandmother and a good daughter. It's just too much.*

Belinda's Check-In has several rich opportunities to highlight learning. She shares a vulnerable example of using the skill of mindful observing in the chaos of caregiving. As the facilitator, you might ask if any other group members might comment on their response to hearing Belinda share, and whether they have ever experienced something similar. This can help normalize Belinda's experience and build group cohesion. Despite starting her Check-In noting how difficult the week was, Belinda was able to successfully use one of the mindfulness skills. You notice, however, that she ends her Check-In with a statement about feeling guilty and down about herself. As the facilitator, this may be an opportunity to highlight the success Belinda had in utilizing the skill in a realistic and meaningful way, while encouraging her not to forget to also bring in the mindfulness skill of no judgment.

Tobias' Check-In response to Session 3: *Before this session, I was already seeing how stopping to check in on my feelings and thoughts gave me more chances to find a calming breath. So the Chinese Handcuffs became a good shorthand for my usual ways of getting into a fuss so quickly when another pressure was added to my day. My whole body was like that straw tube tightening unless I took time to slow down, stop, look at what's happening, and ... breathe. Before the Mindful Pause and the Stationary Meditation, we tried, I thought the best way to handle disturbing thoughts or memories was to ignore them. I didn't realize that relaxing and allowing emotional experiences to simply come up and be seen were all that's required sometimes to let them go. This is something I will have to play with more as it is so opposite of what I'm used to. It's almost too simple to believe it can be effective. The Moving Meditation continues to give a sense of clearing the mind and calming. I plan to use more of the videos at home since I like more active mindfulness exercises. Last week I also did something that was suggested today as a simple thing to do during the day: Rather than keep up my afternoon rush to the next patient, I stopped to make eye contact with a small child in the hall and to listen to her as to why she was there. It took about 5 minutes, but I walked away smiling.*

Like a few participants, Tobias is demonstrating the layered learning of mindfulness skills and practices. He quickly notices how pausing to observe his experience fits in with the way mindfulness encourages stress responding in Session 3. Images like Chinese Handcuffs made the concept of mindless and mindful responding more vivid. It is not surprising that he found mindful noticing of remembered emotional experience a bit strange. We often overcomplicate the challenge of recognizing and releasing such experiences by keeping our attention on avoidance or by ruminating on them. This is why Jan, the facilitator, set up these exercises as experiments that one can continue to play with over time. She avoided efforts to convince participants of this way of handling emotional experiences in exchange for "Try it and see what you experience." This is the basic approach to facilitating learning all aspects of mindfulness. Lastly, Tobias is learning to see the power of savoring positive experiences, too often treated as unimportant or a waste of production time.

Key Concepts

- The way a person *responds* to stress impacts whether that stress can be digested and released or grows in intensity and becomes chronic.
- Mindfulness creates space between the automatic inner reaction and a more intentional mindful response.
- Mindful responding fosters the ability to meet stress in the moment without fueling additional stress in the future.

Session 3 Guide: Mindful Responding

<u>Aim of Session 3:</u>

- To introduce the concept of mindful responding to stressors using the base skill of mindful observing.
- To practice mindful pausing and observing reactive thoughts and emotions, releasing them as opposed to fueling them, and choosing one's response from this stance.
- To relate mindful responding to the caregiver context.

Check-In

Aim: To continue to follow participants' exploration of mindful attitudes and practice in between Session 2 and Session 3. Highlight and validate attempts at mindfulness.

Suggestions: Review Session 2 suggestions. Stay attuned to budding mindful observing skills reported. Draw out not only the form of mindfulness explored but the resulting experience arising from it. Keep in mind, participants new to mindfulness often minimize their attempts at formal or informal practice and maximize their lack of success. Check-Ins give the facilitator the chance to express acceptance and highlight what went right, even if that is only the willingness to try and meet difficulties with awareness. Also, listen to Session 3 themes that may be expressed spontaneously. Participants may have noticed the impact of mindfulness on stress levels, for example. Briefly link the connection between noticing stress experiences in the body, ways of dealing with stress, and the outcome. Note that this is the theme for today. It is usually better to teach from participants' experiences that are shared and make organic connections to the theme rather than teach out of context.

Mindful Pause: Noting and Letting Go of Stress Reactions in the Caregiving Role

Aim: To provide an experiential context for practicing mindful observing of stress reactions, particularly in the body, and the way attention can be reset to release stress spirals. To continue to sharpen participants' internal sensations and the value of attending to them.

Suggestions:

1. Begin with guiding participants' attention to body sensations ("Let's begin with bringing awareness to whatever is going on in your body, simply noticing how sensations may arise and change"). Then shift to awareness of breathing, "much like we did in our mindfulness of breath as an anchor in the last session"). Settle in for a while.
2. "Now let's try an experiment. Open a space inside to allow a recent memory of a *moderately* stressful experience to come forward. Perhaps it had something to do with your caregiver role, or some other event. See it clearly. You may notice thoughts, emotions, or body sensations associated with it. Note them but put your primary attention on what happens in your body as the memory sharpens. Just mindfully *observe*."

3. After a moment or two, "Now see if it is possible to redirect your attention to your breathing again. Just notice breathing sensations as clearly as you can in a relaxed focus." After a moment or two, bring the Mindful Pause to a close.

Discussion/Sharing

After completing the mindful pause, ask for what was noticed. "What did you notice in your body when the stress memory became vivid? And what did you notice in your body as you shifted to focusing on breathing?" If participants give general or abstract ("I felt myself getting upset") responses or try to analyze what happened ("I think just thinking about the memory made me anxious"), ask about specific sensations that arose ("Could you say more about what you specifically felt in your body?"). In this way, you are helping people stay close to actual experiences in a mindful sense, rather than speculate about or judge the experience.

Highlighting the Session Theme: Mindful Responding

- Guiding question: What difference do you notice between emotionally reacting to stress and mindfully responding? What difference does mindfully savoring positive experiences make in overall stress levels?
- Guiding image: Chinese Handcuffs
- **Part A: Seeing the vicious circle of reactive struggle and resistance toward stressors**
  - "Let's begin with an image. Many of us played with a Chinese Handcuff as children, the six-inch woven straw tube. Put your index finger of both hands in the ends, and then you are then invited to escape. As the person pulls harder and harder to release the fingers, the tube closes in tighter and tighter, trapping the fingers. Why is this a good image for the way we get caught up in our reactions to stress?" The facilitator might ask the group for a few responses. Highlight the impulse to escape, resist, and tense up. Notice that failure to escape and feeling trapped often escalates more of the same ineffective coping reactions, spiraling stress rather than subduing it. This is what we call vicious circles: It is not the stressor that is the problem or even the stress feeling itself; it is the way we try to cope with it that makes it worse. As one tries to escape or get control over the stress, various things increase, like negative, anxious, or angry thoughts, emotions of fear or anxiety or depressed defeat, and bodily sensations of rapid heartbeat, shallow breathing, and muscular tension. Participants might reflect for a moment on the ways this might show up in caregiver stressors. Is there another way to respond in which emotions are less likely to get stuck or to spiral?
- **Part B: Mindful Responding to Stress and Pleasant Experience**
  - One counter-intuitive response to fingers stuck in a Chinese Handcuff is to pause, notice reactions and the urge to resist, then breathe and elect to move one's fingers toward each other. Slowly, then, fingers work gently with each other to slide off the handcuff, which no longer tightens when it isn't pulled. Can this be applied to our everyday stress? Perhaps, with patient practice.

- We might call this "catch and release" versus "fight and resist." "Think about your situation, particularly as a caregiver. What do you recognize as your Chinese Handcuffs? Do you try to suppress emotions as an escape? Do you get caught in obsessing about the future or ruminating by chewing on past hurts or resentments?" Ask for a few examples from participants. "Would you be willing to experiment with mindful responding as part of your experiment with mindfulness practices? When you feel stress rising, pause and breathe, then choose your response, which includes *not* responding. **Catch** the stress reaction, **release** the effort to struggle, and **choose** a response. "Questions or comments?" In the next session during Check-In, the facilitator might listen to what people tried in their mindful responding.
- Another way to destress our lives is to mindfully savor and fully experience positive feelings. For example, feelings of gratitude might spontaneously arise in the course of caregiving, which we either bring into focus or ignore. If brought into focus, we bring a kind of nourishment to ourselves.

Moving Meditation:

This movement practice introduces three simple mindful movements that can be completed while seated. With each movement, participants should pair the breath with each part of the movement and focus on the breath and the body as an anchor for attention. See the included video for demonstrations of each of the following movements.

- **The flower:** Extend arms out long, take and inhale and curl arms in to touch your fingertips to your shoulders. Exhale and extend the arms back out long. Repeat.
- **Mindful head rolls:** Inhale and drop the ear towards the shoulder, and roll the head counterclockwise towards 3 o'clock. Exhale and roll your head around to 9 o'clock. Repeat.
- **Sunrise:** Start with arms at your side. Inhale and lift your hands up into prayer above your head. Exhale and slowly lower arms back down to the starting position. Repeat.

Brief inquiry and sharing: What did you notice while completing the movements? Which movement did you enjoy the most? How easy was it to focus and pay attention while completing the mindful movements?

Stationary Meditation: Mindful Emotional Processing

Aim: To demonstrate how emotions might be mindfully digested rather than ignored to avoid an accumulation of congested emotion, which may then surface as fatigue, anxiety, resentment, or depression.

Suggestions: This is a three-phase meditation:

1. "It begins with an invitation to hold oneself with care and kindness and self-compassion. Now create an open space inside as you simply follow your breath

... in and out ... in and out. Let go of any need to be in control or to fix anything." After a few moments,

2. "Now, again, without trying to solve or fix anything, simply allow any emotional experience that was part of your recent past to come to you on its own. When it does, see it, feel it, acknowledge it. Then let it recede as you open for the next experience. Observe with curiosity and with faith in your natural mind and body's ability to digest these experiences without your direct help.
3. After several moments, "Now allow yourself to return to following the breath ... in and out. As you do this, see what happens when you bring warm attention to the feeling of holding yourself, palm over your heart. And just be for a moment." End with the poem "The Space in Patience".

Brief Inquiry/Sharing

"What was your experience with this exercise?" "How challenging was it to simply allow the memories and their feeling tones to be present without comment?"

Summary and Suggestions for Formal and Informal Practices during the Week

Aim: To review and summarize concisely the session themes, guiding questions, and image. To stimulate continued experimenting with formal and/or informal mindfulness practices. To provide participants with resources for their mindfulness perspectives and practices.

Suggestions: Link the parts of the session to the theme of mindful responding. Pose the guiding question and suggest Chinese Handcuffs as a useful image for reactive coping and mindful responding. Most people love images as easy-to-remember metaphors for insight.

Additional note: For this session, ask participants to bring a small food item that would fit the palm of their hand. This will be used for a mindful eating exercise in the next session. Bring raisins or grapes as a backup for those who might forget.

Handouts/Resources:

- Session 3 Participant Summary
- The poem "The Space in Patience"
- Mindful movement video
- Three simple mindful movements

Session 3-Facilitator's Contemplation: What happens during awareness without judgment?

Session 3 Participant Summary: Mindful Responding*

Guiding Question: What difference do you notice between emotionally reacting to a stressful experience and mindfully responding to it? Can actively savoring positive experiences affect your quality of life and stress?

Aim of Session: To introduce the way mindful observing creates a different and more effective way of responding to stress experiences.

What did you notice in the **Brief Mindful Pause: Noting and Letting Go of Stress Reactions?**

What did you notice in the **Moving Meditation: Flower, Head Rolls, and Sunrise?**

* Lumpkin, M., Collins, M.H., & Jarrett, R.B. (2026). Mindful self-care for clinicians and caregivers: A group facilitator's guide. Academic Press.

What stood out for you in the **Stationary Meditation: Mindful Emotional Processing?**

The Vicious Circle of resisting or giving into one's stress reactions and their spirals: Without intending to, we often intensify our stress experiences by trying to think our way out of them, fight to control them, or simply feed our reactions by obsessing and ruminating.

Mindful Responding to Stress/Positivity: Pause to become aware of your internal experience instead of losing yourself in emotional reactivity, stepping back to slow down, breathing mindfully to recenter, and releasing your grip on judgments and self-talk. From there, you are freer to choose your response rather than act out emotional impulses and habits. Catch-Release-Choose. We can also catch and choose to savor positive experiences fully.

Guiding Image of Chinese Handcuffs: If you put your index fingers in the straw tube of the Chinese Handcuffs and then pull and struggle to free yourself, the tube only tightens around your fingers. But if you pause, relax, breathe, and gently move your fingers forward, the tube opens. A good image for reactive versus mindful responding to stress.

In this session, you were invited to feel the way the mind and body jointly experience stress. And you are perhaps reflecting on ways you met stress in your life, reactively or mindfully. You had a chance to see how simply allowing past emotional experiences to come up in memory and be handled with simple mindful attention is one way to permit the body to process and release stored tension. By creating space for awareness without judgment, you may have noticed how this can shift your relationship with difficult emotions. With continued practice, you can cultivate a sense of control and presence in moments of stress, transforming from reactivity to responsiveness.

Suggestions: Continue to experiment with your chosen practices of formal and informal brief moments in your day. Audio and Video meditations are available to you for your explorations during your week. See if you can test out the way mindful responding to stress might work in your life and the challenges of your caregiver role. For the next session, bring a small food item with which to explore mindful eating.

List mindfulness practices you would like to try this week:	☑

The Space in Patience
(Martin Lumpkin, 2025)

A swirl of rush and urge inside of me.
Time's a tightening vice.
So much to think about, to do.
The mind spins, the body tightens.
There is no off switch.
Madly pushing buttons
speeds the spin, torques the tight.
In the midst of this storm inside,
I stop under a tree and
look around.
In the midst of this storm –
I seek shelter in a pause. Just a pause.
Just a crack no larger than a sliver,
let's through a beam of light.
A small space opens and slowly widens.
A space to see and feel, a space to hold what is happening.
Breath slows.
A soft enfolding patience touches rush and urge.
Little by little. Wait.
Little by little. Wait.
Until there's a letting go.
And patience births a space to live in,
breathing me into being.

Lumpkin, M., Collins, M.H., & Jarrett, R.B. (2026). Mindful self-care for clinicians and caregivers: A group facilitator's guide. Academic Press.

Three Simple Mindful Movements

Movement 1: The Flower

Extend arms out long, take and inhale and curl arms in to touch your fingertips to your shoulders. Exhale and extend arms back out long. Repeat.

Lumpkin, M., Collins, M.H., & Jarrett, R.B. (2026). Mindful self-care for clinicians and caregivers: A group facilitator's guide. Academic Press.

Movement 2: Mindful Head Rolls

Inhale and drop ear towards shoulder, and roll head counterclockwise towards 3 o'clock. Exhale and roll head around to 9 o'clock. Repeat.

Lumpkin, M., Collins, M.H., & Jarrett, R.B. (2026). Mindful self-care for clinicians and caregivers: A group facilitator's guide. Academic Press.

Movement 3: Sunrise

Start with arms at side. Inhale and lift hands up into prayer position above head. Exhale and slowly lower the arms back down to starting position. Repeat.

Mindful Emotional Processing Transcript

[The art of facilitating these kinds of meditation is balancing verbal guidance with quiet spacings to allow an experience to unfold. Clues might come from experiencing the meditation yourself.]

This stationary meditation can be done sitting or lying down ....So, finding your position, letting relaxation spread throughout the body. We'll work today with emotional memories to see how mindfulness works in such a simple and direct way with our emotional experiences ... from the past or occurring in the present moment.

Settling in ... feeling yourself in this body ... opening a space ... bringing a kind of hospitality to yourself ... soaked in care and kindness ... for, this is taking care of you ... by allowing emotional experiences to be gently digested ....not left in undigested or congested states ....meeting emotions not with suppression, stuffed until they overwhelm us or ....getting entangled in them and feeding them through obsessing or ruminating.

Is it possible to see our emotional experiences clearly ....and allow them to release in their own way?

You might find memories taking various forms ... some may be visual (seeing what happened) ... some might be auditory (hearing talk and sounds of interactions that took place) ... or perhaps the memory is embedded as feeling tones arising in the body itself ....just be aware of these variations as you allow your way of remembering to naturally come forward ...

Taking a moment now ... clearing a space by breathing in a sense of spaciousness in the body ....and breathing out in this soothing and calming rhythm ... of this breathing ....bringing quiet attention to ... just breathing ... just settling in ... without expectations or the need to be in control or to fix anything ...

And now ... allowing some recent emotional experience to come to you without having to reach for it ... perhaps an experience of moderate intensity rather than high intensity ... you'll find you are filled with natural urges to remember if a space is created ... allowing now ... a memory to come forward ....the work of mindfulness is simply to meet it, to hold it in mind ... without trying to fix or add to it without our thoughts ....when you do experience the memory, face it and simply see it with curiosity ....acknowledging it as though nodding to it ..."yes, I see you" ..."you're there"

Allowing yourself to simply investigate the memory and its impact on the body ... where does it reside and resound in the body? What parts of the body might be involved?...just noticing ... just seeing ... taking no position of judgment ... treating thoughts about the memory as just thoughts ....seeing them if they arise and letting them go ...

When you are ready … allow this memory to move on, whether or not you feel you are finished with it ….settling in … for one more memory as you create a breathing space. And now, waiting and … receiving the next memory … coming on its own … simply seeing it ….or hearing it … or feeling it in the body ….What's it like to simply perceive it without adding any reaction to it? Stepping back … acknowledging it … experiencing it with clarity and acceptance … noticing how the body responds to it … What's this like?

And now … allowing this memory to move on as you refocus on the body and breath … perhaps with whatever residual impact you feel from this exercise … and simply breathing ….feeling the way your body responds to breath … holding yourself with care and kindness. We might have an ending gesture of putting the palm of one hand over the heart (literally or figuratively) … touching yourself in this way for a moment … and just be … for a moment … as we end with a poem called Patience (facilitator reads poem) ….now taking a moment to feel what this exercise did for and to you ….ending with an invitation to see if there is a place for this mindful way of relating to emotions in your own life … in meditation or daily life … (ending with a gong or a countdown for 1–3)

Session 4—Self-Care and Nourishment

Session 4 focuses on the concept of self-care from a bio-psycho-social perspective, including how to monitor, strengthen, and implement self-care practices. The section also includes a written description of experiential practices for the session. The idea of "tending your garden" is used as a metaphor for self-care. The aim of Session 4 is to provide a framework for understanding the concept of self-care, in addition to providing guidance for mindful implementation of self-care practices into daily life.

Mindful Self-Care for Clinicians and Caregivers. https://doi.org/10.1016/B978-0-443-29821-9.00009-1

"In the Garden of Tulips and Daffodils"—Tulips and daffodils bloom in the Collins—Wood Garden—a gentle reminder to tend your own inner garden and make space for vibrant colors and budding life.

Session 4 Facilitator Quick Guide: Mindful Self-Care

Session 4 Theme: The Need and Impact of Attending to One's Own Self-Care

Check-In:
- Check in to allow participants to share mindfulness practices since the last session.
- Focus on allowing participants to observe and assess their current stress level, with attention paid to stress that relates particularly to caregiving.

Mindful Pause: Mindful Eating
- Introduce mindful eating to assess present-moment awareness by connecting with all the senses stimulated through the process of eating.
- Demonstrate turning an everyday task, such as eating, into a mindful practice.

Discussion/Sharing
- "How is this different from the way you usually attend to eating?"

Highlighting the Session Theme:
- **Guiding Question:** "What comes to mind when you hear the word self-care?"
- **Guiding Image:** Tend Your Own Garden. How is your garden doing?
- **Part A: Bio-Psycho-Social Approach to Self-Care** Caring for oneself includes a focus on physical health (biological), mental well-being (psychological), and social connection to others/spiritual connection to a higher power (social).
- **Part B: From a Place of Self-Love and Acceptance:** Self-care is the embodied action of self-love and acceptance. Often, loving others comes easily, but extending love and care to ourselves can be more difficult.

Moving Meditation: Mindful Walking
- Introduce the concept of mindful walking and paying attention to the sensations of each step, as well as awareness of the present moment while walking.
- The attitudes of nonstriving and observing are practiced while walking, focusing attention on the sensations in the body.

Brief Inquiry:
- "What stood out to you in this experience?"

Stationary Meditation: Progressive Muscle Relaxation
- Participants focus on tensing a group of muscles as they breathe in and releasing the muscles as they breathe out to promote relaxation and present moment awareness.

Brief Inquiry:

- "What did you notice in your experience in this meditation?"

Summary and Suggestions for Formal and Informal Practices During the Week:

- Summarize the session theme and the way its exercises are related to it
- Encourage continued exploration based on personal interests in mindfulness practices

Handouts:

- Session 3 Participant Summary
- Session 3 Mindful Walking Audio Recording
- Session 3 Progressive Muscle Relaxation Audio Recording

Session 4 Introduction: Mindful Self-Care

Session 4 introduces and explores a foundational concept of this intervention and group: *self-care,* and incorporates the metaphor of *tending your garden.* As a broad concept, self-care refers to engaging in behaviors or practices that promote physical and psychological well-being (Maranzan et al., 2018). Self-care is best personalized to the individual and may include varied hobbies; activities that promote relaxation; practices that care for physical health, such as exercise, nutrition, sleep, and hygiene; or experiences that cultivate joy, play, or wonder. What these activities share is a purpose and goal of supporting and promoting mental and physical well-being. For individuals who serve in a caregiving role, much of their daily time and energy is consumed with caring for others. Self-care requires some level of focus on the self to care for oneself and, therefore, may be mistaken for being selfish, indulgent, or unnecessary when compared to the value a caregiver places on caring for others. The goal of this session is to not only introduce the concept of self-care but also to discuss some barriers to self-care, including difficulty prioritizing one's own needs when caring for others is valued and needed.

The image of *tending your garden* is introduced as a helpful metaphor for the task of self-care. It is easy to understand why, if a garden is to bloom, it must be tended to. Flowers, trees, and grass cannot grow without the tender loving care of a gardener who lavishes attention, picking leaves, watering, trimming hedges, and removing weeds and pests. Many of us quickly forget, however, that our own body, mind, and soul also require care, time, and attention as well if we are to flourish or, at least, avoid withering. Group participants are asked to stop for a moment and imagine, *"How is your garden doing?"* This will cultivate a greater sense of awareness when it comes to the current state of their self-care and areas that need attention.

Just as a gardener tends plants each day, the goal of self-care is to encourage regular and prioritized practices that are integrated into daily life. Self-care looks like daily choices: a decision to reschedule and/or delay a phone call with a family member when you know it will be draining; a decision to take an extra-long shower with wonderful smelling soap; a decision to sit for an extra 10 minutes while drinking your morning coffee; a decision to trade a new work project for one already assigned, when time is already overcommitted; a decision to delegate and ask for help when needed; a decision to forgive yourself for snapping at your mother when she asked a question; a decision to go to bed 20 minutes early instead of doing the dishes; a decision to change how you speak to yourself, accept yourself, and practice a mindful affirmation, "I am enough today, exactly as I am." These decisions and priorities, small yet mighty, are self-care.

What makes self-care even more powerful is a recognition of the driving force behind each of these small acts: self-love and acceptance. Self-care that comes from a place of self-love and acceptance has the potential to fundamentally change your relationship with yourself and the world. Learning to care for yourself has the potential to be transformative, particularly within living out your values, which includes caregiving. With each self-care decision or practice, take a moment to remember the reason you are choosing this, not because you "have to" or "should," but because you truly love yourself and want to care for your body, mind, and soul. This priority is one of your cherished values. This purposeful action of self-care, carefully integrated regularly into daily life, has the potential to buffer against caregiver fatigue, burnout, and other negative emotions.

A helpful way to think about self-care is to organize it in a biological–psychological-social model, highlighting each of the three different categories. "Biological" speaks to caring for one's physical well-being and could include things such as sleeping, taking medications, attending doctors' appointments, drinking water, exercising, or eating nutritious food. "Psychological" includes caring for one's mental health, which could include attending counseling, joining a support group, practicing relaxation strategies such as meditation, mindful coloring, or listening to music, spending time with people who cherish you, and limiting social media and time on technology. "Social" highlights the values of connection and the fact that humans value connection with others, including friends, family, pets, spirituality, community, or nature. This bio-psycho-social model can be a helpful way to assess and experiment with different areas of self-care and identify one that could be improved with a small, manageable self-care goal.

The mindful eating exercise in this session provides an opportunity for participants to practice doing an everyday task, such as eating, in a new way—mindfully. Eating is a primary function that we often engage in mindlessly, like eating a bag of chips on the couch and not realizing we finished the entire package. Participants may connect with the experience of mindless eating triggered in response to stress or another uncomfortable emotion not involving hunger. This can highlight the disconnect that often occurs between our mind and body. The mindful eating exercise is designed to be a brief experience of eating a single bite of food, like one grape, a raisin, or a cracker, very slowly, and focusing attention on the various physical sensations that occur while eating. The mindfulness skill of observing without judgment is practiced as participants look closely at the item of food using all the senses, noticing color, texture, temperature, and focusing on the experience of the food in their mouth. Participants may also utilize a Mindful Pause before eating, which could be a moment of gratitude for the food, a pause to appreciate the colors of the food, and an acknowledgement of everything that went into bringing this food to your table. The pause could also include aspects of spirituality, with a prayer or other spiritual practice prior to eating. Disrupting the automatic default mode of mindlessness with intentionality, awareness, and present-moment focus is the goal of this exercise.

The moving and stationary meditation practices introduced in this session serve as ideas of self-care practices participants can engage in throughout the week. The mindful walking audio provides an easy illustration for individuals to take a mindful walk, either outside or around the home, and spend a few moments connected to the present moment while walking. The progressive muscle relaxation audio provides participants with an exercise they can complete during moments of stress to take a few moments to release tension and promote relaxation and/or sleep. As these exercises are introduced, work to frame them within the theme of self-care practices.

At the end of this session, invite participants to discuss ideas about how they might practice self-care during the next week and share with each other suggestions for integrating self-care practices into daily life. After facilitating and discussing ideas and answering questions, distribute handouts and close the session.

Some Takeaway Points

The concept of self-care has been mentioned and discussed since the first group week; however, in this session, self-care is formally defined as engaging in behaviors or practices that promote physical and psychological well-being. Self-care can often feel daunting, as it seemingly represents an impossible standard of practice that feels unattainable. The concept of self-care can also, at times, feel invalidating, as if to suggest that the simple solution to burnout is getting a massage or taking a walk. Self-care is not selfish or frivolous, and it also does not have to involve a vacation or extensive time away. The image of *tending your garden* is introduced to encourage thinking about self-care as simple, mindful practices that can be integrated into daily life. Self-care can be organized into biological (physical health and well-being), psychological (mental health and well-being), and social (our connection with others and the world) categories. This model can be a helpful framework for reflecting on different aspects of self-care, identifying strengths and opportunities for growth, and setting self-care goals.

Here is Tobias's response to the Session 4 Check-In: *I was disappointed I didn't do more of the mindfulness exercises on my own. I let busyness take over. Yet, just knowing how to look at my needs to pause more and see how my tendency to multitask and stay in the speed of my thoughts causes most of my stress has been enlightening and encouraging. Now that I think about it, I have chosen to go for a slow walk after work, listening to birds and feeling the breeze. So, I guess I did something!*

Tobias gives us common experiences in learning to practice mindfulness. First, he says he had intentions to practice more, but found he dropped the ball. This is why we normalize the ups and downs of practice, avoiding a self-judgment of failure. Second, he realized that having a mindful perspective on stress was empowering. And third, he remembered he did choose to incorporate mindfulness in his day by taking a walk. Participants often forget or minimize the simple things they do until asked to share their experiences. It seems we are better at remembering our slips than our successes.

Belinda responds to Session 4 in this way: *When I first heard the phrase "self-care," my initial thought was, "I barely have time to care for my mother and grandson; how can I possibly have time for myself?" It was helpful, though, to hear a new way of thinking about self-care, with more of a focus on small daily actions that could become self-care with a simple shift of intention and the addition of mindfulness. It's hard not to feel like I'm being selfish if I take time for myself, even just for a few minutes. I think those guilty thoughts and feelings may be the biggest thing getting in my way at times. It was helpful to hear other group members share feelings the same way, which made me feel less alone. When we practiced the mindful eating exercise in a group, it was eye-opening. I realize how different it felt to slow down and taste a piece of food. It made me realize that I don't even take time for myself to truly eat, enjoy, and taste my meals. This week, I really want to work on a few small self-care steps that can be sustainable over time.*

Belinda's initial response to the discussion of self-care highlights some challenges to discussing this concept and how it may be initially perceived by group members. You can see, however, how her thoughts evolve and transition throughout the session, with a more nuanced understanding of self-care and the addition of mindfulness. She also begins to recognize how her own thoughts *about* self-care, including judgment and guilty thoughts, may be barriers to engaging in self-care. Bringing in mindful, nonjudgmental awareness and a focus on taking small steps towards self-care are ways that Belinda was able to start becoming more open to self-care and creating space for these actions in daily life.

Key Concepts

- Self-care that comes from a place of self-love is even more powerful.
- One way to organize self-care is to think about a bio-psycho-social model: focusing on three aspects—biological (physical health), psychological (mental health), and social (relational health).
- Purposeful self-care has the potential to buffer against caregiver fatigue, burnout, and other negative emotions.

Session 4 Guide: Mindful Self-Care

Aim of Session 4:

- To provide a framework for understanding the concept of self-care and implementing self-care into daily life.
- To discuss self-care from a bio-psycho-social perspective.
- To monitor self-care and strengthen self-care practices.

Check-In

Aim: Check in with participants about mindfulness practices they engaged in throughout the week. Provide caregivers the opportunity to connect, share, and learn from one another. It may be helpful to prompt caregivers to check in regarding their current stress level.

Suggestions: Caregivers spend much of their time and energy focused on other individuals' needs through the caregiving process. This Check-In serves as an opportunity for each caregiver to turn their focus inward and observe their own emotions and levels of stress. In this way, the Check-In serves to increase insight into stress and set the stage for discussing self-care, which is the focus of this session.

Mindful Pause:

Aim: Complete a mindful eating exercise together in session to highlight mindfulness themes and demonstrate turning an everyday task, such as eating, into a mindful practice.

Suggestions: From the previous session, participants were asked to bring a small food item to the session, whether in person or virtual, something they can hold in the palm of their hand. The facilitator should have some small food items on hand, like raisins or grapes, if some group members forgot to bring theirs. Utilize the mindful eating script provided to guide participants through a mindful eating experience. Before starting the exercise, it can be helpful to acknowledge that the experience may feel awkward or different and to encourage participants to lean in with curiosity and openness. As a Mindful Pause, this is a very brief exercise.

Discussion/Sharing: "How is this different from the way you usually attend to eating?"

Highlighting the Session Theme: Self-care

Guiding Question: What comes to mind when you hear the word self-care?

Guiding Image: *Tending your garden* offers an image to go alongside a definition of self-care. Anyone who has gardened before and grown trees, shrubs, flowers, or even grass knows that plants cannot grow without water, food, and sunlight. Often, for a garden to flourish, one must remove weeds, provide fertilizer, and protect against insects or predatory animals. If we think of our individual "self" as a garden, consider the question, "How does your garden look right now? Is it green and lush, or maybe wilted and dry?" As caregivers, we are often highly focused on tending another person's garden, a person who is not able at this time, for whatever reason, to tend their own garden. It begs the question, "What are you doing to tend to your garden?"

In the following section, request participants to write down their own private responses to a series of questions. Provide participants with paper and a pen or pencil. Have them write a key phrase to mark each question as it is read. The goal is to engage participants directly, rather than rely on lecturing. Responses are kept as a reference for each participant to review daily. Ask a question and allow a moment to write a response. Introduce the bio-psycho-social/spiritual dimensions as sections of one's garden. Tending all sections is important for a healthy garden.

Part A: Bio-Psycho-Social Approach to Self-Care

- **Physical Health**
  - The foundation of self-care is caring for your physical health. The following questions directly impact your mood and energy.
  - "How would you rate (1 = very poor to 10 = excellent) your sleep quality? Your approach to healthy eating? Is your daily exercise or physical movement daily quality? Your sleep? Your attention to medical check-ups and follow-ups? Now take a moment and look at any area rated six or below. What would you like to see yourself doing to enhance the quality in these places?"
- **Mental Health**
  - Mental health can be impacted by chronic stress, and mood symptoms might include depression, anxiety, or difficulty sleeping.
  - "How would you rate your usual mood and stress levels? How would you rate your practice of tapping into your center of calm and contentment? If your ratings are six and below, what would you like to see yourself do, including mindfulness practice, to increase your sense of well-being on a daily or weekly level?"
- **Social/Spiritual**
  - **Connection**: Humans are relational beings, and we need connection as part of self-care. This connection may be with family, friends, coworkers, pets, and/or with a higher power through religion or spirituality. This varies by person, and the facilitator should be directed by participants' preferences.
  - "How would you rate the quality of your support system? Your positive connection with something larger than yourself? Are there ways you might practice to reach out and energize your support system and/or spiritual section of your garden?"
  - **Boundaries**: Healthy boundaries remind us that while we can listen and show empathy to others, we are not responsible for fixing them, or making them happy, or always putting ourselves last.
  - "How would you rate your practice of attending to your needs, along with the needs or demands of the person(s) you caretake? Your practice of putting healthy limits on what you can and cannot do? What would you like to see yourself do more of or less of in these two areas?"

Part B: From a Place of Self-Love

- Self-care is the embodied action of self-love. Often, loving others comes easily, but extending love and care to ourselves can be more difficult. Negative, judgmental thoughts may get in the way, or guilt and shame regarding whether we deserve time for self-care.
- "How can you accept this focus on self-care as permission to turn warm attention to yourself if you have had difficulty doing so in the coming week? How can you move toward permitting yourself over time in the coming week?"

Moving Meditation: Mindful Walking

Aim: Discuss the concept of mindful walking and how participants can integrate this practice into their daily routine.

Suggested Instruction: Find a place to walk. It could be in a hallway, outside, in a large room, or in a park. Start by bringing your awareness into the present moment, perhaps with a few deep breaths. Pay attention to each step, including the mechanics of lifting the foot, forward movement, placement of the heel, ball, and toe, and then pushing off the toe. Notice any shifting of the body that occurs as you take each step, in addition to any change in balance. Focus on breathing as each breath comes in and goes out. Notice any movement from side to side. If you find it useful, you can count your steps, perhaps, to 10 and then start again. If you are walking in a small room, walk to the end and then turn slowly, taking small steps to turn and face the other direction, and then slowly walk back. The goal is to focus your attention on each step you take and the tiny movement that connects one step to the next. Focus on the sensation of walking and notice anything that stands out to you.

Brief Inquiry and Sharing:

"What stood out for you with this experience?"

Stationary Meditation: Progressive Muscle Relaxation (PMR)

Aim: Teach participants a simple Progressive Muscle Relaxation (PMR) exercise that can be utilized throughout the day. In PMR, participants focus on tensing each of the major groups of muscles as they breathe in and releasing the muscle group as they breathe out to promote relaxation and present moment awareness. Muscle groups are worked to promote a sense of relaxation throughout the body. PMR helps relieve tension that can fuel anxiety and stress, and caregivers are encouraged to practice this technique as needed throughout the day (refer to PMR audio or guide participants using the PMR transcript found in this session materials).

Brief Inquiry and Sharing:

"What did you notice during this exercise?"

Summary and Suggestions for Formal and Informal Practices during the Week:

Aim: Review and reinforce concepts discussed in the group, particularly self-care and the image of *tending your garden,* and the bio-psycho-social definition.

Suggestions: Caregivers are encouraged to consider ways they care for physical health, mental health, and social/spiritual well-being. Techniques are introduced that can be integrated into daily life, including mindful eating, mindful walking, and setting boundaries, in addition to other mindfulness practices that have already been taught. Caregivers are encouraged to think about their own intentional self-care practices that come from a place of self-love.

Ask, "What will you plant in your garden this week?"

Handouts:

- Participant Summary
- Progressive Relaxation Audio
- Walking Meditation Audio

Session 4-Facilitator's Contemplation: What do you need?

Session 4 Participant Summary: Mindful Self-Care*

Guiding Question: What comes to mind when you hear the word self-care?

Aim of Session: To introduce the concept of self-care as a mindful and multidimensional practice of engaging in purposeful strategies that promote health and well-being.

What did you notice in the **Brief Mindful Pause: Mindful Eating?**

What did you notice in the **Moving Meditation of Mindful Walking?**

* Lumpkin, M., Collins, M.H., & Jarrett, R.B. (2026). Mindful self-care for clinicians and caregivers: A group facilitator's guide. Academic Press.

What stood out to you in **Progressive Muscle Relaxation?**

A Bio-Psycho-Social Approach to Self-Care: Caring for oneself includes focusing on physical health (biological), mental well-being (psychological), and social connection to others/spiritual connection (social).

Self-Care from a Place of Self-Love: Self-care is the embodied action of self-love and acceptance. If self-care practices are the prioritized, purposeful actions we take, self-love is the intention behind the actions. Often, loving and caring for others comes easily, but taking the time to care for ourselves can be more difficult.

Guiding Image of *Tend Your garden*: The image of a garden can be used as a metaphor for self-care. Imagine a garden that represents you at this moment. Tending to a garden requires many actions that help keep the garden flourishing, lush, healthy, and vibrant. Take a moment to reflect on the state of your garden. What do you notice about it? What areas perhaps need more attention and care? How is your garden doing?

In this session, you may have experienced tension, frustration, or hopelessness that emerged when thinking about finding time to practice self-care. While there are many ways to practice self-care, an important piece is finding ways to practice self-care that are manageable and feasible. Think about a specific and reasonable self-care practice you can integrate this week. Start small and build over time. Ask for help and/or delegate if and when needed. Say no and reschedule if that is helpful.

Suggestions: Please continue your own exploration and experimentation with your chosen meditations and options from the list of informal daily practices. Feel free to use audio and video resources.

List mindfulness practices you would like to try this week:	☑

Lumpkin, M., Collins, M.H., & Jarrett, R.B. (2026). Mindful self-care for clinicians and caregivers: A group facilitator's guide. Academic Press.

Mindful Eating Script

To complete this exercise, make sure you have a small bite of food: a raisin, grape, or berry works well, but you can use any small item of food that you can hold in the palm of your hand.

"To begin, start by finding a comfortable position in your chair. Make sure your feet are firmly on the ground, and your back feels supported in the chair. Take a moment and connect to your breath and your body. Scan your body starting from your head and moving down to the tips of your toes, and notice any areas of tightness or tension. If you find an area of tension, try to soften or release that area. Notice any thoughts, emotions, or sensations you are experiencing. Close your eyes for a moment, if you would like. Take a deep inhale, feeling the belly rise, then exhale, feeling the belly fall. And again, inhale—feel the belly rise—and exhale—feel the belly fall.

"Take a moment to notice any sensations in your body. Notice if you are feeling hungry or full, thirsty or content. Become aware of these sensations without judgment, and simply notice, with curiosity, whatever you are experiencing at this moment.

Now bring your attention to the item of food. Hold the food with your thumb and forefinger, or place it in the palm of your hand. Look at the food and try to imagine you are seeing this item of food for the first time, and you have never seen anything like it before. Notice the color, shape, and size. What do you observe about the food? What stands out to you? What seems unique? If you were to describe this food to someone who had never seen it before, what would you say?

As you look at the item of food, imagine everything that was a part of bringing this food into your hand today: water, soil, sunshine, people who harvested, factories that packaged, trucks that transported, a building that stored the food, and a person who purchased the food. Take a moment of gratitude for all the many people, places, and resources responsible for the creation of this food.

Close your eyes for a moment and focus on the physical sensation of the food in your fingers or in your hand. Move the item of food around and feel the texture; notice any bumps, ridges, or smooth areas. Notice the temperature; is it warm or cool? Does the temperature seem to change as it sits in your hand? Notice whether the food is wet, slimy, sticky, and squishy, or dry and brittle. With only your fingers, do you think you could identify this food item?

Now bring the piece of food up to your nose and hold it a few inches away. Take a nice inhale and notice any aromas. Do any memories arise? Any sensations? Maybe your body reacts with your stomach growling or your mouth watering. Now place the piece of food in your mouth, but do not chew yet. Let the piece of food be in your mouth; roll it around with your tongue. When you are ready, take a slow bite and notice the sensation in your mouth—the burst of flavor. Focus on the taste you experience. Notice how the food changes and dissolves. Notice how the flavor changes. Slowly swallow whenever you are ready and imagine the path of the food going down into your esophagus and into your stomach.

Now bring your attention back to the breath; focus on the slow inhales and exhales. Inhale deeply and feel the belly rise; exhale fully and feel the belly fall. And when you are ready, you can open your eyes.

Progressive Muscle Relaxation Script

This script is designed to guide individuals or groups through a full-body progressive muscle relaxation (PMR) practice. The intention of this exercise is to increase awareness of tension in the body and promote deep physical relaxation.

Please be gentle with your body during this practice. If any part of the exercise doesn't feel comfortable, you may skip it. Always listen to your body. It's also normal for your mind to wander—simply acknowledge those thoughts and gently bring your attention back to your breath and the present moment.

Getting Started

Find a comfortable position. You may choose to sit in a supportive chair or lie down—whatever feels most restful for your body.

Close your eyes if that feels right to you, or soften your gaze and let it rest gently.

Begin by bringing your attention to your surroundings. Notice any sounds you hear—soft or loud—just observing without judgment.

Deep Breathing to Settle In

Let's begin with a few deep breaths to ground the body:
Inhale deeply through the nose, hold briefly at the top,
Exhale slowly and completely through the nose.
Repeat:
Inhale... hold...
Exhale fully...
One more time:
Inhale deeply...
Hold...
Exhale slowly and completely...

Progressive Muscle Relaxation Sequence

We will now move through the body, tensing each muscle group on the inhale, holding the tension briefly, and then releasing on the exhale.

Feet and Toes

Inhale: Curl and clench your toes and the arches of your feet.
Hold the tension...
Exhale: Release and let go. Notice the difference.
Repeat once more.

Calves

Inhale: Tense your calves by pointing or flexing your feet.

Hold...
Exhale: Let the muscles relax completely.
Repeat once more.

Thighs and Knees

Inhale: Squeeze your thighs together and tense around the knees.
Hold...
Exhale: Let them soften.
Repeat once more.

Glutes

Inhale: Tense and squeeze the glutes.
Hold...
Exhale: Let go of all tension.
Repeat once more.

Abdomen

Inhale: Pull your belly button toward your spine. Engage your core.
Hold...
Exhale: Release the abdominal tension.
Repeat once more.

Chest

Inhale: Expand your chest and tense the muscles as you hold the breath.
Hold...
Exhale: Let your chest soften.
Repeat once more.

Back

Inhale: Squeeze your shoulder blades together, as if pinching a pencil between them.
Hold...
Exhale: Release and relax your upper back.
Repeat once more.

Hands and Arms

Inhale: Curl your hands into fists.
Hold...
Exhale: Release the tension.
Now include the entire arm:
Inhale: Squeeze your fists and tense the forearms and upper arms.

Hold...
Exhale: Let the arms fully relax.

Shoulders

Inhale: Shrug your shoulders up toward your ears.
Hold...
Exhale: Let the shoulders drop away from the ears.
Repeat two more times, feeling the shoulders grow heavier with each release.

Face

Inhale: Scrunch the face—tighten your lips, eyes, forehead.
Hold...
Exhale: Let your entire face soften.
Repeat once more.

Full Body Scan

Now gently scan the body from head to toe.

Notice any lingering tension. If one area still feels tight, you may choose to repeat that muscle group, tensing and releasing once more.

Visualize a warm wave of relaxation slowly washing over your entire body—from the top of your head, down your face, chest, arms, torso, hips, legs, and all the way to your toes.

Allow yourself to rest in this feeling of calm and stillness.

Closing the Practice

Take a few more deep breaths:
Inhale...
Exhale...

Allow yourself to fully experience this peaceful state, with nowhere to be and nothing to do in this moment but rest.

Acknowledge this time you've taken for yourself—to care for your body and mind.

When you're ready to return:

Gently wiggle your fingers and toes.
Bring some light movement back into the body.
Notice the sounds in the room around you.
And when it feels right, gently open your eyes.
Take your time reorienting to the space around you.

Session 5—Mindfulness and Relationships

Session 5 focuses on a mindful approach to relationships, including setting intentional and adaptive boundaries with others while practicing empathy. The sessions include a written description of experiential practices for the session. The aim of Session 5 is to apply mindfulness principles to interpersonal interactions and expand on techniques that can be applied within relational settings and experiences.

Mindful Self-Care for Clinicians and Caregivers. https://doi.org/10.1016/B978-0-443-29821-9.00010-8

"Ducks in sync sharing space" - Martin took this picture at White Rock Lake in Dallas. He loved the sense of bonded attunement to each other. Perhaps we humans have something to learn when relating mindfully to each other.

Session 5 Facilitator Quick Guide: Mindfulness and Relationships

Session Theme: The Rewards of Mindful Listening and Responding to Restore Heartfelt Connection and Boundaries

Mindful Pause: Mountain and Finding Your Ground

- Connect the mountain image to the goal of finding stability within the pressures of caregiving.
- Allow about 5 minutes for this pause.
- Follow the session guide for a model or script.
- Suggest taking this mountain sense of groundedness into mindful listening.

Highlight the Session Theme: Mindful Relationships

- Guiding questions: How might mindful listening to ourselves, our care person(s), and others help us stay balanced, grounded, and more able to navigate the challenges of caregiving? How might frequent mindful pauses of listening to yourself help keep healthy boundaries and find your *own* life amid caregiving?
- Session images: Mountain as stability and Inner Lake as a sanctuary of calm and clarity.
- Part A: The Impact of Mindful Attention and Listening to Others.
  - Check-In Exercise in mindful listening and responding.
  - Facilitator asks reflective questions to extend the exercise into daily life.
- Part B: Practicing healthy boundaries: Listening mindfully to yourself.
  - The meaning of healthy versus unhealthy boundaries.
  - Questions to promote reflection on the state and need of participant boundaries.
  - The poem "Lake Loons", using the inner lake as a place of self-renewal.

Moving Meditation: Finding and moving from inner mountain

- A nonverbal experience of groundedness and boundaries.
- Video or transcript is available to model or use in session.

Brief Inquiry and Sharing:

- What was noticed in the Mountain pose?
- What stood out in the Golden Ball?

Stationary Meditation: Breathing It All In

- Guided meditation on sensing one's precious being in general and as a caregiver.
- Audio or transcript is available to model or use in session.

Summary and Suggestions for Formal and Informal Practices during the Week

- Summarize Session 5 theme as it was exhibited in the various session exercises.
- Invite explorations, but keep it simple, in mindful listening with others.
- Invite experiments in setting boundaries.

Handouts:

- Session 5 *Breathing It All In* audio
- Session 5 Movement Video
- "Lake Loons" poem
- Participant Summary

Session 5 Introduction: Mindfulness and Relationships

Mindful attending and responding skills can be brought into the realm of day-to-day relationships, where caregivers spend a significant amount of time. Up to now, sessions have focused on the caregiver's relation to her or himself. How can mindfulness be applied to the arena of communicating and connecting with the care person(s) to navigate tensions and to savor moments of closeness? How can these skills help in managing and enriching contacts with friends, family, and professional caregivers? As it turns out, the capacity to observe oneself, step back into the big picture, and then to respond from that perspective is crucial to diluting stress and enhancing positive connections. It can be critical to avoid burnout and instil resilience, and maintain focus on what matters.

Session 5 looks at the following theme: How listening and being listened to mindfully are ways to steer our relationships into calmer waters and find one's own center of renewal. Listening to ourselves attentively becomes the basis for building healthy boundaries and giving oneself permission to and space for self-care. This permission is needed for Session 6 in its invitation to nourish oneself with mindful moments during the day.

The following experiences of the psychologist Carl Rogers gently portray the multiple aspects of mindful listening in the context of caregiving. As the founder of Person-Centered Therapy, he practiced and studied the impact of empathic listening with both the therapy patient and the therapist. For the patient, such listening led to deep feelings of being validated, accepted, and led further to insightful listening to herself. For the therapist, therapy became an intimate and rich journey of connection (Rogers, 1980). In later years, Rogers himself became a caregiver to his critically ill wife. It humbled him. Always self-reliant, he found a new need to be heard in his struggles with others: "I like to be heard" (Rogers, 1980). He found caregiving a mixed blessing in expressing love on one hand and falling toward burnout by neglecting his own needs for renewal: "I realized that it was necessary for my survival to live *my* life" (Rogers, 1980). The famous therapist found he needed boundaries, not unbroken self-sacrifice. He needed to live *his* life as well as give care. He writes of this discovery in his book, *A Way of Being* (1980). It echoes the experience of many caregivers.

When caregivers experience the demands of too little time and too little energy, listening can be reduced to information exchanges at best and rushed brevity at worst. Irritability and frustration can tumble into relational friction that leaves either party very happy. The longing to be heard and acknowledged may fester in both caregiver and care recipient. The practice and value of mindfulness resuscitate the heart of listening as an act of connection. It can revitalize the listener and the listener. Appreciation blooms in what may have been a dry spell of just doing tasks. Caregivers need to feel not just functionally effective but touched by the other. They also need to be heard, their inner worlds felt by another. This is what mindful listening and responding offer, and why it is a skill worth honing.

As facilitators prepare for this session, it may help to keep in mind that we are extending mindfulness skills developed in previous sessions. In a sense, there is a double mindful focus in the present: awareness of one's own feelings and sensations, and awareness of the other's verbal and nonverbal expressions. It is like having a background awareness of various thoughts and sensations while primarily focusing on the sensation of breathing in the meditation below, *Breathing It All In* (Jarrett, 2022). Like all skills, the art within the skill can be refined over time by practice. The intent of the session is to give participants a taste of this mindfulness skill and to inspire its exploration in daily life to see what might come out of it. One way to express this kind of listening is connecting with the other person while staying connected to oneself. It is in contrast to so much of our usual kind of listening, which is often full of emotional reactions and judgments and habitual actions. Two things may come out of old ways of reacting: First, tension, if present, is increased both inside and between oneself and another, and second, opportunities to pause and enjoy open moments of relaxed intimacy are missed in the pressure of obligations. Ideally, participants learn to decrease the first and increase the second.

In contrast to former sessions, the Check-In is brought in after the initial Mindful Pause. This is done to allow the Mindful Pause to set a tone for the session's focus on keeping one's physical, mental, and emotional ground stable while dealing with various demands. Then the Check-In is used for its usual purpose of sharing, as well as its opportunity for participants to get an initial sense of mindful listening and responding.

For the Mindful Pause, the mountain image evokes a sense of finding one's base or ground of stability in the midst of changing life events, like seasonal or weather changes. Mindful awareness of body sensations as one releases usual tensions into relaxation is followed by the addition of a mountain image of one's own making. In this way, a broad base of body awareness is combined and given dimension through witnessing the mountain image and, eventually, feeling oneself as a mountain. The aim is to create a brief practice to call upon in times of challenge. The Session 5 Guide lays out suggestions for facilitating this mindful pause. Although the pause has several parts, it is helpful to remember that it is a pause of around 5 minutes and not a longer meditation.

After the Mindful Pause, the suggestion can be made to use it as a brief way to find a sense of stability when needed, along with other brief practices according to one's preferences.

Then the mountain theme can be brought into the next section: Highlighting the Session Theme: Mindful Relationships. This might be done through the Guiding Questions: "How might mindful listening to our care person(s) and others, as well as ourselves, help us stay balanced, 'mountain' grounded, and more skillful in navigating the challenges of caregiving? How might mindful pauses of listening to ourselves foster healthy boundaries in finding our *own* life in the midst of caregiving?" The mountain image evokes strong grounded-ness, and the image of the lake, from the "Lake Loons" poem, creates a sense of an inner sanctuary of stillness and peace.

Part A the Check-In has two uses. On the one hand, it offers an opportunity to share a moderately intense experience involving some interaction with another person and how one handled it. On the other hand, it provides an opportunity to empathically listen and briefly respond to another participant's sharing. By engaging in the exercise, participants can feel the impact of another's attentive listening and practice this type of listening while observing its impact. It helps to keep the exercise simple rather than allow it to appear complex. The Session Guide explains how to set up this exercise for both in-person and virtual contexts. Timing and marking the time periods are key to keeping the experiment on track and not drifting off into other kinds of talk and sharing. At the end of the Check-In exercise, the facilitator, depending on the size of the group, might ask for two or three responses to "What was your experience in listening in this way and being listened to in this way?" The facilitator has the opportunity here to model mindful listening and responding. The section on Facilitator Reflections offers possible questions to expand the use of these skills. Participants might offer their reflections on each question asked. Part A will take some time, and to let it sink in, it does not need to be rushed. The facilitator may summarize key observations by participants at the close of this section.

In Part B, mindful listening is offered to oneself as a way to know directly how one feels and what one may need to keep a balance between giving out and taking in nourishing experiences. One way to guide this part is to have participants close their eyes in openness to mindful listening and reflection as the facilitator offers thoughts and questions to ponder. The aim is to have participants quietly consider how well they listen to themselves and permit themselves to create time for their own nourishment and renewal. Boundaries are often sacrificed as one gives all attention and energy to daily tasks and responds to care person's needs, finding a kind of dispirited exhaustion at the end. One way to field suggested questions and comments for reflection is to state them slowly and clearly, followed by a brief pause. Part B is concluded with the question, "Can you sense the image of the inner lake as your place for renewal?" and a reading of "Lake Loons." Repeating the poem allows for deeper hearing.

The Moving Meditation and Stationary Meditation internalize the experiences of groundedness, boundaries, and self-appreciation time. The Moving Meditation of Finding and Moving from Inner Mountain comes from Qigong's stabilizing alignment and slow, flowing movement so conducive to relaxed mindfulness. Mountain pose arcs back to the Mountain Mindful Pause. It invites a solid standing as one releases gravity and natural alignment for strength without tension. The modified Golden Ball from Qigong orchestrates a series of gentle, mindful movements, including gestures of opening to receive energy and pushing away obstructions as dimensions of good boundaries. The Stationary Meditation practice of *Breathing It All In* is a meditative experience, including appreciation of oneself and others, in general and in the context of caregiving. Participants are guided through aspects of their past and into their present evolution as a caregiver. The aim is to engender a sense of one's very precious being unfolding over time and up to the present. An attitude of not only self-acceptance but of deep self-appreciation infuses this meditative journey. Both meditations have either audio or video with transcripts to practice facilitation or to use in the session as guides. The meditations are each followed by brief inquiries and participant feedback.

The last transition concludes with the Summary and Suggestions for Formal and Informal Practices during the Week. The Suggestions offer a way to summarize the session's themes. It ties together earlier session skills of mindful observation and responding as they are now woven into mindful listening and relating. Exploring the need for strong boundaries rests upon the turn of this special way of listening to oneself. Mountain and Lake can now be taken as images to be called upon when evoking stability or one's inner sanctuary amid life pressures. Mindful pauses to tune into oneself can be practiced in various ways, whether learned on one's own or in past or present sessions. Taking pauses to refresh and revitalize oneself extends into Session 6. Resources include audio/video guides to meditation, a Session Summary for participants, and the poem "Lake Loons". Session 5 might end with a silent reflection on "What would you like to see yourself do more of or less of in the next week?"

Some Takeaway Points

Prior sessions have been laying the groundwork for self-care through mindful ways of connecting with inner experience to savor nourishing experiences and to soften the impact of stress. Self-care is expanding its dimensions for participants. In Session 5, yet another aspect is added: Mindful listening to oneself and to others. Mindful listening to oneself is crucial for establishing boundaries by listening for needs to say no, to energy-depleting demands to shepherd one's vital reserves, and to say yes to self-focused refreshing. This is harder than it sounds. No one gives a set of instructions for how much or how little to give in caregiving. The other aspect is mindful listening to others, particularly one's caregiver. Reacting to ongoing demands or to pressures to do a competent job can result in reactive listening, where little is heard except one's own judgments and emotions. Mindful or empathic listening requires that we become present-centered, aware of our own feelings while staying open to another's attempt to communicate themselves. The results of mindful listening are often lower conflict and increased closeness, which rewards both people. This, too, is a mindful skill to be honed and practiced over time.

Listen to Belinda's response to the Check-In: *Focusing on self-care this week was difficult, but I was able to start small, like we talked about in group and focus on a few first steps. I decided to take a mindful shower each day, and for 10 minutes focus on the feeling of the water and the scent of the soap and redirect my thoughts back to the present moment every time they drift away to think about the day ahead. The second self-care practice I focused on was a Mindful Pause at the end of each day as part of my nighttime routine. Usually, I tumble into bed at night and scroll on social media for 15 minutes before falling asleep exhausted. This week I created an evening routine. I lit a candle, put on lavender-scented lotion, and read for 15 minutes. It didn't take any additional time, but the intention behind it felt completely different. I'm not sure whether I can keep up these new habits, but I think they helped me feel more centered, relaxed, and focused on myself, which is something I have struggled with for a long time.*

Belinda shares the success she had this week in implementing a few simple self-care practices into her daily routine. She highlights an important insight that the intention behind the self-care action was important and changed the experience of simple everyday tasks. The fact that Belinda selected realistic and attainable self-care actions is also important because she was able to have success this week practicing the skills. She also noticed how powerful small mindful steps can be, and that self-care does not have to consume large amounts of time.

Here is Tobias' response to Session 5: *I have to say that as I have been learning to slow down and pay attention more, I have been less impatient with co-workers and patients under my care. That being said, the focus on listening more carefully in this session seems to be taking me to another level. The Mindful Pause to feel my inside ground or "mountain" felt good. Like some of the earlier Qigong movements, I liked focusing on being stable and balanced no matter what is going on around me. I hope I remember to refer to this pause in the rushed part of my work. The Check-In exercise in listening. Wow, it was hard not to move into giving advice or encouragement! Yet I could tell the other person being listened to felt more at ease simply by being heard. I wonder how often I overdo my comments to others in my life who are trying to tell me something important to them? The part on healthy boundaries was also a helpful reminder. I think the more I just stop to feel what's going on, the better I'll be at knowing when I'm overloading myself. The Moving Meditation took up the mountain image again, giving a pleasant sense of slowing down and downward to feel again what balance is like. The Stationary Meditation was an interesting experience. I rarely look backward over my life, and this exercise, along with the breathing meditation, reminded me of being in a larger life than my narrow current one, like appreciating my journey as a loving parent might.*

Tobias is actively embracing the invitations to try out mindfulness in his life. Mindfulness is becoming a part of his value system, offering ways to deepen his quality of living. Self-care is becoming legitimized. He is open to engaging in session exercises. And he is wondering about how to translate this into daily life because he knows how easy it is to get lost in the rush of the day. He already appreciates the need to listen to himself more as he comes into this session. He also has noticed that the more mindful he is, the more available he is to others. Now he wonders if mindful listening, giving more space to the other person, can improve the way he relates in more of his relationships.

Key Concepts

- Mindfulness skills can be applied both to our experience connecting with oneself, as well as to relational experiences with others.
- Mindful listening strengthens relationships, deepens connection with loved ones and care partners, and helps buffer stress.
- Mindful listening means staying present and aware of our own thoughts and feelings while giving our full attention to another person as they communicate.

Session 5 Guide: Mindfulness and Relationships

Aim of Session 5:

- To cultivate healthy ways of navigating the ups and downs of caregiving and introduce the essential practices of mindful listening.
- To clarify, through examples and practice, the power of empathic connecting to care for persons and others.
- To encourage sensitive management of one's own boundaries.

Theme: Now we are going to explore how our mindfulness practices might be applied to our day-to-day dealings with our care person(s) and others in our lives. We will look at how listening, being listened to, and hearing ourselves with a mindful presence are ways to navigate our relationships into calmer waters. First, we will carve out the need to listen to ourselves in order to have healthier boundaries and savor the privileges offered to caregivers.

Mindful Pause: Mountain and Finding Your Ground

Aim: To evoke a sense of standing firm in mindfulness through using the image of a mountain's stability and equanimity while surrounded by weather and seasonal changes. To relate this brief pause to finding your ground or center from which to listen openly and to feel centered in your own boundaries.

Suggestions: This is meant to be a brief five-minute exercise with the idea that it can be extended in time or practiced in short moments for personal use in the future.

Invite participants to begin: "Settle into a comfortable but stable seated posture, feel grounded, and experience the weight of the lower body and the upward support of the arising spine. Now join your breath to this stable body by breathing into the head space … the neck space … from chest to deep belly … and down the legs, into the feet. Let this feeling of groundedness sink in for a moment."

Add the mountain image: "We are grounding ourselves in ourselves like a mountain. Can you see an image of a mountain vividly in its majestic base and height?"

Blend mountain and self: "Can you feel in some way the mountain and you coming together? Feel yourself as an inner mountain? Feel the sense of its dignity, grounded, and stability in the midst of all kinds of weather, whether sun, rain, snow, or wind? As clouds and birds move around it, it does not move."

Relate mountain/self to the capacity to find one's ground in all sorts of conditions: "What would it mean to access at times this inner mountain, this kind of resolute firmness during times of stress, challenge, or losing sight of your own needs?" Pause to let this sink in, with the facilitator gently ending the mindful pause with a bell or gong.

"Let's take this mountain sense with us now as we explore ways to listen to others and ourselves without losing ourselves."

Highlighting the Session Theme: Mindful Relationships

- **Guiding Questions:** How might mindful listening to our care person, others, and ourselves help us stay balanced, grounded, and more skillful in navigating the challenges of caregiving? How might frequent, mindful pauses of listening to ourselves help us keep healthy boundaries and find our *own* life amid caregiving?
- **Guiding Images: Mountain and Lake**
- **Part A: The Impact of Mindful Attention and Listening to Others**
  - **Check-In:** This section of Check-In normally initiates sessions, but in Session 5 check-in is delayed allowing it to be used not only to elicit participant experiences during the week, but can be made into an active listening exercise. In this Check-In, participants are divided into dyads and separated in space (or if virtual, assigned to breakout rooms) just far enough to allow a separate space for two people to share. The facilitator can be in one of the dyads if there is an odd number of participants. Dyads are given this format: One of the pair is the speaker who shares with their partner some *moderately* intense experience, which is not more than an 8, with 0 being not intense at all and 10 being maximum intensity. The experience is described as what happened, how the participant reacted, and what the participant chose to do or not to do from their reaction. This is timed for 5 minutes. Then the facilitator signals with a gong or bell to stop and to allow the other participant in the dyad to respond. This response is limited to summarizing the shared experience in terms of what happened, how the other participant felt about it, and what the other participant chose to do about it. The listening participant is asked to connect with the speaker more through the heart center than the head. The goal is not to add interpretations, advice, or other commentary but to mindfully attend to and connect with the other participant's report and feeling just as they are. This is timed for 3 minutes. Then, for two timed minutes, the first participant reports what it feels like to be heard in this way. The second part of the Check-In simply reverses participant roles and is timed in the same way. At the end, the facilitator might ask a few people to respond to the question: "What was your experience in listening in this way? And being listened to in this way?"
  - Facilitator reflections: "What would be the implications of listening to another or one's care person(s) in this way? How might it differ from more reactive, emotional ways of listening and responding? How would finding our inner mountain be a way for us to bypass urges to react simply and to create a space for listening? In our busy, often harried days, might we miss times taken for deeper connections with others, with our care person(s)? How might pauses for mindful listening and sharing impact us, giving us something beyond caregiver duties?" These questions are fielded to stimulate participant reflections. They might elicit thoughts from various participants and can be woven into the overall mood of reflection.
- **Part B: Practicing Healthy Boundaries: Listening Mindfully to Yourself**
  - When we have good boundaries, we can connect with others while staying connected to ourselves.

- There are times when self-care asks us to take time to listen attentively to our minds and bodies. What are we being told about our state of energy or our emotional state? We may find we are being told to separate and renew, refresh in what nourishes us, including times of being listened to by others. Do we have the inner to practice saying "no" to outward demands to turn toward ourselves? How can we attend to self-care needs we explored in Session 4 without such mindful listening to our own feelings?
- **"Lake Loons" poem:** Listen for the image of the inner lake as a place of centering and renewal in the poem. How easy it is to be scattered and separated from this inner lake! Read the poem twice, slowly, meditatively.

Moving Meditation: Finding and Moving from Inner Mountain

Aim: To provide a nonverbal experience of groundedness with the gestures of opening; to connect with something outside; and boundary maintenance of separating from what blocks vitality.

Suggestions: Use these slow, flowing Qigong movements to help participants engage in experiencing body movement sensations coming from a mountain-like base of grounding. The emphasis is on feeling the body in motion as a strong alignment allowing for received energy, and time to push away obstacles or tensions. Standing Mountain Pose reminds us of the mountain image and its rootedness. Movements from that base then open out to connect and push away to separate as primary experiences of dynamic boundaries. See the included video for use in facilitator practice or in-session guidance.

Brief Inquiry and Sharing: What did you notice about the sense of feeling grounded? Were you able to connect and bring in, as well as push away to say "no" to what obstructs you?

Stationary Meditation: "Breathing It All In"

Aim: To pause for mindful reflection on how participants became and continue as caregivers.

Suggestions: The facilitator aims to cultivate an authentic appreciation for how caregivers are precious.

Brief Inquiry and Sharing: What came out of this meditation for you?

Summary and Suggestions for Formal and Informal Practices during the Week

Aim: To integrate the session into various exercises around the theme of mindful listening to oneself as part of listening to others.

Suggestions: Summarize some form of the following: "Practicing mindfulness formally and informally grows skills needed in mindful listening. One learns gradually to observe one's feelings and reactions, choose responses rather than act on impulse, and watch what happens nonjudgmentally. Listening mindfully in the moment extends as a gift of validating the other's feelings. That is what Carl Rogers meant when he said, 'I like to be heard.' It opens rather than closes a door. The full skill here is to connect to the other while remaining connected to oneself. In addition, listening mindfully to oneself is the first step toward affirming one's own boundaries and the right to have a separate life at times for renewal."

Invite participants to experiment with mindful listening to the care person(s) during the week and to observe what happens both in themselves and in their person. It is not an easy skill, as it often goes against our usual ways of half-listening and reacting. Also, through mindful pauses, see what it is like to take time to tune into yourself. How am I feeling? What do I need to refresh and renew? Am I able to say no to outer pressures to create some time and space for myself? Remember the inner mountain for stability and feeling solid or grounded. Remember the inner lake for finding your quiet center amid whirling life around.

Handouts:

- Session 5 *Breathing It All In* audio
- Session 5 Movement Video
- "Lake Loons" poem
- Participant Summary

Session 5-Facilitator's Contemplation: What is between you and another?

Session 5 Participant Summary: Mindfulness and Relationships*

Guiding Questions: How might mindful listening to ourselves, our care person(s), and others help you stay balanced, grounded, and skillful in navigating the challenges of caregiving? How might frequent pauses for mindful listening to yourself and others help you keep healthier boundaries and find your *own* life amid caregiving?

Aim of Session: To introduce the practice of mindful listening to others and oneself to calm tensions, deepen connections, and set healthier boundaries in the demands of caregiving.

What did you notice in the **Mindful Pause: Mountain and Finding Your Ground?**

What did you notice in the **Check-In Mindful Listening exercise?**

* Lumpkin, M., Collins, M.H., & Jarrett, R.B. (2026). Mindful self-care for clinicians and caregivers: A group facilitator's guide. Academic Press.

What resonated with you in **Practicing Healthy Boundaries**?

What stood out for you in **Finding and Moving from Inner Mountain?**

What might you have become aware of during the meditation "**Breathing It All In**"?

The Impact of Mindful Attention and Listening to Others: When tired or under pressure, we might not fully listen to the other person through our filters of judgment and old reactions. As a result, tensions between us may mount and, at times, opportunities for deeper connections are missed. Mindful listening is a practice of clearing an inner space to attend to the other's present moment's verbal and nonverbal messages. Mindful responding can be as simple as feeding back to the person what they are communicating, minus our reactions and interpretations. The result is giving the gift of being heard and validated, a rare gift in the modern world.

Practicing Healthy Boundaries: Under the pressure and strain of caregiving, we may fail to listen mindfully to ourselves and thus miss cues of stress, emotions, and needs for self-care. Burnout and a sense of being overwhelmed can result. Taking pauses to tune into your state of mind and body allows you to hear what you need to know about your energy and limits. Healthy boundaries mean giving yourself permission to stay connected to yourself and to take time for your own separate needs for renewal. This can be done in brief pauses in your day or time out for nourishing activities like reading or gardening, or letting yourself be supported by others.

Guiding Images: Mountain for stability and Inner Lake for a place of calm

In this session, you looked at how mindful listening and responding might appear and what they might offer in dealing with others in your challenging life as a caregiver. You were also invited to consider the state of your boundaries in caregiving, how you balance having a life of meeting another's needs and of meeting your own. These are long-term practices in which even a little can make a large difference.

Suggestions: Without pressuring yourself to be perfect, why not experiment with listening to another and yourself in small steps? See what they practically yield. See if these skills contribute to the kind of relationship you would like with your care person (s). And see if pausing to tune into yourself gives you clues about self-care. Experiment, explore, and try not to make this into any kind of chore because you really don't need another one or two, do you? Play with the meditations you are attracted to through the audio or video resources.

Week I want more of (fill in blank) and less of (fill in blank).

MORE OF	***LESS OF***

Lumpkin, M., Collins, M.H., & Jarrett, R.B. (2026). Mindful self-care for clinicians and caregivers: A group facilitator's guide. Academic Press.

LAKE LOONS

(Lumpkin, 2014, p.5)

Be quiet.
Be so still
your body breathes
in the space left by
honking geese of thoughts
now fading over the horizon.
Be so still
the feeling (that small tightness)
of yourself dissolves into
the waters of the host of things
around you now
moving, standing, sounding, breathing. Be so still you are quietly held
in this Holding always under the noise of the world piercing our bodies,
silencing and scattering the loons from their lake.
Be so very quiet
and still
that the shocks
fall from your body
like impotent arrows
as you turn and wing
back to the lake
you left
and
light.

Lumpkin, M., Collins, M.H., & Jarrett, R.B. (2026). Mindful self-care for clinicians and caregivers: A group facilitator's guide. Academic Press.

Session 5: Moving Meditation Transcript

Hello … and welcome to Session 5's Moving Meditation. As you know, Session 5's theme of listening to others and listening to ourselves. And listening to ourselves is about finding our own inner base. Our own sense of groundedness. We called it the "inner mountain." And we're going to explore what this "inner mountain" might feel like if we bring it into a brief meditation. And then we're going to explore what the boundary-work of taking care of ourselves is by opening ourselves up to what nourishes us and pushing away what blocks or obstructs us. What we need to say yes to in order to reset ourselves, and what we need to say no to in order to remove what weighs us down and pulls us into turmoil and blockage.

We're going to be using qigong again—surprise, surprise. Qigong has that wonderful sense of movement that the ancient Chinese gave us – that so works well with mindfulness and bringing a kind of attuned body sense into the body and its flowing movements. It's a wonderful way to savor bodily experiences.

So, let's begin. Let's start with moving into the "mountain" – our inner mountain, so to speak. Begin with feet spaced about hip-length apart. I have on my socks, I like standing in – also like to do this with bare feet. But you can do this in your shoes, if you choose. And just for a moment, let the feet sink into the earth – sink into the floor – spreading their own deep-feeling roots into the ground. To hold you gently, not tensely. A kind of firmness that also combines a sense of relaxation. And coming up through the legs, feeling the knees unlock, and feel the sense of the spine releasing upward – not pushed up, but released up. So that the emphasis is on finding a kind of stability that is cradled in relaxation. A sense of stability that is ours, our natural endowment, but also has to be cultivated. We'll bring our hands cupped in a way in front of the navel area, like we're holding a ball. This is the golden ball that we use in labeling a set of movements. We can imagine this golden ball as a kind of energy that we're bringing toward the body. We can imagine it joining the breath as the breath drops into the deep bowl of the belly … and joins the region of the hands near the navel to remind us where our true center of gravity is. It is so different from being pulled up in constricted breathing, pulled into our heads where noise and scatteredness often overruns us. In contrast, the a deep sense of resting in this mountain sensation. Letting yourself feel that for a moment. The breath makes contact with the body. The sense of allowing the body to evermore let go. And reminding yourself that you have an inner mountain when you need it.

And now, for the second part, we'll do a little boundary exploration. We'll take this modified golden ball exercise and bring it into the body … ahhhh … what we need, what renews us, what gives us refreshment, what gives us new vitality—or rest. And we'll also explore the boundary skill of saying no, pushing away what blocks us, what pulls us down. These are the two essential movements: breathe in, ball opens and expands; ball collapses as we now concentrate on the feeling of moving out of us what obstructs us. And on top of all that, feeling and savoring the sense of flow in this moving body. Simply become mindful now of being in this kind of current. Are we doing it—or is it doing us? Feeling the body open (when it may have been constricted before) and feeling the body doing what it needs to cleanse. We might think of this as a yes and we might think of this as a no.

Returning now to our mountain pose. Feeling that inner stability that secures us, no matter what is happening outside or inside us. There is simply the ability to stand in the midst of all kinds of weather. And breathe. And be.

I wish you good practice. I hope you will be intrigued enough to play with this. It is always available and is so simple. Stopping during the day to find it. So, I wish you good practice and stable mountain-ing.

Meditation: "Breathing It All In"

By Robin B. Jarrett Autumn 2022.

Take a moment, if you will.
Clear your mind as you might.
Steady yourself comfortably, wherever this is.
Wiggle around, until you feel yourself here.
Enjoy the move.
Pause for the present.
Take time to look around.
See it.
Hear it.
Taste it.
Feel it.
Remind yourself of the strength and firmness of you, grounded here, strong, in the present.
Take a moment, one for you.
Focus for a second, on you.
Find yourself in this moment.
Remind yourself that you are present.
Now if, comfortable, close your eyes.
Breathe slowly and deliberately, in and out.
Feel the air pass gently through you.
Consider for a moment the life-giving parts of breathing.
Consider the simplicity of breath.

(Pause)

Now, let's journey to the past.

(Pause)

Slowly, begin to imagine yourself as an infant,
breathing in and out.
Imagine yourself, all new,
fresh.
Rediscover your hands.
Rediscover your feet.
Imagine yourself with everything in front.
See yourself as that precious baby, a blessing to the world.

(Pause)

Now journey again to the past, think of yourself growing, changing.
Imagine yourself as a toddler,

breathing in and out.
Imagine yourself –
all curious, ready to explore.
Imagine you taking in every new, simple thing
delighting in each day.
drifting into sleep each evening.
rising in the morning with the wonder of all that is ahead.
Now, keep growing, notice yourself, a young child,
exploring and learning.
falling and rising.

(Pause)

Bring into your mind's eye, yourself as a teenager.
Breate in your adventures
your experiments,
your excitement about new possibilities, again curious.
Ready to go. Ripe. Full.
Now keep growing and think of yourself today.
Strong.
Present,
in this moment.

(Pause)

Pause now, and relish all that you are, have become, and have ahead.

(Pause)

As you reflect, begin to think about a few of the people who brought you to the now …

… those who fed you,
… those who nurtured you,
… encouraged you, and
… those who showed you something.
In your mind's eye, let them form a circle around you.
Feel them present,
with you in this moment.

Now enlarge your circle even more.
Bring in or focus on
those who taught you about caregiving and all that it holds.

(Pause)

Remind yourself about what they gave you and
why you give the caring.

(Pause)

Now, bring yourself back to the now, breathing in all that is present in this moment.
Feel yourself here.
Breathe in all that you were,
are,
will be,
and all that you give
and leave for others.
See yourself— that precious, dear one, a blessing to the world.

Session 6—Mindfulness in Daily Life

Session 6 focuses on integrating mindfulness into everyday life, exploring ways to incorporate both formal and informal mindfulness practices into your daily routine. The session also provides a written description of experiential practices for the session. The goal of Session 6 is to help participants translate the concepts and techniques learned throughout the course into routines that align with their personal values and lifestyle.

Mindful Self-Care for Clinicians and Caregivers. https://doi.org/10.1016/B978-0-443-29821-9.00011-X

"Autumn's Embrace" - Marielle took this photo during her maternity leave, on one of her daily walks around the neighborhood with her newborn baby. It was a mindful pause to notice the colors of Fall.

Session 6 Facilitator Quick Guide: Mindfulness in Daily Life

Session Theme: Integrating Mindfulness Skills, Theory and Practices into Daily Life.

Check-In
- Have participants share how they incorporate mindful moments into daily life.
- The emphasis is on small, meaningful times that seem to make a difference.

Mindful Pause: Mindful Moments or "Glimmers".
- Highlight the value of noticing small mindful moments that occur in daily life.
- Allow about 5 minutes for this pause.
- Follow Session Guide for a model or script provided in materials.

Highlight the Session Theme: Mindfulness in Daily Life
- Guiding Questions: How might life be different if you were able to include mindfulness practices into every day?
- Guiding Image: "Snowfall".
- Part A: Creating a mindful space
  - Intentionally creating spaces in your home for mindful reflection can help facilitate the opportunity to practice mindfulness.
- Part B: Changing your relationship to the Moment
  - Mindfulness encourages us to experience the moments of life, connect to people and places, set down distractions and acknowledge emotions without judgment.
  - From this perspective, mindfulness is less about formal practices and more about a way of living, and a way of being.

Moving Meditation: Mindful stretching
- Mindful stretching can be done at your desk or at home for a brief mindful break.
- Video or transcript is available to model or use in session.

Brief Inquiry and Sharing:
- "What stood out for you with this experience?"

Stationary Meditation: "Five-Minute Time Out"
- A brief guided imagery for a mindful time out.
- Audio or transcript is available to model or use in session.

Summary and Suggestions for Formal and Informal Practices during the Week

- Summarize Session 6 theme.
- Invite explorations in mindful living and participants' thoughts or reactions.
- Invite examples of how participants may begin integrating mindfulness practices.

Handouts:

- Session 6 Mindful Stretching Video
- Session 6 "Five-Minute Time-Out" Audio
- Session 6 "A Mindful Glimmer" Script
- Session 6 Participant Summary

Session 6 Introduction: Mindfulness in Daily Life

Session 6 focuses on an essential next step in the cultivation of mindfulness for self-care: integrating techniques, practices, and concepts into everyday life. While previous sessions have focused on specific mindfulness skills or themes, this week encourages participants to consider a broader question of how mindfulness can become a part of daily living. Often, when busy caregivers think about mindfulness, self-care, or meditation, there is a misconception that practice requires large amounts of extra time for an hour of meditation or a daily yoga session, and this may feel impossible to achieve. Mindfulness, however, can truly fit seamlessly into everyday activities, in small moments between tasks, and become a way of experiencing life. While some individuals may be able to carve out time for formal mindfulness practices such as Qigong or meditation, cultivating informal practices of mindfulness may be even more rewarding.

This could look like a mindful lunch once a week, with no distractions or taking three slow mindful breaths in between patients if you are a health professional. Informal mindfulness might be noticing your thoughts, feelings, and body sensations after a difficult phone call with a loved one and taking a moment to observe and check in. It might mean five extra minutes in the morning sitting on your front porch, sipping coffee, and observing a beautiful tree. The ability to build small mindfulness practices into your day and notice mindful moments that are right in front of you means mindfulness can be accessible regardless of time constraints. Session 6 is an opportunity for participants to think about the many skills they have learned over the course of 5 weeks and consider ways these can be included regularly in daily life.

One idea highlighted in this session is creating a mindful space that can serve as a reminder to slow down, observe, connect to the moment, and practice self-care. This might be a favorite chair with a table next to it, with a beautiful plant and a gratitude journal. It could be a meditation corner with a pillow, yoga block, and lavender essential oil. It could be a bowl of mindful grounding stones on your desk at work, and a Post-it note that says "Breathe" taped to your computer screen. It could be a few intentional items set on a bedside table, including a favorite affirmation on a note card, a photograph of a relaxing place, and a book to read mindfully before bed. Small reminders in your physical space can be a powerful way to include mindfulness in daily living. The intentionality of creating mindful spaces in your home also serves as a form of self-care, allowing a few items to serve a special purpose just for you.

The Mindful Pause in Session 6 asks participants to share thoughts on a Mindful Moments or "Glimmers." Examples might be the first bite of a chocolate chip cookie straight out of the oven, watching a sunrise over the ocean and seeing the golden dome peak above the horizon line, hearing "I love you", embracing a family member after a long separation, grasping a friend's hand in a moment of need, hearing a baby laugh, seeing your partner smile. Prompting the group to share examples highlights the idea that mindfulness is more about noticing and connecting to moments that are already occurring, rather than creating or scheduling new experiences. Often, the moments mentioned by people have a universal quality to them and surprisingly range from the most unique and profound ("The moment I held my baby for the first time") to the simple and seemingly mundane ("The smell of a fresh cup of coffee on a rainy morning"). Examples shared by participants may represent moments of connection with others, which can harken back to Session 5 on mindfulness and relationships, while others may offer opportunities to discuss and review past skills, including observing or nonjudging. Importantly, this session encourages participants to find ways to use the skills they have learned to integrate mindful experiences into daily life.

Session 6 may also be the participants' final session of MSCC, if the group is 6 weeks without the additional optional Sessions 7 and 8. If this is the final week, it may be important to take a few minutes to discuss next steps and allow participants to set intentions moving forward regarding mindfulness. One way to introduce this topic is by discussing values, the reasons participants signed up for the course, what they find valuable about mindfulness, and what they value in their work as a caregiver. The topic of values can sometimes be difficult to introduce, but it may be helpful for participants to think about their "why" for wanting to learn about mindfulness. For example, you might ask a participant, "Why did you want to learn about mindfulness?" They might say, "Because I want to be less stressed out." You might then ask, "Why do you want to be less stressed out?" They may respond, "Because I want to enjoy my life and live longer." You could continue to probe with, "Why do you want to live longer? What things do you want to be able to enjoy?" The individual might ponder and respond, "I want to enjoy this time I have with my mother while she is living with me. I know the time we spend together as I care for her is valuable, and I don't wants to miss out on these moments. I also know she needs me, so I want to make sure I live long enough to care for her and my husband." In this way, questions help guide the individual to a deeper level of understanding the value *behind* practicing mindfulness or self-care. Connecting small mindful practices to a deeper value creates meaning and purpose, which can motivate individuals to truly commit to integrating these practices into daily life.

Guiding question to caregivers: "What will you bring to yourself to sustain and nourish you in your daily life?" This question is posed to allow individuals to consider how daily practices can be integrated to contribute to self-care.

Relevance to Caregiving: Caregivers lead busy, stressful lives and practicing mindfulness amid chaotic schedules can be a challenge. Session 6 focuses on helping caregivers adapt mindfulness principles and practices into realistic strategies that can be implemented in daily life. Additionally, this session focuses on committed action based on values and works to connect mindfulness practices to caregiver values, which will increase motivation.

The Moving Meditation and Stationary Meditation in Session 6 focus on simple practices that can be easily integrated into daily life. The movement practice is a five-minute mindful stretching video that can be completed in an office or at home. The five-minute audio recording is a brief guided imagery that can serve as a brief mental time-out.

At the end of this session, invite participants to discuss ideas about how they might integrate mindfulness into daily life. After facilitating discussion and answering questions, distribute handouts and close the session.

Some Takeaway Points

Each week, various techniques, practices, and strategies have been discussed that may assist participants in accessing the present moment and practicing mindfulness. Session 6, however, focuses less on the "what" and more on the "how" and "when" of mindfulness practice. The goal is to focus on helping participants find ways to integrate mindfulness into their everyday life and routine, so it becomes part of living. An important takeaway from this week is that small, mindful moments can be equally as powerful as formal practices. Also, finding ways to turn everyday tasks into mindfulness practices, such as transforming a daily walk into a mindful walk, can make it easier to practice mindfulness regularly. A primary goal of this week is to focus less on concepts and theory and more on the practical challenges that caregivers face as they work to add mindfulness into their daily routine. If the facilitator models problem-solving and creativity through the discussion, this can encourage participants to feel inspired and encouraged that mindfulness can become a part of daily living.

Listen to Belinda's response to Session 6: *One of my biggest fears signing up for these sessions on mindfulness was wondering how in the world will I have time to practice mindfulness when I can barely find time to shower? I appreciated that we spent a lot of time this week talking about ways to make mindfulness feasible and something doable every day. I liked hearing examples from Tobias and the other group members about ways they have brought mindfulness into their routine, and it made me feel encouraged that I could do the same. The idea of creating a mindful space in my home resonated with me, and I decided to clean out a corner of my room with my favorite chair and create a mindful sitting area. I put a candle on the nightstand, brought all my essential oils upstairs, and laid out a book I've been wanting to read for a while now. I've started taking 20 minutes in the evening to light a candle, read, and take 10 diaphragmic breaths with my essential oils before bed. It feels like my safe place, and a small piece of comfort at the end of the day.*

Belinda shares a common fear that many participants may have when starting a mindfulness group, which is that mindfulness is unattainable or impractical for a busy caregiver. Taking time in Session 6 to discuss this concern and encourage participants to find ways to integrate mindfulness into their daily routine ensures that mindfulness translates beyond the confines of the weekly sessions. Belinda gives a wonderful example of how she has created a simple daily routine and curated a specific mindful space in her home. She also shares how valuable it is to hear and learn from other group members and brainstorm together ways to practice mindful self-care amid competing demands as a caregiver.

Tobias' response to Session 6 shows how a professional can integrate mindfulness into the job setting: *This session put a point on what I have been trying between sessions recently. Like the English, I have been having afternoon tea in the staff lounge at around 3:00 in the afternoon. I like the ritual of getting out my teapot, putting tea in the strainer, heating the water, and then slowly savoring each sip of tea. It is my daily mind cleanse! I don't think about anything else while I'm doing this. My breathing slows down, and my rush-rush-rush emotions cool. Sometimes I invite people to join me, but often not. The other thing I want to mention is how much I likes the five-minute imagery meditation today. I am a visualizer, so this was made for me. I can see how I can pause and open a mental window to that meadow and floating clouds. My body just let's go into it and tension melts.*

Tobias demonstrates how personal mindfulness practices and choices evolve seamlessly over the course of the session. His tea ritual is adapted to his taste, his environment, and the pace of his day. You can feel how absorbed he is in this practice and how he slowly savors it. The outer practice must be met with inner mindfulness for this to work. The facilitator wants to listen not just to the "what" of the practice but also the inner "how" to help guide participants into this way of practicing. Tobias also responded well to the brief imagery-based meditation. Not everyone is a visualizer like he is, so a variety of practices are introduced to choose from over time.

Key Concepts

- Small mindful moments can be just as powerful as formal practices.
- Finding ways to turn daily activities into mindfulness practices can help integrate mindfulness into everyday life.
- Create a mindfulness space in your home as a reminder to pause and focus on the present moment.

Session 6 Guide: Mindfulness in Daily Life

Aim of Session 6:

- To cultivate strategies for integrating techniques and themes from sessions 1-5 into daily life.
- To discover ways to practice mindfulness in a way that feels accessible and attainable for the caregiver.

Check-In

Aim: Introduce the session theme in the Check-In by asking participants to reflect on ways they have begun to bring mindfulness skills and practices into daily life. Participants might reflect on successes or challenges they have experienced thus far.

Suggestions: At this point in the group, participants have been exposed to a number of formal and informal mindfulness practices, as well as a variety of techniques and skills. Although discussion of how to find opportunities to practice mindfulness has been ongoing throughout the group, this session and the Check-In at the beginning allow for more focus on the practical aspects of integrating mindfulness into life as a caregiver. The opportunity for participants to share, as well as to listen and learn from others, allows for a rich environment of learning and growing. Facilitators may go around in turn and ask participants to each share one example of how they have tried to incorporate mindfulness into their day, or if caregivers have not yet been able to do this, perhaps an idea of how they might start to do this.

Mindful Pause: Mindful Moments or "Glimmers"

Aim: To highlight the value of noticing small mindful moments or "glimmers" of joy, peace, gratitude or meaning throughout your day. Discuss how paying attention mindfully allows you to identify and savor these moments without the mind hijacking your focus away from them. By acknowledging these moments and being present with them, you can shine a light on mindful moments that can be restorative and begin to change daily experiences.

Suggestions: Use the script provided or create your own Mindful Pause reflection that allows participants to consider a mindful moment or "glimmer" they can recall and guide them to picture the moment in their mind while connecting with each of the five senses.

Discussion/Sharing: After completing the Mindful Pause reflection, ask participants to share examples of the mindful moment they recalled during the exercise, or another "glimmer" they recall experiencing this week. It can also be helpful to help participants explore what about those moments in particular causes them to stand out, or perhaps how they felt when savoring or taking a moment to fully experience that moment.

Highlighting the Session Theme: Mindfulness in Daily Life

Guiding Question: "How might life be different if you were able to include mindfulness into every day? What parts of your day could benefit the most from a mindful pause, or savoring a mindful "glimmer"?

Aim: Questions that encourage caregivers to think about the benefits of practicing mindfulness help increase motivation to practice integrating these mindfulness practices. It also allows for reflection about what this could look like for caregivers as they identify small ways that mindfulness could be practiced day to day.

- **Guiding Image: "Snowfall"** (Collins, 2024)

"Snowfall" offers an example of a mindful moment, a written reflection to be read to participants of a mindful moment experienced by stepping outside on a snowy day. Often, moments in nature stand out as experiences that bring us back to the present and capture all of our senses. The reflection below of the image of a snowfall can be used as an example for participants to help highlight a mindful "glimmer" or mindful moment in nature.

Snowfall

Marielle H. Collins (2024).

"The world is quiet with a muffled silence, the air is crisp and fresh. Snow is falling here. Each flake drifts lazily from the sky, dancing its way to the earth. The world feels slower and everything has been wrapped in a blanket of powdery white. I take a breath in and feel the cool air fill up my lungs. As I breathe out I see it linger in the air. For a moment I close my eyes and feel the cool stillness – soft, peaceful, suspended."

Part A: Creating a Mindful Space

- Mindful reminders in your space can be a helpful way to keep at the front of participants' minds the skills, techniques, and principles learned throughout this course. Also, intentionally creating spaces in your home for mindful reflection can help facilitate the opportunity to practice mindfulness. Often *remembering* to stop and breathe, observe the moment, or connect with the body can be the biggest challenge, and a thoughtfully curated physical space can assist with this. Mindful spaces can range from the simple Post-it reminder on your desk to the intentionally created meditation room or corner. Introduce this concept and then encourage participants to discuss ways in which they might curate a mindful space in their home. As a caregiver, much attention may be paid to creating safe and functional spaces for others, and this provides an opportunity to identify and discuss what it might look like to intentionally design a space for oneself and for mindful self-care.
  - Example: Think about your home or your area of work, the spaces where you spend the most time. Are there any areas for relaxation, reflection, or moments of mindfulness? If not, what would it look like to try and create a space? What

thoughts or emotions come up for you as you think about the possibility of doing this? Do you feel guilty? Excitement?

Part B: Informal Mindfulness – Changing Your Relationship to the Moment

- Mindfulness allows us to focus on one moment at a time, without judging or needing to change the experience. It encourages a slowing down, intentionality, and a focus on the moments of life that often are missed or ignored. In a world where multitasking has become common, and everyone is bombarded with input constantly from social media, technology, and life responsibilities, mindfulness represents a significant shift in how we experience each day. It's a radical shift to decide to connect, observe, and respond to a moment, check in with thoughts, emotions, and body experiences, and practice self-care. Instead of hurrying through life, checking out with technology, numbing emotions, and coping through distraction, mindfulness encourages us to experience the moments of life, connect to people and places around us, set down distractions, and acknowledge our emotions without judgment. From this perspective, mindfulness is less about formal practices and more about a way of living, and a way of being.
  - Example: Introduce the acronym **STOP,** where **S** (Stop) means to pause during the busy day. **T** (Take a breath) utilizes a moment of mindful breathing to bring the focus back on the present. **O** (Observe) checks in with thoughts and feelings. **P** (Proceed Mindfully) means to choose the best way to proceed in the day. This skill can be used as a way to connect, observe, and respond throughout the day and respond more mindfully to emotions we experience. Facilitators may teach this skill and then ask participants to think of examples of when they might use this during their experiences of caregiving as a way to practice a mindful pause in the day.

Moving Meditation: Mindful Stretching

Aim: To introduce a mindful stretching series that can be done while sitting at a desk, at a bedside in a hospital room, at the kitchen table, or on the porch.

Suggestions: Mindful stretching can be done anywhere and is an example of a simple and practical practice that can be easily integrated into daily life. A key principle is focusing on breathing throughout the stretching and maintaining focus on the present moment throughout. See the mindful stretching video for a follow-along practice.

Brief Inquiry and Sharing:

"What stood out for you with this experience?"

Stationary Mindfulness: "Five-Minute Time-Out"

Aim: To demonstrate how a brief five-minute guided imagery meditation can serve as a powerful mental break during a busy week.

Suggestions: This brief guided imagery utilizes the power of imagination to create relaxation and a sense of calm. Encourage participants to focus on the experience of the senses as they picture the nature image. You can utilize the script or recording provided or create your own guided imagery meditation using the same format.

Brief Inquiry and Sharing:

"What did you notice during this exercise?"

Summary and Suggestions for Formal and Informal Practices during the Week

Aim: To review and reinforce the concepts discussed in the group, particularly ways participants can bring mindfulness into daily life seamlessly. Participants can hear from one another and share ideas for simple yet powerful ways to add mindfulness practices into daily life.

Suggestions: In this summary, a discussion of challenges and opportunities for mindfulness practices, particularly within the caregiving experience, may be shared. As Session 6 may be the final session, based on group structure, it may be helpful for participants to share thoughts on an intention about how they hope to practice mindfulness moving forward. The past 5 weeks have served as an introduction to mindfulness concepts, as well as a trial period for working to include these techniques in daily living. Session 6 allows participants to take stock of what has worked well or not worked over the past weeks and consider how they might continue to create mindful experiences going forward. If Session 6 serves as the last session of the group, be sure to allow extra time at the end for a reflection of the group experience, what participants have learned, and how this group has changed their thoughts and perspective. Also, participants often bond over the course of a group and therefore allowing time at the end of the session for acknowledgment, appreciation, and good-byes may be important.

Handouts:

- Session 6 Mindful Stretching Video
- Session 6 "Five-Minute Time-Out" Audio
- Session 6 "A Mindful Glimmer" Script
- Session 6 Participant Summary

Session 6-Facilitator's Contemplation: What is mindfulness during daily living?

Session 6 Participant Summary: Mindfulness in Daily Life*

Guiding Question: "How might life be different if you included mindfulness into every day?"

Aim of Session: Discuss strategies for integrating mindfulness techniques and themes into daily life and practice mindfulness in a way that feels accessible and attainable.

What did you notice in the **Mindful Pause: Mindful Moments or 'Glimmers'?**

What did you notice in the **Check-In** while reflecting on your current mindfulness practices?

* Lumpkin, M., Collins, M.H., & Jarrett, R.B. (2026). Mindful self-care for clinicians and caregivers: A group facilitator's guide. Academic Press.

What resonated with you in **Creating a Mindful Space?**

What stood out for you in **Changing Your Relationship to the Moment?**

What stood out for you in **Five-Minute Time-Out** meditation?

Lumpkin, M., Collins, M.H., & Jarrett, R.B. (2026). Mindful self-care for clinicians and caregivers: A group facilitator's guide. Academic Press.

Creating a Mindful Space: Mindful reminders in your space can keep skills and techniques at the forefront of your mind. Creating intentional spaces in your home for mindful reflection can facilitate mindfulness practice. Often *remembering* to stop and breathe, observe the moment, or connect with the body is the biggest challenge. Mindful spaces can range from the simple, like a Post-it reminder on your desk, to the extensively curated meditation corner.

Changing Your Relationship to the Moment: Mindfulness allows us to focus on one moment at a time, without judgment. It encourages slowing down and focusing on the moments of life that often are missed. In a world where multitasking has become common and we are constantly bombarded with input, mindfulness represents a significant change in how we experience each day. Mindfulness encourages us to connect to people and places around us, set down distractions, and acknowledge our emotions without judgment. From this perspective, mindfulness is less about formal practices and more about a way of living, and a way of being.

Guiding Images: The “Snowfall” image can be used as an example of a mindful moment or “glimmer” that can be restorative, simple, and found in daily life. Take a moment to reflect on a mindful moment or “glimmer “that was a part of your day or week. Think of one you perhaps did not stop and highlight, or felt too rushed to pause and savor.

Suggestions: In this session, we discussed ways to integrate mindfulness into daily life, and ways in which mindfulness can be practiced in formal ways like meditation, mindful movement, etc. and also informal ways that are more about mindful living and a different way to connect with the moments of life. This week, we invite you to think about a few more ways you can bring mindfulness more fully into your daily life.

List mindfulness practices you would like to try this week:	☑

Lumpkin, M., Collins, M.H., & Jarrett, R.B. (2026). Mindful self-care for clinicians and caregivers: A group facilitator’s guide. Academic Press.

Mindful Stretching: Transcript

Welcome to your mindful stretching video. For this video, all you will need is a chair where you can sit comfortably, at home, at work, anywhere where you can take a few moments for yourself. Let's begin by closing our eyes and setting an intention for this practice. Anything else that's on your mind today, worrying or stressing you, set it aside for these moments. Focus on being present with yourself, your body and your breath for a few moments of self-care.

Begin by gently rotating your body to one side, twisting and looking over the opposite shoulder and feeling a nice rotation through your spine, breathing in and exhaling into the twist. Come to center and twist to the other side again, rotating and looking over that back shoulder, breathing in. Exhale into the twist. Rotate the spine. Come back to the center. Interlace your fingers and press the palms forward and curve your spine, creating a C shape and feeling a nice stretch through the upper back. With each exhale, try to make the stretch a little deeper. Next, reach your arms up overhead and gently bend over to one side and then come back to center. Reach over to the other side and then come back to the center and release. For our next stretch, cross one ankle over your knee and then, if you can, reach down toward the floor. If that stretch feels too intense, stay seated in an upright position. Inhale and exhale. Now switch and cross the opposite ankle over the knee, and again, if you would like, you can gently reach your arms down toward the ground, or you can stay seated upright, if that's more comfortable. Breathing in and breathing out.

Next, reach one arm out in front of you and gently pull the fingertips toward you, feeling a stretch in your wrist. Now switch to the opposite side and again, gently pull the fingertips toward you. Breathing in and breathing out.

Now we are going to gently roll the head around to stretch out the neck. Rotate the head all the way around in a circle, and then switch to the opposite direction. Try and make these neck rolls nice and big to release any tension in your neck and shoulders. Now reach your arms up, and then bend one arm back so that your fingertips are in between your shoulder blades. Gently pull on that elbow and lean to one side. Switch and gently pull on the elbow on the other side, and lean the other direction.

Next, reach both arms up high and pull the elbows down in a W shape, feeling the chest opening up. Do this stretch two more times - reach up and again pull down, opening up the chest with a nice exhale. Reach up one more time and pull down, open the chest. Go ahead and take one arm across the body and gently pull it toward you. Exhale into the stretch. Now switch to the opposite side, gently pull toward you.

Now we are going to extend the arms out front and roll the wrists out. Rotate the wrists in one direction and then the opposite direction. Next, open and close the hands and pull each finger into a fist, and then open the hand back out. Now take a big reach up, but stretching the arms up and around, making a big circle. Stretch up high to the sky and release.

Now, go ahead and close your eyes again. End this practice by taking three deep breaths. Inhale, hold at the top – exhale all the air slowly out. And again, inhale, hold, exhale all the air slowly out again. Last time, inhale – hold at the top – exhale all the air out.

"Five-Minute Time-Out" Script

Start by settling into a comfortable position, whether seated or lying down. Close your eyes if that feels right to you, or feel free to soften your gaze. Take a moment to scan your body, and see if there are any places of tension you can soften, or any tightness you can release. Starting at the top of your head and scanning the body down to your shoulders, release any tension in the neck, dropping the shoulders down. Moving down to the chest, release any tightness in the belly, letting the hips relax and feel heavy. Continue your focus down to the legs, the calves, and the feet. Let a sensation of relaxation move through the body. Take a deep inhale, hold at the top for a moment, and exhale all the air slowly out. Again, breathe in deeply, hold at the top, exhale fully. Now allow your breath to find its own natural rhythm, inhaling and exhaling.

With your eyes closed, imagine that you are lying in a grassy field, looking up at a wide, blue sky with soft, puffy white clouds. The sun is shining, and as you lie in the grass, you begin to notice the warm sensation as you feel the sun shining on your skin. In this moment, you are resting here. There is nowhere else you need to be, nowhere you need to go, and nothing else in this moment you need to do. Allow yourself to just BE in this calm and safe place.

Listen for a moment and notice what you hear. Maybe you can hear the gentle rustle of the grass as a breeze blows; maybe you can hear the sound of birds in the background. Allow your body to relax, breathe, and focus your mind on this moment. As you lie here, feel the sensation of the air entering your body, filling up your lungs, and then leaving the body as you exhale.

Feel the sensation of the ground beneath you, holding your body. Allow yourself to release into the earth any stress you may be holding onto. Focus your mind on the breath, the breathing in and the breathing out. In this moment, you are breathing, allow everything else to fall away. Take a moment to look at the clouds above you that are slowly passing by in the sky. Notice how, moment by moment, each of the clouds slowly changes shape. Bring your attention back to focus on the breath. Follow the air in and all the way out. Inhale and exhale.

As this practice comes to an end, slowly bring your awareness back into the room you are in. Begin to notice your body again, and then expand your attention to the room where you are. When you are ready, you can open your eyes.

A Mindful Glimmer *Script*

By Marielle H. Collins (2023).

Take a moment to center yourself.

Take a deep inhale, hold at the top for a moment, and slowly exhale.

Close your eyes if you would like, or you may soften your gaze.

Take a scan of your body and see if you can find any points of tension that you can release, soften, or relax.

If you find a spot, take a breath in, sending your breath to that part of the body, creating space and then exhale and release.

With your eyes closed, bring to mind something that for you represents a perfect moment in time.

It might be a memory with a loved one, a moment of excitement, joy, or contentment.

It could be a moment of wonder or awe, an experience in nature or a simple everyday experience. Allow this moment to come into your mind.

Picture this moment in your mind. Imagine that you are there now.

What do you see?

What do you hear?

What can you feel?

Is there anything you can taste?

What do you smell?

Bring all of this to your mind as vividly as possible. Holding it in the mind's eye.

Take an inhale … and an exhale. And again, inhale and exhale.

And when you are ready, you can open your eyes.

Lumpkin, M., Collins, M.H., & Jarrett, R.B. (2026). Mindful self-care for clinicians and caregivers: A group facilitator's guide. Academic Press.

Author Reflections: Thoughts from a First-Time Mom
By Marielle H. Collins, PhD

One of the unique times in life when caregiving emerges suddenly and completely is becoming a first-time mom. The transition from caring for yourself to caring fully for a helpless newborn, is both incredible and overwhelming.

Nothing truly prepares you for the extreme sleep deprivation, emotional exhaustion, and strange combination of joy and panic. Days and nights blur together between feedings every 1–2 hours and being constantly on alert; the tiny human who brings so much joy and awe also requires constant attention. My sweet newborn did not like to be put down, wanted to be held constantly and always needed something. His only way of communicating his needs was through crying, which, especially as it escalated, sent my nervous system into fight-or-flight mode. The early weeks postpartum felt like a trial by fire, learning to do everything with one hand while holding a baby, trying to sleep in two-hour increments, and mustering the grace to take each day one step at a time.

During this special time, I thought about mindfulness. The advice I heard most often from friends, family, and social media was "This time doesn't last," "Enjoy every minute" and "You can never get these newborn moments back." These words were often delivered with a sense of foreboding, tinged with longing and grief, which inevitably made me feel stressed. Being told that I was already losing something that had barely begun, created a pressured need to desperately hold onto time that was passing. The impending sense of loss seemed to cast a shadow over the beauty of the present, with a temptation to focus on a fear of the future rather than savoring the time I had.

I imagine that people offer this advice to encourage new moms to stay mindful and treasure the moments with their baby. Ironically, though, this advice pulled me out of the present moment, as it stirred up memories of a future time when my baby would be grown, and the contact naps and snuggles a distant memory. Additionally, telling a new mom to enjoy every moment and feel nothing but bliss also sets up unrealistic expectations, leaving room for self-judgment when other emotions surface.

As I began to recognize the conflicting messages I was hearing, I tried to find a new way to be mindful and set aside the pressure of foreboding joy. What helped me most was paying attention to the moments as they presented, and to the various emotions as they came and went. While I still found myself grappling with fear, anxiety, sadness, and frustration - the sweet moments came too. When they did, I focused on being present, connecting with my baby and trying not to focus on the future. I also made an effort to carve out small moments of self-care, even when it felt almost impossible.

From just one mother's experience, here are three ways I integrated mindfulness:

- *Focusing on each one of my senses in the moment, as I rocked my baby to sleep in the nursery: the smell of my newborn baby's head, the feel of his soft velvety cheek against my cheek as I held him on my shoulder, the rhythm of the rocking chair going back and forth, the sound of the white noise machine whooshing in the background, the sound of my voice as I sang a lullaby, the color of his blue eyes peering up at me, the tiny smiles that danced across his face as he fell into rapid eye movement sleep. Connecting with each of these senses helped me stay present, not miss the moments, and avoid falling into the trap of thinking about the future.*
- *Making sure, no matter what, to take a shower every day as a small but essential act of self-care. Those five to 10 minutes to myself helped me feel like a person again when I was losing my sanity. Whether it was a one-hour nap after being awake all night, a quick 10-minute shower, or watching a comforting television show at 3:00 a.m. while breastfeeding, these small moments made a difference.*
- *Giving myself permission to feel every emotion that steamrolled through the postpartum period: notice it without judgment, label it, and let it pass. Allowing to come and go the frustration of sleepless nights, the anxiety about "Am I doing this right?" and "Are my emotions are normal?" and the occasional feelings of loss, all lived amidst the moments of newborn joy.*

If I could offer any guidance to a new mom from the trenches, it would be this: It's impossible to predict how you'll feel, and whatever emotions arise are completely valid. While it's tempting to fall into the trap of "foreboding joy" and try to hold on to every fleeting moment, remember that these stages, changes and growth are part of a natural rhythm, one that women have experienced since the beginning of time. Trust the process and live the experience.

Do what you need to get through the day, and make time (however small) for yourself, even if it's just 5 minutes. The intention behind how you use that time, and your perspective on its purpose, can matter more than the amount of time itself. Hold space with curiosity and compassion for the myriad emotions that come each day. Let go of the "shoulds" to create space to be present each day. There will be precious moments buried in the midst of difficult ones, when you find the special moments, notice them, and collect the jewels along the way through the rambling forest of Motherhood.

Session 7—Discovering Your Way to Mindfulness

Session 7 provides a review of previous themes and practices, and serves as an opportunity to strengthen mindful self-care strategies and implementation into daily routine. The session also includes a written description of experiential practices for the session. The aim of Session 7 is to reinforce and deepen the mindfulness concepts and techniques learned throughout the course.

Mindful Self-Care for Clinicians and Caregivers. https://doi.org/10.1016/B978-0-443-29821-9.00012-1

"An Old Walking Bridge"— Martin tried to bring a sense of this old bridge to the feeling of transition in one's journey... from introductory explorations in mindfulness and self-care to the commitment to keep on the path with the resources selected in one's backpack. The journey that never really ends.

Session 7 Facilitator Quick Guide: Discovering Your Way to Mindfulness

Session Theme: Strengthening Mindfulness Skills, as outlined in Sessions 1 through 3. Reflecting on one's own Individual Path of Growing Mindfulness

Mindful Pause: Finding Myself, My Living Breath, and The World Around Me

- Summarize the aim of the Mindful Pause, as this is only one example.
- Notice how attention can intentionally shift to various present moment experiences.
- First shift: Finding Myself by placing attention on one's present inner bodily state.
- Second shift: My Living Breath, as the familiar focus on the inner feeling of breathing.
- Third shift: The World Around Me opens the senses to the outside around you.

Brief Sharing

- Participants share a word or brief phrase to describe the outcome of the pause.

Highlight the Session Theme: Discovering Your Way to Mindfulness

- Guiding Question: What are you discovering about what works best for you in opening your doors into mindfulness?
- Guiding Image: Swinging toward the open sky bit by bit in your backyard tree swing.
- Part A: Learning to Swing into Mindfulness Step by Step
  - Begin with the guiding question, and then summarize Sessions 1–3.
  - The guiding image suggests we learn mindfulness through step-by-step practices.
- To help each person connect with their own story of mindful development to this point, read Tobias in An Interlude: The MSCC Journey (finishing at the end of the 11th paragraph under Tobias … "My path to burnout was taking a turn.")
- Part B: Discovering Your Way to Mindfulness
  - Check-In: using Tobias' story to look at our own still-unfolding journey into mindfulness.
  - Ask participants where they began, where they are now, and where they would like to go in the future.
  - What formal and/or informal practices have come to have a meaningful impact?
  - Seek opportunities to highlight emerging mindful attitudes and skills in accessing mindfulness, emphasizing the long-term process with ups and downs in this growth.

Moving Meditation: Session 1 Qigong and Free Form Qigong

- Mindfulness of breath, body, and the flow of gentle movements from Session 1 Qigong.

- At the end of Session 1 Qigong, add a brief exploration of free-form Qigong in which participants let go of a given format and release into spontaneous movements.
- This practice combines a familiar practice with a new twist at the end.

Brief Inquiry and Sharing

- Ask about what came out of this experience of mindful moving.
- Was there a difference between the set forms and the free form movement experience?

Stationary Meditation: Brief Body Scan with Mindfulness of Breath

- This practice combines two separate sitting practices into one to see how one might enhance the other.
- Review the audio and/or transcript of the Body Scan in Session 1, then use a briefer, selectively focused Body Scan of the bottom of the feet, thighs, small of the back, stomach, shoulders, neck, palms of hands, and ending with the feel of the body as a whole.
- Transition to Session 2's Mindfulness of Breath as an Anchor, beginning with "Entering the final phase as finding and centering on your breath…" in the audio or transcript.

Brief Inquiry/Sharing

- Ask about what stood out in this combined Body Scan and Mindfulness of Breath meditation.
- Ask about what aspects of the meditation seemed most helpful in centering your attention in the present.

Summary and Suggestions

- Briefly summarize the session theme as reflected in the story of Tobias: How are participants understanding the nature of their journey to learn the basic Session 1-3 mindfulness skills?
- Ask participants to think about how to bring consistency to the mindfulness practices they have chosen as their favorite forms.
- Wonder about what each will choose to use, choosing informal and/or formal practices during the next week.
- Briefly go over the Session 8 theme of self-care (integrating Sessions 4–6), reminding them that it will be the last session, but the beginning of the challenge of continued practice.
- Read the poem "It Takes A While" to the end.

Handouts:

- Session 1 Qigong Movement Video

- Session 1 Body Scan with Session 2 Mindfulness of Breath Audios.
- "It Takes A While" poem
- "Bringing Mindfulness to Daily Life," a handout from Session 1.
- Tobias

Session 7 Introduction: Discovering Your Way to Mindfulness

Sessions 7 and 8 are special review sessions, pulling together the themes of Sessions 1 through 6. They serve two purposes: First, to deepen former sessions by adding practice and reflections on the nature of growing mindfulness, and, second, to provide a way to make up missed sessions. Session 7 integrates Sessions 1 through 3 with a focus on the path to learning basic mindfulness skills. Session 8 looks at the theme of mindful self-care, moving through Sessions 4 through 6. Together, the last two sessions put a cap on the journey through the prior sessions, a kind of mountain top view. Along with familiar practices, the sessions add some new twists to meditations in order to stimulate continued exploratory play with ways to learn mindfulness.

A bigger picture of the path to mindfulness can more fully emerge in these last two sessions. The Buddhist notion of *dharma* incorporates the aspects of understanding the teaching, the various practices, and the experience that arises from them. What might be called the "way of mindfulness" is an unfolding process that has parts blended into a whole: the experience of mindfulness, the practices/attitudes that sharpen the skill of entering mindfulness, and the framework of mindfulness as a way to look at our situations and possible responses to them. These aspects were there all along in the sessions, although some were explicitly carved out more than others. As the facilitator, you have been a source of exhibiting the whole blending by the way you express mindfulness in your guidance and responses. While many participants in the sessions may have entered mindfulness training with a sense of acquiring techniques, most begin to appreciate something larger at play as they progress on the path. Mindfulness as a *way* enfolds techniques within a container of attitudes, insights into a style of living, and some selected practices to strengthen their skills of accessing this natural but often underprized state of awareness. Techniques morph into practices that become guiding experiences. Sessions 7 and 8 draw the curtain back to reveal this pattern of development to lift it into view.

An Interlude: The MSCC Journey, in an earlier part of this book, was written for both facilitators and session participants. For participants, only the section through the Tobias vignette is used. It briefly summarizes the benefits of mindfulness for caregivers and provides a picture of how one develops mindfulness skills over the MSCC course. The vignette about Tobias personalizes one person's experience over time. The story of Tobias is not meant to be a prescription. It is meant to stimulate reflections about one's own accumulating growth in skills and understanding over time in the course. It is an appreciative view of a journey meant to continue long past the ending of the sessions. The aim in using the Tobias story in *The MSCC Journey* is to inspire participants to continue walking the evolving walk within their own story.

Session 7 begins with the overall aim of Sessions 7 and 8, with Session 7 reviewing the theme of developing basic mindfulness skills sequenced in Sessions 1 through 3. A *Quick Summary of Sessions 1 through 3* gives you, the facilitator, a brief rundown of what was covered. The *Aim* of Session 7 in the session guide covers the gist of a helpful introduction expressible in your own words. In this session, participants can experience examples of informal practices like Mindful Pause and formal practices of Movement and Stationary Meditations. Those who missed any of Sessions 1 through 3 have a chance to experience some of the themes and practices they missed. This can come in the form of Informal and Formal Session 7 practices that incorporate prior practice elements like Body Scan, Mindfulness of Breath, or Mindful Pause. The Tobias vignette may also uplift prior session themes, such as mindful responding to stress. For those who did not miss any of Sessions 1 through 3, Session 7 provides a kind of repracticing basic practices with a few new elements, such as combining Body Scan and Mindfulness of Breath, and familiar Qigong with the addition of a free-form ending. A central session experience is the reflection on one's story of cultivating mindfulness skills and insights. The Check-In is placed later in the session to stimulate the sharing around one's own Tobias-type journey. The aim here is to inspire each other to appreciate growth and encourage future growth.

The Mindful Pause in Session 7 is similar, yet slightly different from the one in Session 1. Although formal meditation often gets the most attention in mindfulness programs, it is helpful to underscore the power of simple, brief ways to shift into mindful moments in one's day. These are often the practices of choice of many participants. Participants are encouraged to see their informal practices as critical to infusing mindfulness into their days. They are also encouraged to reshape these session practices in any way that becomes user-friendly, and yet results in momentary shifts into mindfulness.

The session theme has the guiding question of "What are you discovering about what works best for you in opening your doors into mindfulness?" The question is now asking participants to look at what they are discovering in their own experience to be of help, rather than focus on some new content of skill, or practice. This is a transition toward supporting one's own authority, rather than seeing oneself as a successful or perhaps unsuccessful follower of someone else's model. Without this transition, we will ignore the fact that participants will select in very personal ways what is uniquely useful for them, no matter how strong an ideal model is presented. And this should be the way we look at their outcomes. The guiding image of "Swinging Toward the Open Sky" hopefully captures the sense that one is building one's own swing from the prior sessions' materials, and that progress in swinging the learned skills toward the open sky of mindfulness is progressive, bit by bit. The supportive attitude of such swinging is more in line with exploration and play than tense striving for mastery or for some result.

At this point, An Interlude: The MSCC Journey is brought into play. In it, the Tobias vignette is the facilitator script. Present it as a way to reflect on the path to learning mindfulness skills that have been taking place. It is important that the Tobias vignette not be seen as an ideal, but rather as one person's unfolding experience over time, which may share some similarities with participants' own experiences. Although this will be a handout (see Tobias in handouts) at the session end, you offer to read a section, ending with the 11th paragraph in the "Tobias" section. Ask participants to listen mindfully and openly, to allow aspects of their own journey to arise in the mind and be noticed. Pause when finished reading and ask those present to think about what brought them to the session, to remember where they began, where they feel they are now in developing mindfulness practices and ways of responding on their own, and where they see themselves going on their future path to strengthen mindfulness in their lives. The Check-In initiates the sharing. The facilitator can now listen for opportunities to highlight and reinforce participant discoveries. The Check-In closes with the facilitator summarizing shared group themes. Group members are invited to see their journey as long-term, with ups and downs, to be taken in stride as part of the process. They are encouraged to trust themselves to continue selecting and experimenting with practices they are drawn to.

The two formal mindfulness practices of Moving and Stationary Meditations are shown as previously presented practices, incorporating some novel additions. The Moving Meditation is taken from Session 1 Qigong. The novel aspect ends with self-generated, spontaneous movement done in the flowing style of Qigong but freed from prescribed forms. The Qigong form of feet planted with knees straight ahead can be continued while the upper body just lifts, curves, and turns in one's own way. Facilitators might practice this free form on their own just to get used to doing it unselfconsciously. The Stationary Meditation is a combination of an abridged Body Scan and a shortened Mindfulness of Breath from Sessions 1 and 2. The session guide suggests which parts of each to use in guiding the meditation.

The Summary and Suggestions in Session 7 end the session with participant reflections of their mindfulness skills journey, with encouragement to continue practicing in one's own way. The poem "It Takes A While" supports the session theme in an inspiring way. Handouts include Tobias, which will be used in Session 8. The Participant Session Summary encourages notes on the session experience and a reminder of what the session covered. The poem is also handed out for personal use. And audio/video resources for the formal meditations are again presented and encouraged. The handout "Bringing Mindfulness to Daily Life" is distributed again, since it is the only resource for listing possible informal practices.

Some Takeaway Points

Focused on basic mindfulness skills and practices from Sessions 1 through 3, Session 7 inspires participants to review and reflect on what they have learned about the nature and benefits of mindfulness and its basic practices. For some, this is a review with dimensions added to prior practices to savor and try on. For others, this is an opportunity to experience what was missed in a prior session or two. The Tobias narrative provides a framework for participants to review where they started, where they are now, and where they want to be in the future. This is a time to appreciate the journey of learning and to choose one's own set of practices, from prior sampling of several possibilities. Each person shapes his or her own preferred formal and/or informal mindfulness practices, not some standard set for everyone. The aim is to integrate mindful self-care with caregiving into everyday life. We will now hear from Yolanda, a young caregiver to a child on the autism spectrum, and Steve, a middle-aged man caring for his wife, paralyzed by a stroke.

Yolanda responds to Session 7: *I hated that I missed the second session because I wanted to learn more about this sitting breath meditation I've heard so much about before this session. This session gave me a chance to see what it was like. And I did like it! It brought me to a calm place that I wish would go on and on. And the Qigong uplifted me and made me smile. I loved the part where I just moved like my own dance. I hadn't realized movement can be mindful! Hearing Tobias's story was a treat. I thought about my own start as an overwhelmed mom, just wanting some relief that wasn't a pill. I really didn't know what mindfulness was until we were taught to place our attention on something in the present, something different from my usual worry and planning. The mindful pauses and meditation gradually brought this home to me. I am taking these pauses into my dealings with my son. I've had times of change, from resenting him to taking a breath and laughing at us both. The key for me is to snap out of old thoughts and just open my eyes to just what's happening, not going beyond it, the past, or into the future.*

Yolanda gives us several points to ponder. She was able to catch up on the experience of sitting meditation with the breath that she wanted but missed in a prior session. She got the sense of play in the spontaneous part added to the Qigong meditation. Tobias stimulated her own sense of a growing, conscious awareness of her development. And she is telling us about her attraction to Mindful Pauses with her son as a likely adopted practice in the future. Her last sentence captures her basic grasp of what moves through all mindfulness skills. As a facilitator, these are all potential aspects to validate.

Here is Steve's response to Session 7: *Tobias got me thinking about where I've been and where I am heading. I started this session with such a heavy weight on my heart. I can now see it was grief over losing so much of my wife, and anguish over how to give her the care she needs. I was totally unprepared for how to make good decisions, like when to call her doctors or how to tell if she is getting better or not. I didn't know if I should push her to recover or let her be. No wonder Angina hit me so many times. These sessions helped me see that I am not alone and to see how so much of my stress comes from my own unchecked reactions. Compared to others, I feel I am a slow learner here. But going back over earlier meditations, I can see how I can move into a relaxed attention a little better. The Mindful Pause today made more sense as a simple way to check in with myself and know how I'm doing. I like moving more than sitting. So, I think I will continue to watch some of the Moving Meditations to see which ones I like best. I like walking and getting outside to the garden. Now I know how to use these to slow down and let go of my worry mind.*

Like so many, Steve knew he was suffering, but he did not spend time with himself to know why. As he listened to others in the group and learned to focus more attention on inner feelings, he came to appreciate the unacknowledged grip of grief mixed with heavy self-doubt over how to be an effective caregiver. These mindful insights help make sense of what can seem senseless. And this allows for greater acceptance of the source of suffering. Steve feels he is a slow learner and may struggle to see his development over time. Yet, the experience of repeating aspects of earlier mindfulness practices surprised him. The group and the facilitator gave him a mirror he was not holding up to himself. And from this, Steve is encouraged to select practices that suit him and fit into his lifestyle. Steve is making mindful practice his own.

Key Concepts

- Mindfulness deepens and develops in caregivers over time.
- Identify a few mindfulness techniques that resonate with you to encourage long-term use.
- Approach mindfulness as a lifelong journey—expect lapses, and gently return to the practice when they occur.

Session 7 Guide: Discovering Your Way to Mindfulness

Aim of Session 7

To bring the first three sessions together in a kind of review, and allow participants to connect and deepen the core practices presented in them. For those who missed a session, this review puts what was missed in its larger context and provides a way to explore aspects of missed practices. For Session 7, participants will situate mindfulness in the world of caregiving and clarify the attitudes that foster mindfulness. They can see again the formal and informal types of mindfulness practice to encourage personalizing one's choices of practices.

Mindful Pause: Finding Myself, My Living Breath, and The World Around Me

Aim: To present the pause as an informal practice that is such an accessible way to shift into mindfulness at any time. Pauses are brief but effective ways to become aware of one's inner state, directly felt, of a simple anchoring sensation to follow the breath in the present, and of a fresh perception of one's surroundings. This is but one of many ways to pause as a way to wake up to sense and to feel what is actually happening, rather than losing ourselves in thought and fantasy. We can use Mindful Pauses to savor experiences in ways that nourish us and as ways to work free from stress reactions.

Suggestions: Summarize the Aim of the Mindful Pause. Then invite participants to discover what is in the experience for themselves in an exploratory way, patiently noticing what is happening as they gently redirect their attention. The first part of Finding Myself places attention on one's inner state. How are you feeling in your body at present? Bring simple observing without judging or mental commenting, if possible. Briefly notice thoughts, if there, but keep primary attention on body sensations. Let a word or phrase come up that captures some or most of the way your body is telling you how you feel. Now shift attention to your breathing as you allow the body focus to be more in the background. What's it like to follow the flow of your breath in and out when you are not thinking about the breath but are directly sensing it … up close? After around three breaths, shift attention to what you are seeing and hearing around you. Let breathing and body sensations drift to the background as you look and listen simply to see and hear what is there. End by simply feeling yourself in the world around you. Have participants volunteer a word or two reflecting this experience. Remind them at the end that this practice is always available to them as a way to embrace both positive and negative experiences mindfully. This exercise could take around 5 minutes.

Highlighting the Session Theme: Discovering Your Way to Mindfulness

- **Guiding Question:** "What are you discovering about what works best for you in opening your doors into mindfulness?"
- **Guiding Image:** Swinging toward the open sky bit by bit in your new backyard tree swing.

- **Part A: Learning to Swing into Mindfulness Step by Step**
  - Begin with the guiding question, then shift to the swing image. "In the first three sessions, we explored the way we recognize mindfulness and the ways we formally and informally shift into it. We sensed it may enhance the way we live within the ups and downs of our caregiver lives, giving us moments of release and renewal. In Session 1, we looked at our new backyard tree swing of mindfulness and what made it different, and how to begin swinging in it. Over Sessions 2 and 3, we practiced swinging higher, sometimes in brief moments like pauses in the day, and sometimes in longer practices of meditation. We saw how mindfulness can swing us into savoring positive experiences in the present and out of our own spiraling stress reactions. Learning to swing or shift into greater mindfulness takes place bit by bit as we practice. We play with rather than impatiently push or try to control the swing. We are learning to simply open to our experiences without judgment and with kindness and gentleness toward ourselves."

  "Today, we are going to reflect together on your mindfulness journey and then practice our mindfulness swings in Moving and Stationary Meditations. By reflecting on your journey with mindfulness, perhaps you will appreciate where you have come from and where you want to go. Let's begin with one person's journey, Tobias. His story is not meant to be a model so much as it is meant to stimulate you to see your own developing story. We will use the account of Tobias as it relates to Sessions 1 through 3. Then we will use his report in Session 8 as it relates to Sessions 4 through 6 with their shared theme of self-care. After listening to Tobias, let's move into our Check-In as we ponder our own experiences in learning and applying mindfulness in our lives." Then read "Tobias," finishing at the end of the 11th paragraph with "My path to burnout was taking a turn."
- **Part B: Discovering Your Way to Mindfulness**
  - **Check-In:** "Now let's use Tobias to look at our own stories." Invite participants to respond to where they began, where they feel they are now, and where they would like to go in the future. Ask about what informal and/or formal practices they are each drawn to continue. As you listen to participants, see if there are opportunities to highlight in your feedback the mindful attitudes you hear, such as increased nonjudgment, willingness to explore, self-kindness, etc. See if there are ways to summarize the growing skills in shifting into mindfulness and experiencing its effects. This might include practicing Mindful Pausing and responding under stress. And it might also include experiences of savoring moments in one's life. This savoring can be an individual, private moment, or one shared with someone like the caregiver. Try to keep the Check-In to around 20 minutes. The time allowed may encourage asking everyone for their story in small groups, or asking for volunteers, and selectively eliciting a few stories if the size of the larger group permits.
  - **Check-In Close:** Take some time at the end to bring forth a summary of themes heard across participants. This may be a ripe time to suggest the journey of developing mindfulness is a long-term process, with advances and setbacks

being all part of it. Encourage participant selection of a few practices that have meaning to them, making these informal and/or formal practices their own with deepened familiarity.

Moving Meditation: Session 1 Qigong and Free Form Qigong

Aim: To reexplore a familiar movement meditation while playing with a new aspect that encourages trust in one's own intuitive directions.

Suggestions: In this movement practice, participants revisit Session 1 Qigong while adding, at the end, moments of spontaneous, free-form ways of moving. Then the meditation ends, as it does in the video, with hands over the navel and taking notice of the final stillness of emerging bodily sensations. The idea is to practice something familiar to deepen it, as well as something new. The spontaneous movements enhance a sense of letting go as one listens to what the body wants to do. For some or all, it may help to close the eyes and keep the lower body relaxed, but unmoving as a stable base. As the facilitator, you can begin this free-form moving, inviting the group to join you with their own, individual, spontaneous movements. During the free form, invite participants to flow into movement without thinking about the moves as they play, as a way of breaking free from imposed forms. The observing mind simply notices the feel of what arises on its own. Breaking free of imposed forms parallels other times of Mindful Pauses from mental and emotional habits to experience what is always new in the present. The Moving Meditation might take around 15 minutes, with 5 minutes for the inquiry.

Brief Inquiry/Sharing

"What came out of this experience of mindfully moving for you? Was there a difference between the set forms and the free form movement experience?"

Stationary Mindfulness: Brief Body Scan with Mindfulness of Breath

Aim: To show how two forms of stationary practice introduced in the first two sessions might enhance each other when combined. To allow those who missed either Body Scan or Mindfulness of Breath in Sessions 1 and 2 to experience aspects of what was missed.

Suggestions: Review the audio and/or transcripts of Body Scan and Mindfulness of Breath as an Anchor if you, as the facilitator, need to refamiliarize yourself with ways to guide them. Present them to participants as forms of Stationary Meditation that one can choose to do separately or in combined ways, as in today's session practice. In this exercise, the two forms will be combined with Body Scan as a way of initiating mindfulness of body sensations, which can also help relax the body and mind before the focus on breathing. For some, this combination makes the Mindfulness of Breath meditation easier. In this meditation, Body Scan will be abbreviated by reducing what is covered in the body areas. Begin with a sitting Body Scan and use the following body areas for noticing and focusing on the bottom of the feet, thighs, small of the back, stomach, shoulders, neck, and palms of the hands. End the Body Scan section with a brief noticing of how the body now feels. Then transition to find the breath. In the audio or transcript, this part picks up on the last phase of the meditation, which begins with "Entering the final phase as finding and centering on your breath..." Of course, as the facilitator, you can use your own words to present this phase or choose to refer to the transcript as a guide. The overall meditation should take around 15 minutes, leaving 5 minutes for the inquiry.

Brief Inquiry/Sharing

"What stood out to you in this combined Body Scan and Mindfulness of Breath? What aspects seemed most helpful in centering your attention in the present?"

Summary and Suggestions for Formal and Informal Practices during the Week

Aim: To underscore Session 7 as a way of integrating Sessions 1 through 3, while adding a couple of new practice elements. To stimulate reflections on where participants feel they are and where they might like to continue to grow basic mindfulness skills as sessions wind to an end.

Suggestions: Encourage participants to think about their journey into the growth of mindfulness, as Tobias did. How do they want to bring consistency to their mindfulness practices? Which practices most appeal to them to adopt in some form? Informal mindfulness practices, such as those found in our session practice, like Mindful Pauses, or in the handout "Bringing Mindfulness to Daily Life," are surprisingly powerful, brief ways of seeding the benefits of mindfulness in everyday living. One or two formal practices may become one's steady companion in bringing more balance to caregiver worlds. And for most of us who value it, mindful practices, attitudes, and perspectives merge into lifelong support. Post-it reminder notes, readings in mindfulness, YouTube and online talks, and workshops are but a few of the ways some of us keep mindfulness in mind, streaming into our lifestyles, knowing how easy it is to pave our road with only wishful intentions. End with the abridged poem "It Takes A While." Next time is the final session. It will take up the themes of mindful self-care from Sessions 4 through 6. Ask for any remaining questions or comments.

Handouts:

- Session 1 Qigong Movement Video
- Session 1 Body Scan with Session 2 Mindfulness of Breath Audios.
- "It Takes A While" poem
- "Bringing Mindfulness to Daily Life," a handout from Session 1.
- Tobias

Session 7-Facilitator's Contemplation: How will you nurture curiosity and self-care?

Session 7 Participant Summary: Discovering Your Way to Mindfulness*

Guiding Question: What are you discovering about what works best for you in opening your doors to mindfulness?

Aim of Session: To reflect on your journey in learning basic mindfulness benefits and skills in Sessions 1 through 3, as basic mindfulness practices are revisited along with new aspects.

What did you notice in the **Mindful Pause: Finding Myself, My Living Breath, and the World Around Me?**

What did you notice in the **Mindful Movement: Session 1 Qigong and Free Form Qigong?**

* Lumpkin, M., Collins, M.H., & Jarrett, R.B. (2026). Mindful self-care for clinicians and caregivers: A group facilitator's guide. Academic Press.

What did you notice in the combined **Body Scan and Mindfulness of Breath as an Anchor?**

The Guiding Image suggests that you are learning to swing into the open sky of mindfulness bit by bit as you practice your swings on the practices you have selected to keep in your life. These swings or practices may be your combination of informal mindfulness, such as small shifts like mindful pauses during your day, and/or formal practices like body scan or mindfulness of breath, or moving meditations. What practices do you feel most drawn to? What will help to keep them active and a part of your life? How are you learning to meet stress more mindfully? Are you able to stop and savor positive experiences, rather than busily bypass them?

In **Mindful Self-Care for Caregivers: A Review**, you met Tobias as he reflected on his mindfulness journey through these sessions. How did his story stimulate you to see where you began, where you are now, and where you want to go in growing your mindfulness skills?

Suggestions: Continue to create your mindfulness toolbox of a few practices that appeal to you, and take them into your next week. Consciously seek a mindful response to stress when it arises. Savor more beautiful moments in your life on purpose. Look over the handouts for inspiration.

List mindfulness practices you would like to try this week:	☑

Lumpkin, M., Collins, M.H., & Jarrett, R.B. (2026). Mindful self-care for clinicians and caregivers: A group facilitator's guide. Academic Press.

Tobias

I am an emergency department (ED) nurse (RN) and have been for the past 11 years of my career. On top of the usual variety of crises, COVID-19 knocked us all for a loop at work. But I am still here and have survived—still loving what I do. Not too long back, I was afraid love would crumble under the strain of caring for so many patients so sick, and I now know, not just the strain itself, but the way I was handling the strain.

The time of downward-crashing strain was a gathering storm of long work weeks, overcrowded wards, and a greater number of deaths. All of us in the ED no longer walked; we ran. COVID was the new predator, and its attacks left us feeling helpless many times. We watched and held the hands of dying patients isolated from their families. Heartbreaking. I remember going home after a long day and looking at loads of undone chores I was too tired to do. I would crash and wake up to rush off to work. I had no real life outside the hospital. Friends and family, my parents and sister, were on hold. To make things worse, I was not able to say no to coworkers needing coverage or supervisors pressing for overtime. I was in a race that had a life of its own, including my life. I was always tired or wired from coffee, energy drinks, and fast food. Looking back, I was living in a mix of being always on edge while sinking into lower and lower morale.

Inside, I was tense. My edginess could spiral into irritability and, unfortunately, temper bursts. My head was always buzzing nonstop. I couldn't stop thinking about my longer and longer list of things to get done. I knew I was not at my best, and I can now see I was feeling bad about that, adding more pressure and resentment, although I couldn't say who this was toward.

One day, I noticed, as I was getting coffee, an announcement of a new session on the staff bulletin board. It was a series of training meetings called Mindful Self-Care for Clinicians and Caregivers. I thought, "Who has the time?" Then I noticed it was at the end of my shift for a little over an hour each time, and only once a week. It wasn't just a relaxation session. I already knew about those techniques. This new session seemed to teach skills to use during the day to better balance and even out. Okay, why not? Let's see what's behind this mindfulness thing I've been hearing about for a while. So, I went.

Now that I have gone through all eight sessions, here's what stands out to me 6 months later. It's hard to capture all the phases I went through learning what I did. I can say that what I learned happened gradually, and with a lot of encouragement from my teachers and session mates. Maybe it was because I had to unlearn old familiar ways I had thought about and reacted to things, emotions, and thoughts in my life.

The session of 10 people was a mix I didn't expect. My session mates were an internist, several nurses, a rehabilitation therapist, three at-home caregivers of their chronically ill spouses or parents, and an elementary school teacher. Our different backgrounds soon blended into surprisingly common experiences—the heavy load of caregiving that seemed to swallow our daily lives. In each session, we began by

Lumpkin, M., Collins, M.H., & Jarrett, R.B. (2026). Mindful self-care for clinicians and caregivers: A group facilitator's guide. Academic Press.

talking about our experiences, playing around with different aspects of mindfulness as we understood it, and its practices. This, quite frankly, kept me inspired by hearing of others' discoveries and, sometimes, struggles.

From the first session on, we jumped into practicing and experiencing mindfulness. It was not at all academic, as I half expected. The very first question blew me away: "How do you know you are being mindful?" I could say that I, although mindfulness was about calming myself by not worrying so much. But I soon found out I just didn't know. I wanted its benefits of being calmer, but did not know what being mindful felt like. Through some session exercises, I did recognize mindlessness! It was the state I'd been living in! It was a tense body, frantic emotions, and a hyperactive mind, always thinking and always talking to or at myself, criticizing or complaining. Wow. Then over the next three sessions, we were given exercises and short guided meditations to step into the shallow end of the mindful state and gradually go deeper. It was inspiring that this could be done, but not always easy. For example, I tried to focus only on body sensations in one of the meditations by fighting back my thoughts, trying to make my mind quiet. But I learned that fighting thoughts only made them bigger! I thought I'd never learn to do this. Our teachers understood this and said everyone goes through this, and encouraged us to relax, not fight our minds, and try "just noticing." That this noticing is the beginning of mindfulness—this stepping back to look at what's happening in and around us without the old jumping into mind talk.

In each session, we were learning how to stop and pause for a moment to tune into our breaths, our eyes and ears, our body's feelings and sensations. We were guided through sitting meditations and moving meditations. In between sessions, we were asked to explore and experiment with the exercises and practices that most attracted us, not being pressured to do more homework than we felt up to. Short practice times in the day were just as valuable as longer meditations. We were encouraged to practice as a way to really learn mindfulness, but we were left free to choose what to work on. Session mates often tried different practices than each other, yet we shared our experiments in the group, learning about ones we may not have tried. I tried out the guided recordings they gave us, finding I really liked the Body Scan. I tried pausing a few times in my day to stop my usual rush and notice how my body felt and how I was breathing. I am a multi-tasker, so a few times a day, I just focus my attention on only one thing at a time. I also liked taking little breaks at the hospital to just stop outside and see the sunshine on things. There were certainly days I forgot to do any of this, but I learned to feel good about the times I did remember.

I have to admit that for a while, learning to feel when I was tense and taking pauses to breathe or settle my focus for a moment on something pleasant, like really tasting my coffee or watching a kid play in the waiting room, seemed to be challenging enough to remember, yet pretty refreshing when I did. I felt I was being given a special secret that is simple to see if you know what to look for.

A big test of my beginning mindfulness skills was using it to directly deal with stress and anxiety in a new, and hopefully better way. First, I had to see what I normally didn't see—my usual way of reacting to stress! Before I knew about mindfulness, I focused only on what was outside me, pushing my buttons. So many things did. For instance, when too many patients demanded my attention while I had a list of other things to do, I thought, "Why now of all times?" or "Where's the help around here?" or "Why can't patient X for once just be more cooperative?" At the end of the day, I could be edgy, exhausted, or just nervously wired. The day was a blur, a jumble of so many things I seemed to carry around in one big lump inside.

But I was learning something in a mindfulness session that sort of surprised me. Most of my stress really came from the way I automatically stoked my own reactions, rather than the actual stressor I was reacting to. It was my thoughts about patient X that were feeding my stress, making it bigger. Once I stepped back to notice what was happening, it was a bit embarrassing how obvious it was. I began to accept patient X as he/she was, as well as my reactions.

All the work learning to pay more attention to more of the moments in my life began to pay off when I wanted to bring mindfulness to my stress. I started by noticing when I was feeling stressed. I usually ignored this before until the stress in me got too big. For me, my neck and shoulder muscles would tighten, my chest felt taut and small, and my breathing was more like gasping. I would then see my stress thoughts tumbling around and how I was being pulled into them. And I could feel myself gradually going from irritated to pissed off. The way I talked to myself was critical and hard. I learned over time not to judge these reactions, to only pause to see and feel them. Then, the next step was to stop feeding the stress spirals by the angry way I talked to myself, slowing down, and being more patient with myself. I would focus on my breathing, fully feeling the way it loosened and filled more of my body. Then I would decide on the best next action to take—and move on. It became like putting a bit of space between my tense emotions and the response I really wanted to make to the situation. Rather than chewing someone out, I would wait, feel what was happening, breathe, and either say nothing or something kinder. Man, it took a while to remember to do this in the heat of the moment! And I still go back to my old ways at times, but that's okay. This is practice for the long haul, and I like the refocusing me. When being more mindfully attentive, I felt stress draining out of me more easily, and I felt a new kind of confidence. My path to burnout was taking a turn.

I want to mention a couple of other mindfulness learnings that were kind of bonuses to these sessions. One was on how to be more sensitive to others, taking moments to connect rather than move past. As I began to pay more attention to my own feelings, I was surprised to find I was not as good at attending to other people as I thought I was. Yes, I often heard information or facts, but I didn't stop to take in feelings and real concerns. No wonder some of my patients and coworkers had a sense that I had too little time or too much to do to really hear and connect with them. And, honestly, I was getting less and less emotional income from my work as a caregiver. So one of my practices was to reinvest a little time, pausing again to feel myself and feel the other person I was with. This meant stopping some busy work for a moment and turning my focus to what a patient was saying and what feelings were around the saying. I found my patients didn't complain as much to get my attention when the real attention was already there. I would often feel a patient relax when they sensed I was hearing them. And my reward? I felt moved by the connection and reminded of why I want to give care.

Another bonus was taking my own self-care. In session, we looked at what a balanced life is like, and what personal needs and interests are often buried under caregiving for others. But they were crying out for recognition from me. Trench mentality had narrowed my life to work with little left over. When I stepped back to see this, I felt a kind of sadness. What had I done to myself? Then the question was where to start. It was helpful to think of self-care like a pie chart sectioned off into different zones or pieces. In the biological part, I knew I needed to eat better, sleep longer, and return to jogging in my neighborhood. And meeting friends for softball on Saturdays hit both the physical and the social parts of the pie. A small thing I started doing was sending friendly energy to baristas in my neighborhood coffee bar. It helped start the day in a good way. The psychological zone I chose was changing the way I talked to myself—with less criticism and a softer, kinder tone. This led me to take better care of my time, saying "no" more often to pressure to work longer hours. The spiritual part of the pie I am still exploring. I am considering joining a monthly online group supported by a local bookstore. They select a range of spiritual outlooks and ways to walk a more soulful path in life. None of this was possible until I stopped my mindless rat race and listened quietly and patiently to myself. It took a while to feel myself below the noise in my head and numbed-out body.

Today, I am overall calmer and more contented in my life. I run less from the past and wait less for a future; the present is where I seek to live and pay attention. In the beginning, mindfulness was in bits and pieces, seen just as a collection of techniques for better coping. But over time, mindfulness has come to mean a whole way of looking at fuller living and ways of caring for this life I have been given. I began to connect these dots over time. I would practice different meditations and exercises in pausing in the day, often feeling their possibilities in session, but not noticing a clear benefit on my own stressed life until the practices seemed to settle into me. It might take two or 3 weeks of experimenting before I would wake up 1 day and feel my mind clearer, my mood more positive, and my energy smoothing out. I can see why the teachers warned us against expecting too much too soon, rather than just playing with the ideas and practices in a looser way.

I have had times when I relapsed into my old mindless ways and suffered the consequences. But I just see that as part of this learning path as well. Because of these slips, I am more convinced I need the simple power of these practices. I just pick myself up without fuss and start again. I use reminders like sticky notes on mirrors and my computer. My coffee cup says, "Mindfulness Is Not What You Think!" Another cup says, "You Can't Stop The Waves, But You Can Learn to Surf!" I still use the session audios and videos, and worksheets too.

I ran into one of my mindfulness session mates the other day. Noreen, an at-home caregiver, was bringing her husband with advanced Parkinson's to the hospital after he fell and broke a wrist. We chatted about our lives since the session, and how much we miss it at times. She has been meeting with another session mate to practice meditation together every other week and to talk about their other practices. She said she does progressive relaxation at night after tough days, and she does the Qigong movements to wake up and release tension knots during the day. She felt she was slowed down, particularly when with her husband. She teared up a little when she said that. Rather than "doing, doing, doing," she gets a lot out of taking time out to listen, sharing feelings with her husband about their days, and quietly taking in music together. And she was letting friends take her out to lunch at least once a week. She said something interesting: "I take time to check in with my inside self, more often. When I feel sad, I let myself be sad without pushing it away. When I feel uplifted, I let it in like sunshine." We ended up laughing when I reminded her to remember to "savor" the coffee she was holding.

Thank you for letting me share my ongoing trip with mindfulness. I know your trip will have some similar things in it, yet it will be different as well. You, like me, will find certain things resonate for you and stand out. And you will reach for them and take them as your own. Stay inspired.

As Tobias lays out, mindfulness is a rich tapestry with many interwoven threads. It is a way of seeing yourself in your life situation. It is a set of attitudes toward yourself, like patience, kindness, nonjudgment, and willingness to explore rather than grasp at results. It is a way of listening to yourself and others. It is taking time to see and feel your self-care needs. It is meditation practices, taking longer times to strengthen awareness. It is informal mindfulness practices, like the way you pause from the noise and speed within to breathe, to deeply sense and feel the sensations of yourself and the inviting world around you. And it is a way of responding to stress in a more liberating way.

Tobias also reminds us that mindfulness takes hold, deepens, and becomes a part of you *over time*. Learning takes practice and a willingness to just go with the flow and see what happens. You learn to trust your intuitions about which practices you select for yourself. For, as the saying goes, all roads lead to Rome.

So, take heart from Tobias—not as a particular model, but as an illustration of how mindfulness can grow into and change your own individual path. Bringing care to yourself can be as, if not more, challenging as bringing care to others.

Poem: It Takes A While

(abridged)

(Lumpkin, 2014, p.94)

It takes a while
    to release cares and sip your breath like subtle tea.
It takes a while
    to turn from traffic and wander lost with faith in the forest.
It takes a while
    to be convinced it is safe to no longer think of what must be done.
It takes a while
    to let the birds in the tree of your belly and heart sing after the storm.
It takes a while
    to cease making deals in the marketplace and head for the park.
It takes a while
    To lay down the little life to walk into the big.

Lumpkin, M., Collins, M.H., & Jarrett, R.B. (2026). Mindful self-care for clinicians and caregivers: A group facilitator's guide. Academic Press.

Quick Summary Sessions 1 Through 3

Session 1

- Begins with the question: How do you know you are being mindful?
- Monkey Mind, our usual and habitual mode of attention, is distinguished from Mindfulness, choosing to place attention on present experience nonjudgmentally.
- Because of the power of Monkey Mind, we need to practice mindfulness if we want to strengthen it in our lives.
- We begin by using three pillars of mindfulness practice: the present moment, awareness of body/breath/sensory experiences, and bringing the attitude of nonjudgment.
- Participants were exposed to three practices in the session: The Mindful Pause, Qigong movements, and Body Scan as informal mindfulness practices and formal mindfulness practices, both moving and stationary.
- At the end, participants were invited to choose informal, brief practices from the handout Bringing Mindfulness into Daily Life and explore the formal practices they are interested in using audio or video resources.

Session 2

- Engages the question: What difference might mindfully observing our inner experience make in our daily lives, as opposed to inattention to inner experiences?
- Listening to what our bodies are telling us affects our mental and physical health.
- Tuning into our inner sensations and feelings also supports the mindfulness skill of stepping back from being lost in distracting mind chatter and finding greater calm and clarity in the present moment.
- Like Session 1, participants were exposed to three practices: A Mindful Pause, being a journey through the senses, Qigong movements, and Mindfulness of Breath as an Anchor, ending with the poem "Another Little Greek Tale."
- Participants were invited to continue to experiment with informal practices of their choice as well as explore the formal practices they are drawn to, using audio and video resources.

Session 3

- Centers on the question: What difference do you notice between emotionally reacting and mindful responding to stress? How might attending to and savoring positive experiences affect overall stress levels?
- Most stress comes from the way we respond to it. We can either increase stress by being pulled by reactivity, like efforts to struggle like the image of Chinese Handcuffs, or we can decrease it by mindful steps of Catch (observing stress signals), Release (letting go of struggling reactions and focusing on the breath), and Choose (selecting our response with calm and clarity).

- Like Sessions 1 and 2, participants experienced three practices: an exercise in Noting and Letting Go of a Stress Reaction, Pairing Breath and Movement with Flower, Head Roll, and Sunrise movements, and a mindfulness exercise called Mindful Emotional Processing with the poem "The Space in Patience."
- Participants were invited to continue selecting informal and formal mindfulness practices to explore during their week and to try out mindful responding to stress.

Session 8—Minding Your Own Care

Session 8 provides a final review of mindful self-care techniques and strategies learned throughout the sessions to continue strengthening retention of skills. The session also includes a written description of experiential practices for the session. The aim of Session 8 is to review and strengthen mindfulness concepts and practices learned over the course of the prior sessions.

Mindful Self-Care for Clinicians and Caregivers. https://doi.org/10.1016/B978-0-443-29821-9.00013-3

"Sunflower Garden" - This photo of a quiet patch of sunflowers, taken by Marielle on a trip with family to a sunflower farm, reminds us that turning toward the light—like acts of self-care—is a gentle, daily practice in resilience.

Session 8 Facilitator Quick Guide: Minding Your Own Care

Session Theme: Using the image of the "Inner Garden", participants reflect on their self-care needs through the lens of the biopsychosocial model as introduced in Sessions 4 through 6, as well as chapter 2 of this guide.

Mindful Pause: Watering in Your Garden

- Summarize the aim of the Mindful Pause as a use of imagery to highlight self-care needs that call out for our attention and tending.
- Invite participants to close their eyes and envision a garden with a variety of flowers.
- Mention that this garden is one that needs care to grow and flourish, connecting to everyone's needs for self-care.
- Bring to their imagination a radiant sun as attention and the breeze of the breath as the water offered to the garden, feeling your active tending to these flowers.
- Transition to focus on the breath for a few moments, and then come to a close.

Optional

To deepen the Mindful Pause, play the audio labeled *"Switzerland Stream"* from the companion portal. Invite participants to practice mindful listening to the bubbling stream as they visualize their inner garden, allowing sound, imagery, and breath to come together as a moment of self-care.

Brief Sharing

- "What did the image of the inner garden mean to you?"

Highlight Session Theme: Minding Your Own Care

- Guiding Question: What helps to restore your spirit as you give so much of yourself to the world of caregiving?
- Guiding Image: The Inner Garden of self-care needs.
- Part A: Placing Value on Time for Self-Care
  - Begin with the Guiding Question and the self-care theme of Sessions 4-6
  - Merge the image of tending the inner garden with the biopsychosocial areas of self-care and the sense that neglect of this garden leads to depletion and possibly burnout.
  - To help us reflect on each of our pathways to self-care, return to the story of Tobias, beginning with "In each session we were learning how to stop ..." and read to the end of the Tobias section.
- Part B: Minding Your Own Care
  - Check-In: Ask participants to share their self-care journey, what their garden needs are, and how they have tried to tend them.
  - Seek opportunities to validate participants' efforts, needs, and obstacles.

- Seek openings to reinforce attractions to various practices now and in the future.
- Summarize themes shared and your own experience with self-care over the long term.

Moving Meditation: Walking With Wide-Open Awareness

- The aim of this practice is to combine a practice familiar to most participants but with a new element, that of focused, mindful attention to sensations in walking as well as open, mindful awareness of one's environment.
- Using the audio or audio transcript as a guide, invite participants to focus on the sensations of lifting and lowering the feet in a slow walk, reminding them to simply notice and savor the experiences rather than get caught up in "doing it right".
- Later, bring in the element of wide-open awareness to the environment one is walking in, as well as the continued focus on lifting and lowering the feet, synchronizing breath with movements.
- This meditation can easily become a brief, informal meditation each day, given the amount of walking we do.

Brief Inquiry/Sharing

- "Does this focus on walking sensations prompt mindful attention?"
- "How did you respond to adding the open awareness aspect?"

Stationary Mindfulness: Breath Meditation with Lake Image

- The aim is to review participants using the breath as an anchor for mindful attention and to explore the use of imagery in evoking calm and in handling distractions. Some people find imagery helpful, while others may not.
- Refer to the audio or audio transcript of this meditation.
- The breath is a common focus in mindful meditation and worth cultivating both formally and informally in daily pauses.
- The meditation ends with the poem - "Lake Loons" -which will be familiar to most. Poems repeated tend to be heard more deeply. The lake image in the poem mirrors the meditation image as a place of inner refuge.

Brief Inquiry/Sharing

- "Are you becoming familiar with the breath as a meditation object?"
- "Is the lake image helpful or not? Why?"

Summary and Suggestions for the Future

- Briefly summarize the session theme and focus, and practices introduced.
- Underscore the inner garden image grounded in the biopsychosocial model of self-care.
- Introduce the idea of this session as an ending but also as a beginning toward continued growth of minding one's own care.

- Distribute handouts and refer to resources participants might want to consider.
- Go around the group and ask people to share their experience of the sessions, what they have gained, what they want to grow in themselves, and their feelings about sharing this experience with other group members. Include yourself last.

Handouts:
- Session 8: Breath Meditation with Lake Image audio
- Session 8: Walking With Wide-Open Awareness
- Session 8: Participant Summary

Session 8 Introduction: Minding Your Own Care

With Session 8, we step back and take an appreciative look at the garden each person has been cultivating. Practices have been planted and tended in order to give rise to mindful self-care. Throughout MSCC, participants have been enticed to explore, play with, and select forms of mindfulness and self-care that fit their individual preferences. There is no one-size-fits-all presumed in these sessions. How Sally chooses to practice self-care will most likely be different from the way John chooses his favorite practices. As the facilitator, you might want to keep this in mind as a core principle in the varied ways the philosophy and practices of MSCC are taken out of each session's content, ideas, and sharing among participants. You extend an open invitation to experiment with session elements. In Session 8, participants look at the garden of selected practices they carry for future sustenance and nourishment in the intense world of caregiving.

Session 8 pulls Sessions 4 through 6 together in the interwoven theme of self-care. We are both caregivers and care-receivers. Imbalance may disrupt vitality and self-renewal. Caregivers who gather in MSCC groups may have taken up and accepted roles that can eclipse the care-receiver's need and may need restoration and vitalizing care from themselves and from others. Learning the art of embodied listening is a core mindfulness skill in self-care and other care. It is based on sensitivity to body-based signals about our feelings and needs (i.e., physiology) that are often lost under the noise of habitual self-talk (i.e., cognition) and busyness (i.e., behavior). This is not a simple technique to fix ourselves. It is a style of tuning in and connecting to the self below automatic thoughts, receiving clues as to what is needed in one's life now as well as another's. It is a way of living that goes beyond ways of reacting. All mindfulness practices open an interior space for such listening beyond the need to judge and control experiences arising in the moment. These practices lead to living in tune, not out of tune, with ourselves. This intentional flow into calm acceptance and an openness to step out of old habits and into fresh options with curiosity and experimentation.

The guiding image of Session 8 is the caregiver's inner garden. This garden is each person's variety of self-renewal needs imagined as flowers. These parts of ourselves need watering and attentive sunlight, but languishing and depletion can easily occur under the demands of caregiving. In Session 4, needs were presented as various parts of a whole by discussing the biopsychosocial model of requirements for self-care. These parts can be imagined as sections of an integrated garden design. The Bio-is the biological or physical requirements for nourishment, rest, exercise, rest, and relaxation. The Psycho-are the psychological needs for monitoring and resetting stress thoughts and emotions, taking on the mindfulness perspective as a way of looking at life and self-awareness. The Social-section is all the ways we connect with others in affirming and vitalizing ways, and how we build regular positive contacts for renewal.

Some participants may also wish to emphasize their own spiritual content and process depending on their cultural background and preferences. These spiritual practices are embedded in their cultural experience through related social and psychological processes. Facilitators need to keep in mind that the spiritual domain is broad and as personal and unique as each individual. In a diverse group, beliefs may span: completely secular, to a faith in God, or to aesthetic openness to beauty and sense of goodness, without a specific reference or name, to other self-described perspectives. The skilled facilitator models open and mindful acceptance of and curiosity about diverse beliefs expressed and/or experienced. An overarching goal of MSCC is ongoing cultivation of mindful attention to the health of one's inner garden of Bio-Psycho-Social flowers, planted in a personalized spirituality for some, but not all.

A Quick Summary of Sessions 4 through 6 is available for you, the facilitator, to review. In the Session 8 Guide, you will find the Aim of Session 8 available for you to present at the start of the session, emphasizing the session theme, image, and practices. Feel free to express these in your own words. If participants missed any of Sessions 4 through 6, they have an opportunity to experience the theme of self-care through both movement and stationary mindfulness practices, but with added novel elements. The novel elements provide participants who did not miss prior sessions a chance to review, deepen, and sample an added dimension to the practice. Like Session 7, Session Check-In is embedded in the section on Highlighting the Session Theme. In a similar way, it will use the Tobias story to stimulate group members' self-reflections on their own present and future stories of self-care practices.

The Mindful Pause in Session 8 moves right into the image of the caregiver's inner garden. It is a brief meditation using imagery to evoke the feel of inner living needs, awareness of those needs, and acts of tending to those needs. Imagery allows participants to let go of familiar ways of thinking in order to explore more sensory modes of representing parts of themselves. It is more about an experience than an analysis. The powerful image of the inner garden and its need for tending is raised as a simple starting point for the session and as a connecting thread throughout the session and beyond.

The section Highlighting the Session Theme: Minding Your Own Care carries the image of the inner garden forward and poses the question, "What helps to restore your spirit as you give so much of yourself to the world of caregiving?" Using the inner garden metaphor, the biopsychosocial aspects of that garden are reviewed, and ways of tending them are given as examples. The story of Tobias is, again, presented not as a prescription but as a stimulant to each person's story of evolving self-care practices. The Tobias Vignette is picked up from the last session and finished. The Tobias story nicely fills in the context of caregiving as efforts to care-giver to oneself evolve. The Check-In asks participants to reflect and share their own stories of self-care now and into the future. As facilitator, you listen, validate, and look for opportunities to underscore self-care practices, their effects, and the future intentions of group members. One point is to prize the individual's attraction to select practices rather than the expectation of one size fits all.

As self-care involves practices to strengthen mindfulness, movement and stationary practices are offered for exploration. As always, participants are invited to savor these practices rather than strive to get them right. Mindfulness perks up awareness of sensations and feelings that these practices stimulate. The only goal is to *be with* the experience in openness and curiosity. Walking in Wide Open Awareness brings together the focused mindful attention in the walking meditation of Session 4 with an invitation to combine it with open awareness of ones environment. The beauty of walking meditation is its use as a brief moment of mindfulness in everyday life, given the common experience of walking. Adding open awareness to this former meditation extends mindfulness skills by balancing specific attention to some area of experience with a broader awareness of what is happening in and around one. Another image might be the focus on a lone bird flying against a background of the large sky.

The stationary meditation Breath Meditation with Lake Image repeats the common focus on the breath as an anchor to attention practiced in several former meditations. The added element of the lake image introduces the use of an occasional guiding image to renew an inner place of calm and a place of holding all parts of oneself together. Some people may find the use of imagery quite helpful in galvanizing their meditation, while others may not. So, this is offered as a kind of sampling meditation for participants to judge for themselves. The poem "Lake Loons" used at the end of the meditation is a repeat from a former session, perhaps deepening the experience of the familiar.

The Brief Inquiry following the meditation offers an opportunity for participants to put their experience into words, which can help sharpen and clarify the experience. The inquiries also pique interest in the various ways the meditations can be experienced by others. This keeps one open to other possibilities with meditation.

The Summary and Suggestions section for Session 8 is special, given that this is the ending session for MSCC. Aside from a brief summary of the session theme and content, the facilitator moves to inspire group members to appreciate their engagement with the sessions and the practices adopted, and to continue to develop their pathway to self-care. This is perhaps a moment of mixed feelings as participants prepare to graduate and to say goodbye. It may be a time when you, as facilitator, share relevant aspects of your own journey. Encourage the use of various resources from the session, from the internet, and other ideas you may have to support continued mindfulness practice. A warm way to end is to go around the group so person can say their goodbye and a brief sharing of their overall experience with MSCC and how they feel their relationship to caregiving has been impacted.

Some Takeaway Points

Session 8 completes the circle of prior sessions by reviewing the theme of self-care, uniting Sessions 4 through 6. Like Session 7, it provides a chance for participants to review content from sessions they may have missed, as well as gives an opportunity to explore prior practices alongside a few novel elements. The inner garden image highlights the value of utilizing mindful listening to identify one's needs within the biopsychosocial areas of life. Balance in living includes seeing oneself as both a caregiver and care-receiver. Self-care for caregivers has the potential to integrate these perspectives. Again, the Tobias story invites participants to hold a mirror up to themselves to appreciate the whole journey from reaching for help and eventually growing one's own style of self-care practices both now and into the future. There is poignancy in this last session, as an end and as a kind of graduation. We will hear from Yolanda and Steve again as they relate to Session 8 experiences.

Listen to Yolanda's response to Session 8: *I had to miss sessions 2 and 4 because I could find no sitters for my son who has autism. I loved getting a chance to hear about the different areas of our lives we need to keep in focus if we are to stay healthy. I saw how I've let friendships and church-going drop off. I can see how I've gotten more depressed without this support. They need to be a part of watering my garden. Thinking about Tobias, I see how I started just hoping the sessions would give me time with people sort of like me. Now, I am learning to take my own mindful breaks, sometimes doing the progressive relaxation, sometimes sitting and breathing slowly and looking out the window. A knot inside relaxes more and more. I am going to try out the lake image breathing audio meditation on my computer. It seemed to help me go deeper into quiet and relaxation. I will miss these sessions and the friends I've made in them. I hope I will plan better for practice times. Like Jan our facilitator said, I can always begin again and again.*

Although Yolanda missed a couple of sessions, she persisted and did not drop out. The facilitator made it clear that Yolanda was encouraged to come when she can. Sessions 7 and 8 allowed Yolanda to experience some of what she missed as well. Yolanda is realizing how to see self-care in personal ways, like the importance of contact with friends and church. The garden image makes self-care come alive and not be left as a set of ideas. Yolanda is also selecting practices she is drawn to and—importantly—sees that positive experiences from them can reinforce their value. Yolanda is beginning to get the sense that motivation may wane at times, but there is always the freshness of beginning again and again.

Here is Steve's response to Session 8: *I can't believe the sessions are ending. I don't want to slip back into the heavy grind I was in when sessions started. I seemed to get lost in missing my wife as she was and overcome with the load of taking care of her. I get how I let go of my own garden as I spiraled down. I can't let that happen again or I'll fail her and sicken myself. I feel like I have a kind of permission to tend better to myself than before. I will come away from the session with my own little bag of mindfulness exercises. For example, I liked the walking meditation today and how it slowed me down and opened by feelings to the world around me. Having a kind of library of meditations and handouts will keep me trying out different things. Some things I want to do more of, like garden, have coffee away from the house with Bill, eat better and have fewer soft drinks and pizza dinners!, And I want to take time with my wife to really listen to her rather than just do things to take care of her. At the end of the group sessions, I teared up, so touched by how we've been there for each other.*

Steve, like many others, realizes the multi-dimensional nature of mindfulness training and self-care. He values everything from exercises to explore, to clarification of a more mindful lifestyle that values self-care and keeps growing. He has insight into the self-neglect that uproots resourcefulness and self-tending. Steve has a map of where he wants to go. Was it learning to listen, or the way he was listened to by the group and facilitator, that grew into a desire to more deeply connect with his wife? Perhaps both. As a facilitator, it seems important to let Steve and other group members fully feel the journey they have been on and the poignancy of the transition from session to tending one's own garden.

Key Concepts

- Caregiving depends on both being a caregiver and a care receiver.
- Embodied listening sensitizes caregivers to their own needs for balance and renewal.
- Tending one's inner garden means growing and fertilizing one's physical, emotional, social, and possibly spiritual elements when helpful, as defined by the individual.

Session 8 Guide: Minding Your Own Care

Aim of Session 8:

- To provide a summary of prior sessions 4 through 6, uplifting the theme of mindful self-care.
- To invite participants to invest in a deep commitment to self-care by carving out specific ways to enliven and uphold the inner-self behind the scenes of outer action.
- To encourage participants' resolutions to grow and nourish self-care into the future with various approaches, and recognition of the ways participants individually carve out their own path.

Mindful Pause: Watering Your Garden

Aim: To get the group to focus on their inner needs for replenishment and to introduce a simple mindful pause using the image of an inner garden to sense and nourish parts of oneself.

Suggestions: Share the Aim of the Mindful Pause. Invite participants to close their eyes and imagine a garden with a variety of flowers. Some are thriving well; some flowers need tending and nourishing. Allow a moment to let this arise in imagination. Then suggest that this is an inner garden of what needs to grow and stay green inside us to bring us aliveness and uplift. Perhaps it is a need for rest, for healthier eating or recreation, for moments with others, for talking to yourself or treating yourself with greater compassion and kindness, or for spiritual support. But for now, we will leave them as various kinds of flowers trying to grow in you. Your very attention to this garden is the sun, and the water is the breath you breathe into and over your garden. Take time to sun your garden and to water it breath by breath. How does it feel to see and tend this garden? After a few moments, allow the garden to gradually fade. Rest in the breath coming in and out. Then ask them to open their eyes as we transition. At this point, ask the group for their experiences of this exercise and how the image of an inner garden holds meaning for them.

Highlighting the Session Theme: Minding Your Own Care

- **Guiding Question:** What helps to restore your spirit as you give so much of yourself to the world of caregiving?
- **Guiding Images: The Inner Garden**
- **Part A: Placing Value on Time for Self-Care**
  - Begin with the guiding question. Then, "In Sessions 4 through 6, we focused on the ways mindfulness skills expand into recognizing the need for tending to our own care as just as important as tending to our care person's needs. In a sense, this is a need to attend to both the other's physical and emotional outer garden requirements and your own inner garden. The inner garden grows spirit, energy, and renewal if watered, exposed to sunlight, and fertilized. Your garden

also has to have protective boundaries to protect it from overexposure to what can deplete its resources. To tend your garden, you bring physical nutrients like eating well and exercising, for example. You bring psychological nutrients by treating yourself more gently, compassionately, and by seeding your days with large or small mindfulness practices. You bring social nutrients of connection time with others who provide listening and positive energy. You may bring spiritual nutrients in times of ritual or meditation oriented to a sense of a larger Whole. Caregiving to another and to oneself depends upon a kind of mindful listening beyond the temptation to rush, multi-task, and check off the items on our list. Mindful listening means slowing down to sense and feel what is happening in yourself and between yourself and another: What is deeply needed in this moment below the surface?"

  - "Today we continue to reflect on your mindfulness journey through the past sessions. How have you and how will you attend to this living, tender inner garden? We will follow, again, Tobias' story as a way to stimulate your thoughts about your life of self-care. We will pick up his story close to where we left off last session as he describes his own ventures into turning attention to his needs for recovery and renewal. We will use our Check-In as a time to share what you are willing to share about your own unfolding journey. Then, we will practice movement and stationary meditations that build on practices done in past sessions." Read the Tobias Vignette, beginning with the second paragraph on page 3, "In each session we were learning how to stop …" and ending with the end of the Tobias section.

- **Part B: Minding Your Own Care**
  - Check-In: "Let's look at Tobias' story through your own stories." Ask participants to think about their own desires for and practices of self-care. What does their garden need, and how have they tried to tend it? What are the challenges to focusing on this garden, and what are the ways these challenges have been or may be met? To facilitate, listen for opportunities to recognize and validate any practice of self-care expressed and the result it produced. Listen for challenges and obstacles to self-care, recognizing those as well as legitimate forces in one's life and asking about what ways might work with them.
  - Check-In closing: As in the last session, take a little time at the end to summarize themes and practices shared. This might be the place to share your own sense of how mindfulness practice and self-care are long-term, with advances and setbacks held in a perspective of commitment to them. As with mindfulness practices, self-care is quite personal and individual in how it is implemented. What works for a person is what matters.

Moving Meditation: Walking With Wide Open Awareness

Aim: To build upon the prior movement meditation from Session 4's Walking Meditation, expanding it to include not just focused attention on walking sensations but combining it with an open awareness of one's surroundings. In this way, mindfulness follows a specific set of sensations while staying oriented to one's environment.

This, again, is a practical practice that uses times of unconscious walking to shift into a period of mindfully conscious movement.

Suggestions: Facilitate this practice by familiarizing yourself with the audio and/or transcript of "Walking With Wide Open Awareness." Introduce it to review a prior meditation from Session 4 while adding a dimension to it. The goal is to explore bringing mindfulness to the usual habit-driven activity in daily life, that of walking. Two aspects of mindfulness can be experienced in this meditation: attention to specific sensations involved in taking steps slowly and a wider awareness of moving in the space that surrounds you. It would be like walking to your car in a parking lot, aware of two sensations: that of your legs and feet lifting and lowering while staying aware of the area of the parking lot itself. In daily life, we need to both attend to something we are doing and to the feel of the environment we are doing it within. Key elements of the meditation are slowing the speed of walking, focusing on the sensations of lifting up one foot while rolling forward on the other, relaxing rather than tensely trying, remembering to breathe, and staying quietly aware of the space in which you are moving. If you become distracted, simply return attention and awareness to these areas. You might notice distractions from Monkey Mind, often throwing us into imbalance and unsteadiness.

Brief Inquiry/Sharing

"How did you respond to this form of moving meditation? What was it like to balance the focus on body sensations with the surrounding space?"

Stationary Meditation: Breath Meditation with Lake Image

Aim: To practice and reinforce a familiar form of mediation with the added element of a lake image. Some people may find that the addition of imagery in a familiar meditation is helpful in handling distractions, giving the mind just enough stimulation to hold it better in place. The lake imagery carries on the theme of creating an inner space to hold all parts of oneself with openness and kindness, an important aspect of self-care.

Suggestions: Refer to the audio/transcript of Breath Meditation with Lake Image. Most participants will be acquainted with the breath focus in mindfulness. This will give a chance to further develop that resource. The breath has been the most repeated form of focus in formal and informal styles of practicing mindfulness. It is fitting, then, that it is part of the MSCC finale. You will notice that the lake image blends with one's inner space as a place of smoothing out tensions, greeting and accepting inner experiences equally, and holding all parts of oneself together in unity. The meditation ends with the familiar poem "Lake Loons" which evokes this use of the inner lake.

Brief Inquiry/Sharing

"How are you coming to find the breath as a way of mindful focusing? How did you find the use of the lake imagery?"

Summary and Suggestions for the Future

Aim: To summarize Session 8 as an integration of Sessions 4 through 6 on the overall theme of mindful self-care. To see the relationship of the two meditations practiced today as extensions of meditations introduced in earlier sessions, those of Mindfulness of Breath as an Anchor and Walking Meditation. To inspire participants to continue to develop their own self-care practices. And to say appreciative goodbyes to each other as this phase of training ends.

Suggestions: Invite participants to hold and carry their MSCC journey as a prized investment in themselves and in their precious roles as caregivers. This last session might be seen as a graduation to the ever-ongoing continuing cultivation of mindful self-care. How do they want to see their path settle into a style of living? What do you see as the future of a style of meeting stress and of finding times of joy and uplift? This path includes the way the relationship with one's care-person can ignite enlivening connections in which both are fed. Can you see yourself in a style of being more present in life? Ask participants to share their experience of being together in the sessions and of the sessions themselves. Share your own experience of being with them and the privilege of entering their lives. Encourage mindful support groups or support buddies to foster each other's practices and experiences in self-care. These sources may be in existence or may be created by participants, according to what is available to them. Endings are usually poignant, touched with gratitude but mixed with the sadness of parting, and tinged with anticipation of what might happen next.

Handouts:

- Session 8: Breath Meditation with Lake Image audio
- Session 8: Walking With Wide-Open Awareness
- Session 8: Participant Summary

Session 8-Facilitator's Contemplation: How will mindfulness unfold on each of the journeys ahead?

Session 8 Participant Summary: Minding Your Own Care*

Guiding Question: What helps to restore your spirit as you give so much of yourself to the world of caregiving?

Aim of Session: To reflect on your journey in finding self-care practices now and in the future; to explore a mindful pause, moving meditation, and a stationary meditation related to Sessions 4 through 6, with some novel elements added.

What did you notice in the **Mindful Pause: Watering Your Garden?**

What did you notice in the **Mindful Movement: Walking With Wide Open Awareness?**

* Lumpkin, M., Collins, M.H., & Jarrett, R.B. (2026). Mindful self-care for clinicians and caregivers: A group facilitator's guide. Academic Press.

What did you notice in the **Breath Meditation with Lake Image?**

The Guiding Image of the inner garden is one you may want to return to often as you mindfully pause to sense and feel the state of your Bio-Psycho-Social-needs for replenishment and renewal. Each of these needs requires your recognition and permission to feed them in some way. The biological refers to needs for physical energy through diet, exercise, rest, and relaxation. The psychological refers to the need for mindfulness of your stress reactions and ways to reset your inner state toward calm and clarity. It also refers to the need for savoring positive experiences as they show up in life. The social refers to the need for contact and connection with others. For some, the spiritual refers to the needs to turn toward a higher power or to move beyond the small-self into moments of beauty and wholeness. Watering your garden means a special kind of mindful listening to yourself, especially the messages of your bodily sensations and feelings below the constant stream of the Monkey Mind. How do you plan to nourish your one and only precious life?

In **Mindful Self-Care for Caregivers: A Review,** you met again Tobias as he shared his growing awareness of his inner garden needs. How did this story get you to reflect on your path of self-care?

Suggestions: This last session is an end and a beginning. Savor your progress, your graduation, your gratitude for this group, and your inspiration to grow your self-care practices.

From here, I want to see myself regularly practice (in my bio-psycho-social-spiritual plan):

List mindfulness practices you would like to try this week:	☑

Lumpkin, M., Collins, M.H., & Jarrett, R.B. (2026). Mindful self-care for clinicians and caregivers: A group facilitator's guide. Academic Press.

Walking in Wide Open Awareness Transcript

In this moving meditation, we will explore two aspects of mindfulness: present-moment attention to some chosen spot and more open awareness of what surrounds you. We will do this using slow walking

So, let's begin by simply standing, balanced on both feet. Bring attention to your right and left legs and feet. What's going on there? Is it possible to just feel sensations in the legs and feet without thinking about them? Turning on the light of attention to these parts of our body usually taken for granted. These living sensations in legs, in feet.

Pick out a walking path. It can be short or longer. It can be forward a bit, then back, over and over. A repetitive path is simple and one you do not have to think about or plan.

When you are ready, begin by slowly lifting one foot, attentive to the sensations of lifting and moving. Staying focused mainly on your feet and legs in movement, lifting and lowering gives a simpler area in which to pay consistent attention. Refining your focus to lifting and lowering, placing the heel and rolling to the ball of the foot, this moving sense of rolling weight. Eyes looking just ahead of your feet, spine-neck-head released and allowed to extend upward. (Pause) Lifting, placing, rolling, lifting, placing, rolling. Mindfully following your stepping sensations, letting thoughts and distractions go into the background. (Pause) Just here, just now, lifting and lowering.

Now, see if it is possible, as you continue to focus on lifting and lowering, to allow some awareness to extend to the space around you. Attending primarily to lifting and lowering while awake to what is around you. (Pause) The feeling of legs and feet moving, and the sense of the space you are moving through. All-of-a-piece. All together … lifting and lowering in a surrounding space … staying aware of it all. (Pause) When needing to turn, sensing the sensations of turning, and how the feet move in the turn.

One foot lifts while the other foot rolls from heel to ball of the foot, then lifts as the other foot, lowers and rolls. And sensing this space that holds you. Noticing thoughts or mental distractions, if there, and simply accepting them, returning to this mindful walking.

Just in this walking body … awake … lightly aware … curious about what is showing up … in this body … in the space around … just here … just here …

Moving in silence, focused, relaxing, awake.

One foot lifts while the other foot rolls from heel to ball of the foot, then lifts as the other foot lowers and rolls. Sensing this space that holds you.

Coming slowly to a standstill. Taking a moment to feel what has happened. Ending this meditation with a sense of the breath being breathed in the whole body.

Breath Meditation With Lake Image Transcript

Begin with aligning and synchronizing mind and body: Let's try a familiar focus on the breath intermingled with the image of a lake. We'll begin by bringing mind and body together, synchronizing them. So, taking your seat … finding your way into the posture of sitting meditation at ease and awake. Feeling your way into the space of your body sensations. The feeling of your body sitting, giving its weight to the seat. The feeling of your feet and ankles, lower and upper legs joined, meeting at the hips, and rising through the spine, neck, and head. Arms and hands at rest. Feeling supported by your body while letting go of tense areas into a kind of alert relaxation. Feeling this happening in your own way, allowing it to happen without effort or thought. Just a sense of being there in this body field of sensations coming and going. (Pause)

Bringing a kind of willingness to just let things happen as you simply notice what is happening, without judgment or goal. Just being. (Pause)

Noticing this shift into being more mindful … mindful of what is presently happening. No longer absorbed in thoughts or judgments about what is happening … or pulls into the past or future. Letting the Present open out for you. (Pause)

Finding the sensation of your breathing now. Letting the breath gently expand and deepen as it wants, without forcing anything. Following the breath in — and out. In and out. As though riding the waves of this breathing, following the feel of it. (Pause) Accepting the pull of thoughts as they might come, but returning always, again and again, to this breathing … in and out.

Noticing breath like a gentle breeze over the surface of a lake, caressing the surface, smoothing it out, smoothing it out. (Pause) As the lake holds sea plants, fish, turtles, you are holding all parts of yourself, all parts of yourself (sensations, feelings, thoughts) equally … allowing and prizing them all. (Pause) In this quiet, even shy deer come to the edge to drink clear water … like the quieter parts of yourself behind all the usual noise. Breathing in and out this soft breeze, soothing what it touches with care and kindness. Everything held together, held together.

A breathing wrapped in this warm, caring attention, noticing it and whatever else comes to you now on its own. Like fish in the lake or deer at its edges, noticing now what's showing up in you now, what's showing up. (Pause) And breathing the breeze of breath through it all.

And now, just being in this breath, this new and fresh breath, appreciative of its simply being there. You and breath together, until only the breath is there, only the breath is there. (Pause)" Only the breath is there. (Pause) Only the breath … Only this breath …

We will end with a poem. (Read the poem Lake Loons slowly, repeating the last line.)

(Ending the meditation) And now beginning to transition out of the meditation, though not completely ending it. Rather than letting its fragrance linger … its aftereffects. I will count (or ring a chime or bowl) to three, and on the last count, opening the eyes if they have been closed and quietly coming to sense the room. (Count down or ring chimes, bowl, or bells).

Quick Summary: Sessions 4 Through 6

Session 4

- Session question: What comes to mind when you hear the words self-care?
- Looks at how to monitor and strengthen self-care practices.
- The Mindful Pause uses mindful eating exercises, which highlight a small way mindfulness practices might enter daily life.
- The image for self-care of tending your own garden.
- The Bio-Psycho-Social model is given as a map for areas of self-care.
- Mindful Meditations: Mindful Walking and Progressive Relaxation.

Session 5

- Session question: How might mindful listening to our care-person, others, and ourselves help us stay grounded, balanced, and more skilful in navigating the challenges of caregiving?
- Mindfulness encourages empathic connections, listening to one's own inner messages, and setting healthy boundaries.
- The Mindful Pause: Mountain and Finding Your Own Ground.
- Session images: Mountain and Lake as inner qualities of stability and calm.
- Session activity included a Check-In exercise of listening mindfully to others' disclosures.
- Mindful Meditations: Qigong from the base of the inner mountain, Breathing It All In

Session 6

- Session question: How might life be different if you were able to include mindfulness in everyday life?
- The power of small mindful moments.
- Creating mindful cues and space as ways to remember to be mindful.
- Mindfulness as a way of living.
- The Mindful Pause: A Perfect Mindful Moment.
- Session Image: Blooms of the Senses as mindful moments.
- Mindful Meditations: Mindful Stretching and Five-Minute Time Out

Part C

Parting Thoughts and Resources

Epilogue

Reflections of Peace and Water. This photograph was taken (in 2024) by Robin B. Jarrett at Lake Junaluska in North Carolina. The image invites daily mindfulness over a lifetime.

What a pleasure this has been for us to walk with you on your journey toward facilitating mindful self-care for all kinds of caregivers! We hope that the resources in *A Guide* will support you as you inspire caregivers to renew their vigor and to access the rewarding passions found through caring for other persons. Too often, the burdens in caregiving may feel like a journey laden with toil and trouble.

As facilitators, you are caregivers to caregivers. Like us, you, as a facilitator, may have your own current or past experiences with direct caregiving and/or perhaps being a care person yourself—in the hands of other caregivers. It would not be surprising in your role as a caregiver for caregivers that you might experience strong emotions as you work with participants in your group. During these times, you too can rely on mindful practices to ground yourself as the facilitator, anchored in this role.

Throughout the process of collaborating, creating, and writing this book, we found ourselves traversing the fluid boundaries of our own times as caregivers (formal and informal), facilitators of caregivers, and care persons in need of care. We, at times, gave caregiving attention to each other during our own challenges, some completely unpredictable. Our commitment to writing the book became a commitment to each other, as our own group process deepened and became stronger. We continuously asked, how can this opportunity inform mindful self-care? Such lived experience gave us the opportunity and inspiration to dig deeper into our writing about caregiving and the skills underlying mindful self-care. We offer you *The Guide*, developed while we too were touched by mindful practice in these contexts.

Author Reflections: A Caregiver's Journey
By Martin Lumpkin, PhD

My caregiving experience began in 2008, when I gradually discovered that my 88-year-old mother was sinking into dementia. This was a woman who had handled family investments and even roofed a home. A beautiful woman who loved to dance and took pride in her independence since my father died 12 years before. I was not prepared for the erosion of that spirited life.

So, I denied it at first. The slips in her checkbook figures and her anxiety over how to make familiar financial deposits and pay her bills I took as too much worry over accidents. I did not want to see her losing her prized and dependable abilities. I saw accidents accumulating. Her friends at her independent living residence took me aside with concern over changes they saw in her. Then one day, almost in a flash, scales fell from my eyes…and I saw what was there before me. Emotions parked, I saw what needed to be done and did it. My wife, Janet, and I moved her to an assisted living residence near us. I took over her bills and finances and investments. We lined up a new physician and services she needed on a daily basis. Janet was a full partner and support to me as we took on co-caregiving.

When the initial busyness was over, I began to feel what was happening: taking pleasure in giving my mother relief and having her so open to being helped; sadness over her loss of friends and familiar surroundings; fear of not being prepared for the task of taking care of her; and anxiety over losing some of my own freedom. I stepped across a threshold. I was now responsible for another human being for the rest of that being's life.

The healthcare system in America is like Swiss cheese. It has solid places and holes. I learned that the solid places for my mother were generally in acute, sometimes emergency care—as when dehydration produced puzzling mental symptoms that were cured in a short hospital stay. I discovered the holes were in day-to-day care of uneven attention from assisted living staff. This uneven care could be best managed by being a monitoring, yet friendly, presence at her place. In a way, becoming an adjunct part of the staff allowed Janet and me to navigate problems and build alliances. Staff seemed to know which residents were loved and watched over and which were, more or less, abandoned. The latter got the worst care, I believe.

Even though I was practiced in mindfulness, I had to learn it anew as a caregiver. For example, I worried over every aspect of my mother's health in the beginning. When she would refuse to drink enough water, I concocted various devious but, ultimately, ineffective ways to trick her into better hydration. When she would pick out the worst dietary things to eat, I, again, found myself stiffening and lecturing her about her food choices. The irony here is that she was an early proponent of the health food movement when I was a child. I discovered that this anxiety and chronic frustration were results of trying to control what you cannot control. Mindfulness reminded me of the deep value of nonjudgment and acceptance. I stopped the control efforts, accepted that this may have physical costs, and spent more time laughing and playing with my mother. For example, staff contacted me, saying the mother was hallucinating. Mom told me she saw two children in her room who disappeared and that we must find them. I saw her deep concern and did not challenge her. Instead, we took time to look around the facility. We took a break for a drive in the country near us, and she forgot the children on her own. There was no book of instructions about how to handle so many situations. Making peace with uncertainty and the unknown was a gradual process.

I was alone with her on her last night alive in hospice. I sang softly to us both into the early morning.

Martin's story expresses the vulnerability in most of us, no matter how skilled we are in mindful self-care or promoting stable mental health. Like many, he had to see again and again his disconnection from his feelings and needs to reset himself in mindful awareness and choices. Learning MSCC skills and moving forward rests on this perspective of continued awakening when losing one's way, allowing the possibility of better and more sustained caregiving. We leave you with this vision to share with MSCC participants: Practicing mindful self-care is a continual cycle of discovery and rediscovery of its fragility and durability. Accepting this cycle is nothing less than one's own resilience, vital living, and connection with all the senses. Each author—Marielle, Robin, and Martin—walks this path and enjoys the thought that you, too, walk with us. We wish you fulfilling journeys as you facilitate mindful self-care with all types of caregivers located in diverse settings.

Coda

Lake Brienz in the Morning—The glacial stillness of Lake Brienz reflects the power of pausing mindfully for a few moments, amid life's towering demands to find strength; photo taken by Marielle in Switzerland, Summer 2024.

Mindful Self-Care for Clinicians and Caregivers: A Group Facilitator's Guide places a special lens on the plight of caregivers as a way to make their often-invisible lives of self-sacrifice and service visible, as a way to acknowledge the costs of caregiving and the gifts of self-care. All too often, the costs accumulate to the point of stressful burden or burnout. The deep satisfaction and meaningfulness of caregiving can easily be buried under the weight of this complex role. *Mindful Self-Care for Clinicians and Caregivers: A Group Facilitator's Guide* offers to take the caregiver in hand, attempting to make the challenges of his or her world visible and to invite the caregiver to give himself or herself life-nourishing care. This encouragement of self-care is part of a larger effort to create a self-care culture in society and its institutions. The reason self-care is neglected or suppressed is that our larger society too often rewards the opposite. The need for self-care is sometimes seen as a weakness or a selfish desire in a society that idolizes nose-to-the-grindstone pressure to survive and succeed. The very speed of contemporary life undermines unrushed reflective self-awareness. This kind of awareness, we call mindfulness. The kind of awareness we all need to balance extrinsic striving and goals with intrinsic meaning and self-connection. May the journey of MSCC not only reach our vulnerable clinicians and caregivers but also be a voice in a chorus singing to our beleaguered culture...the inner songs of inward listening to ourselves, finding an aliveness no longer silenced by the surrounding noise and the unrelenting pressure to merely cope.

About the Authors

Martin Lumpkin, PhD

Psychologist in Private Practice, Dallas, Texas, USA

Martin Lumpkin, PhD, is a Licensed Psychologist with decades of experience in facilitating growth through psychotherapy and mindfulness training. His insights are described in the book *Into the Music of the World: Living Life Mindfully*. Dr. Lumpkin received his doctorate in Clinical Psychology at Texas Tech University in 1971. He has held staff and administrative positions at Terrell State Hospital, including creating and overseeing the Substance Abuse Program there. He enjoyed 5 years in a management consulting firm (Rohrer, Hibler & Replogle), where he developed the executive and team building skills of managers. Since the 1980s, Dr. Lumpkin has been active in private practice focused on psychotherapy and mindfulness training. He taught at the University of Texas Southwestern Medical Center (UT Southwestern), introducing doctoral students in clinical psychology to psychotherapy and coordinating a doctoral internship consortium between UT Southwestern and Terrell State Hospital. Dr. Lumpkin studied and received extensive training in mindfulness training, including mindfulness-based stress reduction and mindfulness-based cognitive therapy. Since the early 1990s, he has promoted the practice of mindfulness for personal well-being and as a therapeutic intervention. Dr. Lumpkin has been sharing his passion for mindfulness by providing workshops throughout the Dallas–Fort Worth Metroplex.

Marielle H. Collins, PhD

Clinical Health Psychologist

Assistant Professor of Psychiatry, Cleveland Clinic Lerner College of Medicine

Cleveland Clinic, Department of Psychiatry and Psychology, Cleveland, Ohio, USA

Marielle Collins, PhD, is a Clinical Health Psychologist in the Department of Psychiatry and Psychology at Cleveland Clinic, where she serves as Director of Consultation–Liaison Psychology. Her clinical and scholarly work focuses on the psychological care of medically hospitalized patients, with particular expertise in consultation–liaison psychology and the integration of evidence-based psychological interventions within acute medical settings. Dr. Collins earned her doctorate in Clinical Psychology from the University of Texas Southwestern Medical Center and completed a fellowship in Clinical Health Psychology at Cleveland Clinic. Her research interests include mindfulness-based approaches and the role of psychology in interdisciplinary medical care, with an emphasis on improving patient adjustment, coping, and engagement during acute illness and hospitalization. She has led mindfulness workshops, educational groups, and training programs for medical students, residents, faculty, and community organizations. Her work is grounded in mindfulness and emphasizes presence, self-compassion, and resilience in supporting clinicians, caregivers, and patients.

Robin B. Jarrett, PhD, ABPP

Professor of Psychiatry

The University of Texas Southwestern Medical Center, Department of Psychiatry, Dallas, Texas

Board-Certified Clinical Psychologist
Fellow, American Psychological Association
Fellow, Association for Behavioral and Cognitive Therapies
Founding Fellow, Academy of Cognitive and Behavioral Therapies
Fellow, Executive Leadership in Academic Medicine

Robin B. Jarrett, PhD, ABPP, is a Professor of Psychiatry at the University of Texas Southwestern Medical Center where she has studied the role of psychosocial factors and interventions on the course of health, including mood and related disorders. Dr. Jarrett is a North Carolina native, who earned a BA with honors from The University of North Carolina at Chapel Hill. She received her doctorate in Clinical Psychology from the University of North Carolina at Greensboro. Dr. Jarrett is a Board-Certified Clinical Psychologist who has been continuously active in clinical practice and teaching throughout her distinguished scientific career. She offers mindful practices to trainees, patients, and clients. Dr. Jarrett is internationally known for research, education, and practice in psychosocial intervention, particularly cognitive–behavioral therapy. Dr. Jarrett is a Founding Fellow of the Academy of Cognitive and Behavioral Therapies and a Fellow in the American Psychological Association, the Association of Behavioral and Cognitive Therapies, and Executive Leadership in Academic Medicine or “ELAM”. She is certified as a Professional Coach and helps people activate their strengths in the workplace and outside. She enjoys consulting with both individuals and groups. Her favorite spots include Santa Fe, the Texas Hill Country, the Great Smoky Mountains, and Carolina beaches. Her passions include mindful Sundays, time with family and friends, and walking in nature.

Appendix: List of Transcripts, Handouts, and Audio/Video Resources

Listed in the following are facilitator transcripts, participant handouts, and online audio or video materials attached to each of the eight sessions. Transcripts and handouts follow the session guides and introductions in Part B of this book.

Transcripts for Use in Sessions to include:

Session 1 Qigong transcript
Session 1 Body Scan transcript
Session 2 Breath Meditation transcript
Session 2 Qigong transcript
Session 3 Three Simple Mindful Movements (with photos)
Session 3 Mindful Emotional Processing transcript
Session 4 Mindful Eating script
Session 4 Progressive Muscle Relaxation
Session 5 Finding and Moving from Inner Mountain transcript
Session 5 Breathing It All In transcript
Session 6 Five Minute Time-Out transcript
Session 6 A Mindful Glimmer transcript
Session 6 Mindful Stretching
Session 7 Refer to Session 1 Qigong transcript
Session 7 Refer to Session 1 Body Scan and Session 2 Mindfulness of Breath transcripts
Session 8 Breath Meditation with Lake Image transcript
Session 8 Walking with Open Awareness transcript

Handouts to Spark Mindful Daily Practice to include:

Session 1 The Radio and the Open Window
Session 1 Participant Summary
Session 1 Bringing Mindfulness into Daily Life
Session 1 Body Scan Description
Session 1 Qigong Practices: An Introduction
Session 2 Participant Summary
Session 2 Poem: "Another Little Greek Tale"
Session 3 Participant Summary
Session 3 Three Simple Mindful Movements (with photos)
Session 3 Poem: "The Space in Patience"
Session 4 Participant Summary
Session 5 Participant Summary
Session 5 Poem: "Lake Loons"
Session 6 Participant Summary
Session 7 Participant Summary

Session 7 Bringing Mindfulness to Daily Life
Session 7 Tobias Vignette
Session 7 Poem: "It Takes A While"
Session 8 Participant Summary

Portal Contents to Aid in the Facilitation of Mindful Self-Care for Clinicians and Caregivers

Session 1 Qigong video
Session 1 Body Scan audio
Session 2 Qigong video
Session 2 Mindfulness of Breath audio
Session 3 Three Simple Mindful Movements video
Session 3 Mindful Emotional Processing audio
Session 4 Mindful Walking audio
Session 4 Progressive Relaxation audio
Session 5 Finding and Moving from Inner Mountain video
Session 5 Breathing It All In audio
Session 6 Mindful Stretching video
Session 6 Five Minute Time-Out audio
Session 7 Refer to Session 1 Qigong video
Session 7 Refer to Session 1 Body Scan and Session 2 Mindfulness of Breath audios
Session 8 Breath Meditation with Lake Image audio
Session 8 Walking with Wide Open Awareness audio
Session 8 Switzerland Stream Audio

Listing of Mindful Images

1. Rainbows and Rain
2. Path during Journey
3. Sunburst flower
4. Perched watchful owl
5. Light amid the Storm
6. In the Garden of Tulips and Daffodils
7. Ducks in sync sharing space
8. Autumn's Embrace
9. An Old Walking Bridge
10. Sunflower Garden
11. Reflections of Peace and Water
12. Lake Brienz in the Morning
13. Chinese Handcuffs

References

AARP and National Alliance for Caregiving. (2020). *Caregiving in the United States 2020.* Washington, D.C.: AARP. https://doi.org/10.26419/ppi.00103.001

AARP Public Policy Institute. (2023). *Valuing the invaluable: 2023 update.* Washington, D.C.: AARP. https://doi.org/10.26419/ppi.00082.006

Abbit, L. (2017). *The conscious caregiver: A mindful approach to caring for your loved one without losing yourself.* New York: Simon & Schuster.

Aizik-Reebs, A., Shoham, A., & Bernstein, A. (2021). First, do no harm: An intensive experience sampling study of adverse effects to mindfulness training. *Behavioral Research and Therapy, 145*, Article 103941. https://doi.org/10.1016/j.brat.2021.103941

Aldbyani, A. (2024). Exploring islamic mindfulness: Cultural practices and their impact on public health outcomes. *Mindfulness*, 1–7. https://doi.org/10.1007/s12671-024-02485-5

Alzheimer's Association. (2015). 2015 Alzheimer's disease facts and figures. *Alzheimer's & Dementia, 11*(3), 332+. https://www.alz.org/media/documents/2015factsandfigures.pdf.

Ameli, R., Sinaii, N., West, C. P., Luna, M. J., Panahi, S., Zoosman, M., Rusch, H. L., & Berger, A. (2020). Effect of a brief mindfulness-based program on stress in health care professionals at a U.S. biomedical research hospital: A randomized clinical trial. *JAMA Network Open, 3*(8), Article e2013424. https://doi.org/10.1001/jamanetworkopen.2020.13424

American Nurses Foundation. (2023). *Understanding and prioritizing nurses' mental health and well-being.* https://www.nursingworld.org/practice-policy/work-environment/health-safety/disaster-preparedness/coronavirus/what-you-need-to-know/survey- 4/contentassets/understanding-and-prioritizing-nurses-mental-health-and-well- being.pdf.

American Psychiatric Association. (2022). *Diagnostic and statistical manual of mental disorders* (5th ed., text rev.). American Psychiatric Association Publishing.

Anderson, M. R., Kaplan, D. M., & Palitsky, R. (2022). Religious and existential determinants of affective response to a brief mindfulness intervention. *Affective Science, 4*(1), 143–151. https://doi.org/10.1007/s42761-022-00139-0

Aneshensel, C. S., Pearlin, L. I., Mullan, J. T., Zarit, S. H., & Whitlatch, C. J. (1995). *Profiles in caregiving: The unexpected career.* San Diego, CA: Academic Press.

Artress, L. (1995). *Walking a sacred path: Rediscovering the labyrinth as a spiritual tool.* Riverhead Books.

Baer, R. A., Carmody, J., & Hunsinger, M. (2012). Weekly change in mindfulness and perceived stress in a mindfulness-based stress reduction program. *Journal of Clinical Psychology, 68*, 755–765. https://doi.org/10.1002/jclp.21865

Bazazan, A., Dianat, I., Rastgoo, L., & Mombeini, Z. (2018). Factors associated with mental health status of hospital nurses. *International Journal of Industrial Ergonomics, 66*, 194–199.

Bellone, K. M., Elliott, S. C., Hynan, L. S., Warren, B., & Jarrett, R. B. (2023). Mindful self-care for caregivers: A proof of concept study investigating a model for embedded caregiver support in a pediatric setting. *Journal of Autism and Developmental Disorders, 53* (2), 539–552. https://doi.org/10.1007/s10803-021-05113-6

Bianchi, R., Schonfeld, I. S., Vandel, P., & Laurent, E. (2017). On the depressive nature of the "burnout syndrome": A clarification. *European Psychiatry, 41*, 109–110. https://doi.org/10.1016/j.eurpsy.2016.10.008

Bianchi, R., Verkuilen, J., Schonfeld, I. S., Hakanen, J. J., Jansson-Fröjmark, M., Manzano-García, G., Laurent, E., & Meier, L. L. (2021). Is burnout a depressive condition? A 14-sample meta-analytic and bifactor analytic study. *Clinical Psychological Science, 9*(4), 579–597. https://doi.org/10.1177/2167702620979597

Black, D. S., & Slavich, G. M. (2016). Mindfulness meditation and the immune system: A systematic review of randomized controlled trials. *Annals of the New York Academy of Sciences, 1373*(1), 13–24. https://doi.org/10.1111/nyas.12998

Bolton, D. (2023). A revitalized biopsychosocial model: Core theory, research paradigms, and clinical implications. *Psychological Medicine, 53*(16), 7504–7511. https://doi.org/10.1017/S0033291723002660

Britton, W. B., Lindahl, J. R., Cooper, D. J. C., Canby, N. K., & Palitsky, R. (2021). Defining and measuring meditation-related adverse effects in mindfulness-based programs. *Clinical Psychological Science, 9*, 1185–1204.

Brooke, A. (1978). *Hidden in plain sight. The practice of Christian meditation.* Nashville, Tennessee. *The Upper Room.*

Brown, K. W., Coogle, C. L., & Wegelin, J. (2016). A pilot randomized controlled trial of mindfulness-based stress reduction for caregivers of family members with dementia. *Aging & Mental Health, 20*(11), 1157–1166. https://doi.org/10.1080/13607863.2015.1065790

Burns, J. W., Jensen, M. P., Gerhart, J., Thorn, B. E., Lillis, T. A., Carmody, J., & Keefe, F. (2023). Cognitive therapy, mindfulness-based stress reduction, and behavior therapy for people with chronic low back pain: A comparative mechanisms study. *Journal of Consulting and Clinical Psychology, 91*(3), 171–187. https://doi.org/10.1037/ccp0000801

Bykov, K. V., Zrazhevskaya, I. A., Topka, E. O., Peshkin, V. N., Dobrovolsky, A. P., Isaev, R. N., & Orlov, A. M. (2022). Prevalence of burnout among psychiatrists: A systematic review and meta-analysis. *Journal of Affective Disorders, 308*, 47–64. https://doi.org/10.1016/j.jad.2022.04.005

Cheng, S. T., Lam, L. C., Kwok, T., Ng, N. S., & Fung, A. W. (2013). Self-efficacy is associated with less burden and more gains from behavioral problems of Alzheimer's disease in Hong Kong Chinese caregivers. *The Gerontologist, 53*(1), 71–80. https://doi.org/10.1093/geront/gns062

Cheung, D. S. K., Kor, P. P. K., Jones, C., Davies, N., Moyle, W., Chien, W. T., Yip, A. L. K., Chambers, S., Yu, C. T. K., & Lai, C. K. Y. (2020). The use of modified mindfulness-based stress reduction and mindfulness-based cognitive therapy program for family caregivers of people living with dementia: A feasibility study. *Asian Nursing Research, 14*(4), 221–230. https://doi.org/10.1016/j.anr.2020.08.009

Cleveland Clinic. (November 30, 2023). *Caregiver burnout.* https://my.clevelandclinic.org/health/diseases/9225-caregiver-burnout.

Cohen, K. S. (1997). *The way of qigong: The art and science of Chinese energy healing.* Ballantine Books.

Collins, M. H. (2023). A mindful glimmer. In M. Lumpkin, M. H. Collins, & R. B. Jarrett (Eds.), *Mindful self-care for clinician and caregivers: A group facilitator' guide* (Ist Edition). Elsevier, 2026.

Collins, M. H. (2024). Snowfall. In M. Lumpkin, M. H. Collins, & R. B. Jarrett (Eds.), *Mindful self-care for clinician and caregivers: A group facilitator' guide* (Ist Edition). Elsevier, 2026.

Collins, R. N., & Kishita, N. (2019). The effectiveness of mindfulness- and acceptance-based interventions for informal caregivers of people with dementia: A meta-analysis. *The Gerontologist, 59*(4), e363–e379. https://doi.org/10.1093/geront/gny024

Conversano, C., Ciacchini, R., Orrù, G., Di Giuseppe, M., Gemignani, A., & Poli, A. (2020). Mindfulness, compassion, and self-compassion among health care professionals: What's new? A systematic review. *Frontiers in Psychology, 11*, 1683. https://doi.org/10.3389/fpsyg.2020.01683

Coughlin, J. (2010). Estimating the impact of caregiving and employment on well-being. *Outcomes & Insights in Health Management, 2*(1), 1–7.

Cramer, H., Lauche, R., Anheyer, D., Pilkington, K., de Manincor, M., Dobos, G., & Ward, L. (2018). Yoga for anxiety: A systematic review and meta-analysis of randomized controlled trials. *Depression and Anxiety, 35*(9), 830–843. https://doi.org/10.1002/da.22762

Creswell, J. D., Lindsay, E. K., Villalba, D. K., & Chin, B. (2019). Mindfulness training and physical health: Mechanisms and outcomes. *Psychosomatic Medicine, 81*(3), 224–232. https://doi.org/10.1097/PSY.0000000000000675

DeMauro, A. A., Jennings, P. A., Cunningham, T., et al. (2019). Mindfulness and caring in professional practice: An interdisciplinary review of qualitative research. *Mindfulness, 10*, 1969–1984. https://doi.org/10.1007/s12671-019-01186-8

Demina, A., Petit, B., Meille, V., Lebon, F., & Trojak, B. (2023). Interventions combining mindfulness training with non-invasive brain stimulation and their impact on mental health outcomes: Protocol for a systematic review and meta-analysis of randomized controlled trials. *PLoS One, 18*(11), Article e0288692. https://doi.org/10.1371/journal.pone.0288692

Di Mauro, S., Di Giacomo, D., & Gualano, M. R. (2019). Mindfulness-based interventions for healthcare professionals: A systematic review. *International Journal of Environmental Research and Public Health, 16*(19), 3660. https://doi.org/10.3390/ijerph16193660

Dimidjian, S., Goodman, S. H., Felder, J. N., Gallop, R., Brown, A. P., & Beck, A. (2016). Staying well during pregnancy and the postpartum: A pilot randomized trial of mindfulness-based cognitive therapy for the prevention of depressive relapse/recurrence. *Journal of Consulting and Clinical Psychology, 84*(2), 134–145. https://doi.org/10.1037/ccp0000068

Dreeben, S. J., Mamberg, M. H., & Salmon, P. (2013). The mbsr body scan in clinical practice. *Mindfulness, 4*, 394–401. https://doi.org/10.1007/s12671-013-0212-z

Dunn, T. J., & Dimolareva, M. (2022). The effect of mindfulness-based interventions on immunity-related biomarkers: A comprehensive meta-analysis of randomised controlled trials. *Clinical Psychology Review, 92*, Article 102124. https://doi.org/10.1016/j.cpr.2022.102124

Dykens, E. M., Fisher, M. H., Taylor, J. L., Lambert, W., & Miodrag, N. (2014). Reducing distress in mothers of children with autism and other disabilities: A randomized trial. *Pediatrics, 134*(2), e454–e463. https://doi.org/10.1542/peds.2013-3164

Ebbinghaus, H. (1908). *Psychology: An elementary text-book*. Boston: D.C. Heath & Co.

Elayoubi, J., Nelson, M. E., Mu, C. X., Haley, W. E., Wadley, V. G., Clay, O. J., Crowe, M., Cushman, M., Grant, J. S., Roth, D. L., & Andel, R. (2023). The role of caregiving in cognitive function and change: The REGARDS study. *Psychology and Aging*. https://doi.org/10.1037/pag0000766

Engel, G. L. (1977). The biopsychosocial model and the education of health professionals. *Behavioral Science, 22*(6), 207–216.

Engel, G. L. (1980). The clinical application of the biopsychosocial model. *American Journal of Psychiatry, 137*(5), 535–544. https://doi.org/10.1176/ajp.137.5.535

Erdoğan Yüce, G., Döner, A., Bilgin, A., & Muz, G. (2024). The effect of mindfulness-based interventions on caregiver burden, quality of life and psychological distress in caregivers of adults with chronic diseases: Systematic review and meta-analysis of randomized controlled trials. *Worldviews on Evidence-Based Nursing, 21*(5), 528–541. https://doi.org/10.1111/wvn.12736

Erdoğan Yüce, G., & Muz, G. (2020). Effect of yoga-based physical activity on perceived stress, anxiety, and quality of life in young adults. *Perspectives in Psychiatric Care, 56*(3), 697–704. https://doi.org/10.1111/ppc.12484

Family Caregiver Alliance. (n.d.). Caregiver statistics: Demographics. https://www.caregiver.org/resource/caregiver-statistics-demographics/.

Farb, N., & Segal, Z. (2024). *Better in every sense: How the new science of sensation can help you reclaim your life*. New York: Little, Brown Spark.

Feldman, C., & Kuyken, W. (2019). *Mindfulness: Ancient wisdom meets modern psychology*. New York: The Guilford Press.

Fernández-Portero, C., Alarcón, D., Gallardo-Flores, A., Amián, J. G., & Sánchez-Medina, J. A. (2021). Effectiveness of a mindfulness-based intervention program for women family caregivers of older adults. *Healthcare, 9*(9), 1216. https://doi.org/10.3390/healthcare9091216

Freudenberger, H. (1975). The staff burn-out syndrome in alternative institutions. *Psychotherapy Theory Research and Practice, 12*(1), 73–82. https://doi.org/10.1037/h0086411

Frost, R. (1923). Stopping by woods on a snowy evening. In *New Hampshire: A poem with notes and grace notes* (pp. 9–10). Henry Holt and Company.

Frost, R. (2019). New Hampshire. *Vintage Classics*.

Galante, J., Friedrich, C., & Collaboration of Mindfulness Trials (CoMinT). (2023). Systematic review and individual participant data meta-analysis of randomized controlled trials assessing mindfulness-based programs for mental health promotion. *Nature Mental Health, 1*(8), 462–476. https://doi.org/10.1038/s44220-023-00081-5

Gawande, R., Smith, L., Comeau, A., Creedon, T. B., Wilson, C. L., Griswold, T., Cook, B. L., Loucks, E. B., & Schuman-Olivier, Z. (2023). Impact of warm mindfulness on emotion regulation: A randomized controlled effectiveness trial. *Health Psychology: Official Journal of the Division of Health Psychology, American Psychological Association*. https://doi.org/10.1037/hea0001303

Goldberg, S. B., Riordan, K. M., Sun, S., & Davidson, R. J. (2022). The empirical status of mindfulness-based interventions: A systematic review of 44 meta-analyses of randomized controlled trials. *Perspectives on Psychological Science, 17*(1), 108–130. https://doi.org/10.1177/1745691620968771

Goldberg S. B., Segal Z. (n.d.). Mindfulness-based cognitive therapy. American Psychological Association Society of Clinical Psychology. https://www.div12.org/treatment/mindfulness-based-cognitive-therapy/.

Goldberg, S. B., Tucker, R. P., Greene, P. A., Davidson, R. J., Wampold, B. E., Kearney, D. J., & Simpson, T. L. (2018). Mindfulness-based interventions for psychiatric disorders: A systematic review and meta-analysis. *Clinical Psychology Review, 59*, 52–60. https://doi.org/10.1016/j.cpr.2017.10.011

Goleman, D., & Davidson, R. J. (2017). *Altered traits: Science reveals how meditation changes your mind, brain, and body*. Penguin Random House.

Goyal, M., Singh, S., Sibinga, E. M. S., et al. (2014). Meditation programs for psychological stress and well-being: A systematic review and meta-analysis. *JAMA Internal Medicine, 174*(3), 357–368. https://doi.org/10.1001/jamainternmed.2013.13018

Green, A. A., & Kinchen, E. V. (2021). The effects of mindfulness meditation on stress and burnout in nurses. *Journal of Holistic Nursing, 39*(4), 356–368. https://doi.org/10.1177/08980101211015818

Guidi, J., Lucente, M., Sonino, N., & Fava, G. A. (2021). Allostatic load and its impact on health: A systematic review. *Psychotherapy and Psychosomatics, 90*(1), 11–27. https://doi.org/10.1159/000510696

Gustafson, T., & Hemberg, J. (2021). Compassion fatigue as bruises in the soul: A qualitative study on nurses. *Nursing Ethics, 29*(1), 157–170. https://doi.org/10.1177/09697330211003215

Haidar, A., Nwosisi, E., & Burnett-Zeigler, I. (2023). The role of religion and spirituality in adapting mindfulness-based interventions for black American communities: A scoping review. *Mindfulness, 14*, 1852–1867. https://doi.org/10.1007/s12671-023-02194- 5

Heinrich, D. S., & O'Connell, K. A. (2024). The effects of mindfulness meditation on nursing students' stress and anxiety levels. *Nursing Education Perspectives, 45*(1), 31–36. https://doi.org/10.1097/01.NEP.0000000000001159

Hölzel, B. K., Carmody, J., Vangel, M., Congleton, C., Yerramsetti, S. M., Gard, T., & Lazar, S. W. (2011). Mindfulness practice leads to increases in regional brain gray matter density. *Psychiatry Research, 191*(1), 36–43. https://doi.org/10.1016/j.pscychresns.2010.08.006

Hou, R. J., Wong, S. .Y., et al. (2014). The effects of mindfulness-based stress reduction program on the mental health of family caregivers: A randomized controlled trial. *Psychotherapy and Psychosomatics, 83*(1), 45–53. https://doi.org/10.1159/000353278

Hwang, Y., & Kim, J. (2024). Influence of caregivers' psychological well-being on the anxiety and depression of care recipients with dementia. *Geriatric Nursing, 55*, 44–51. https://doi.org/10.1016/j.gerinurse.2023.10.015

Jaffray, L., Bridgman, H., Stephens, M., & Skinner, T. (2016). Evaluating the effects of mindfulness-based interventions for informal palliative caregivers: A systematic literature review. *Palliative Medicine, 30*(2), 117–131. https://doi.org/10.1177/0269216315600331

Jarrett, R. B. (2022a). Conceptual models of emotional states and mindful self-care for caregivers. In M. Lumpkin, M. H. Collins, & R. B. Jarrett (Eds.), *Mindful self-care for clinician and caregivers: A group facilitator' guide* (Ist Edition). Elsevier, 2026.

Jarrett, R. B. (2022b). Breathing it all in. In M. Lumpkin, M. H. Collins, & R. B. Jarrett (Eds.), *Mindful self-care for clinician and caregivers: A group facilitator' guide* (Ist Edition). Elsevier, 2026.

Javadzade, N., Esmaeili, S. V., Omranifard, V., et al. (2024). Effect of mindfulness-based stress reduction (MBSR) program on depression, emotion regulation, and sleep problems: A randomized controlled trial study on depressed elderly. *BMC Public Health, 24*, 271. https://doi.org/10.1186/s12889-024-17759-9

Johannsen, M., Nissen, E. R., Lundorff, M., & O'Toole, M. S. (2022). Mediators of acceptance and mindfulness-based therapies for anxiety and depression: A systematic review and meta-analysis. *Clinical Psychology Review, 94*, Article 102156. https://doi.org/10.1016/j.cpr.2022.102156

Kabat-Zinn, J. (2013). *Full catastrophe living, revised edition: How to cope with stress, pain and illness using mindfulness meditation*. New York: Bantam Books.

Karo, M., Simorangkir, L., Daryanti Saragih, I., Suarilah, I., & Tzeng, H.-M. (2024). Effects of mindfulness-based interventions on reducing psychological distress among nurses: A systematic review and meta-analysis of randomized controlled trials. *Journal of Nursing Scholarship, 56*, 319–330. https://doi.org/10.1111/jnu.12941

Kechter, A., & Black, D. S. (2020). Mindfulness-based interventions applied to addiction treatments. In S. Sussman (Ed.), *The Cambridge handbook of substance and behavioral addictions* (pp. 409–417). Cambridge University Press. https://doi.org/10.1017/9781108632591.040

Kennedy, B. M., Rehman, M., Johnson, W. D., Magee, M. B., Leonard, R., & Katzmarzyk, P. T. (2017). Healthcare providers versus patients' understanding of health beliefs and values. *Patient Experience Journal, 4*(3), 29–37.

Khoramirad, A., Taheri, L., Eskandari, N., & Abedini, Z. (2024). Effect of mindfulness-based neurodevelopmental care on infant outcomes in NICU. *Journal of Neonatal Nursing, 30* (3), 237–242. https://doi.org/10.1016/j.jnn.2023.10.001

Khoury, B., Sharma, M., Rush, S. E., & Fournier, C. (2015). Mindfulness-based stress reduction for healthy individuals: A meta-analysis. *Journal of Psychosomatic Research, 78*(6), 519–528. https://doi.org/10.1016/j.jpsychores.2015.03.009

Kögler, M., Brandstätter, M., Borasio, G. D., Fensterer, V., Küchenhoff, H., & Fegg, M. J. (2015). Mindfulness in informal caregivers of palliative patients. *Palliative & Supportive Care, 13*(1), 11–18. https://doi.org/10.1017/S1478951513000400

Korecki, J. R., Schwebel, F. J., Votaw, V. R., & Witkiewitz, K. (2020). Mindfulness-based programs for substance use disorders: A systematic review of manualized treatments. *Substance Abuse Treatment, Prevention, and Policy, 15*(1), 51. https://doi.org/10.1186/s13011-020-00293-3

Kovach, C. R., Evans, C. R., Sattell, L., Rosenau, K., & Gopalakrishnan, S. (2018). Feasibility and pilot testing of a mindfulness intervention for frail older adults and individuals with dementia. *Research in Gerontological Nursing, 11*(3), 137–150. https://doi.org/10.3928/19404921-20180223-01

Krämer, M. D., & Bleidorn, W. (2024). The well-being costs of informal caregiving. *Psychological Science, 35*(12), 1382–1394. https://doi.org/10.1177/09567976241279203

Kriakous, S. A., Elliott, K. A., Lamers, C., & Owen, R. (2021). The effectiveness of Mindfulness- based stress reduction on the psychological functioning of healthcare professionals: A systematic review. *Mindfulness, 12*(1), 1–28. https://doi.org/10.1007/s12671-020-01500-9

Kunkle, R., Chaperon, C., & Berger, A. M. (2020). Formal caregiver burden in nursing homes: An integrative review. *Western Journal of Nursing Research, 43*(9), 877–893. https://doi.org/10.1177/0193945920979691

Kuyken, W., Warren, F. C., Taylor, R. S., Whalley, B., Crane, C., Bondolfi, G., Hayes, R., Huijbers, M., Ma, H., Schweizer, S., Segal, Z., Speckens, A., Teasdale, J. D., Van Heeringen, K., Williams, M., Byford, S., Byng, R., & Dalgleish, T. (2016). Efficacy of mindfulness-based cognitive therapy in prevention of depressive relapse: An individual patient data meta-analysis from randomized trials. *JAMA Psychiatry, 73*(6), 565–574. https://doi.org/10.1001/jamapsychiatry.2016.0076

Li, X., Ma, L., & Li, Q. (2022). How mindfulness affects life satisfaction: Based on the mindfulness-to-meaning theory. *Frontiers in Psychology, 13*, Article 887940. https://doi.org/10.3389/fpsyg.2022.887940

Li, G., Yuan, H., & Zhang, W. (2016). The effects of mindfulness-based stress reduction for family caregivers: Systematic review. *Archives of Psychiatric Nursing, 30*(2), 292–299. https://doi.org/10.1016/j.apnu.2015.08.014

Liu, Z., Heffernan, C., & Tan, J. (2020). Caregiver burden: A concept analysis. *International Journal of Nursing Science, 7*(4), 438–445. https://doi.org/10.1016/j.ijnss.2020.07.012

Lomas, T., Medina, J. C., Ivtzan, I., Rupprecht, S., & Eiroa-Orosa, F. J. (2018). A systematic review of the impact of mindfulness on the well-being of healthcare professionals. *Journal of Clinical Psychology, 74*(3), 319–355. https://doi.org/10.1002/jclp.22515

Lumpkin, M. (2014a). *Into the music of the world: Living life mindfully*. Amazon CreateSpace.

Lumpkin, M. (2014b). Lake loons. In , *2014. Into the music of the world: Living Life Mindfully* (p. 5). Amazon CreateSpace.

Lumpkin, M. (2014c). It takes A while. In *Into the music of the world: Living life mindfully* (p. 94). Amazon CreateSpace.

Lumpkin, M., & Jarrett, R. B. (2015). Mindful self-care for caregivers (MSCC). *Unpublished manual, Department of Psychiatry*. Dallas, TX: The University of Texas Southwestern Medical Center.

Maranzan, K. A., Kowatch, K. R., Mascioli, B. A., McGeown, L., Popowich, A. D., & Spiroiu, F. (2018). Self-care and the Canadian Code of Ethics: Implications for training in professional psychology. *Canadian Psychology/Psychologie Canadienne, 59*(4), 361–368. https://doi.org/10.1037/cap0000153

Marmot, M. (2005). Social determinants of health inequalities. *Lancet, 365*(9464), 1099–1104. https://doi.org/10.1016/S0140-6736(05)71146-6

Maslach, C., & Jackson, S. E. (1981). The measurement of experienced burnout. *Journal of Occupational Behavior, 2*(2), 99–113. https://doi.org/10.1002/job.4030020205

Maslach, C., Jackson, S. E., & Leiter, M. P. (2018). *Maslach burnout inventory manual* (4th ed.). Mind Garden.

Matko, K., & Sedlmeier, P. (2019). What is meditation? Proposing an empirically derived classification system. *Psychology of Consciousness: Theory, Research, and Practice, 6*(2), 150–171. https://doi.org/10.1037/cns0000182

McClintock, A. S., McCarrick, S. M., Garland, E. L., & Zeidan, F. (2019). Brief mindfulness-based interventions for acute and chronic pain: A systematic review. *Journal of Alternative & Complementary Medicine, 25*(3), 265–274. https://doi.org/10.1089/acm.2018.0351

McPherson, C. J., Wilson, K. G., Chyurlia, L., & Leclerc, C. (2011). The caregiving relationship and quality of life among partners of stroke survivors: A cross-sectional study. *Health and Quality of Life Outcomes, 9*. https://doi.org/10.1186/1477-7525-9-29. Article Number 29(2011).

Medscape. (2020). National physician burnout & suicide report 2020. *Medscape*. https://www.medscape.com/slideshow/2020-lifestyle-burnout-6012460. (Accessed 15 October 2020).

Melnyk, B. M., Kelly, S. A., Stephens, J., et al. (2020). Interventions to improve mental health, well-being, physical health, and lifestyle behaviors in physicians and nurses: A systematic review. *American Journal of Health Promotion, 34*(8), 929–941. https://doi.org/10.1177/0890117120920451

Minor, H. G., Carlson, L. E., Mackenzie, M. J., Zernicke, K., & Jones, L. (2006). Evaluation of a mindfulness-based stress reduction (mbsr) program for caregivers of children with chronic conditions. *Social Work in Health Care, 43*(1), 91–109. https://doi.org/10.1300/J010v43n01_06

Mistretta, E. G., Davis, M. C., Temkit, M'hamed, Lorenz, C., Darby, B., & Stonnington, C. M. (2018). Resilience training for work-related stress among health care workers: Results of a randomized clinical trial comparing in-person and smartphone-delivered interventions. *Journal of Occupational and Environmental Medicine, 60*(6), 559–568. https://doi.org/10.1097/JOM.0000000000001285

Monin, J. K., Levy, B., Doyle, M., Schultz, R., & Kershaw, T. (2019). The impact of both spousal caregivers' and care recipients' health on relationship satisfaction in the Caregiver Health Effects Study. *Journal of Health Psychology, 24*(12), 1744–1755. https://doi.org/10.1177/1359105317699682

Morse, G., Salyers, M. A., Rollins, A. L., Monroe-DeVita, M., & Pfahler, C. (2012). Burnout in mental health services: A review of the problem and its remediation. *Administration and Policy in Mental Health, 39*(5), 341–352. https://doi.org/10.1007/s10488-011-0352-1

Napier, R., Wuinna, S., & Gershenfeld, H. (2025). *Group theory and experience* (8th ed.). Houghton Mifflin.

National Institute for Health and Care Excellence. (2009). *Depression in adults: Recognition and management.* https://www.nice.org.uk/guidance/cg90.

National Institute for Health and Care Excellence. (2022). *Mental wellbeing at work (NICE Guideline NG212).* https://www.nice.org.uk/guidance/ng212.

National Institutes of Health. (2020). *Caregivers.* MedlinePlus. https://medlineplus.gov/caregivers.html.

Nigam, J. A., Barker, R. M., Cunningham, T. R., Swanson, N. G., & Chosewood, L. C. (2023). *Vital signs:* Health worker–perceived working conditions and symptoms of poor mental health — Quality of worklife survey, United States, 2018–2022. *MMWR Morbidity and Mortality Weekly Report, 72*, 1197–1205. https://doi.org/10.15585/mmwr.mm7244e1

O'Connor, K., Muller Neff, D., & Pitman, S. (2018). Burnout in mental health professionals: A systematic review and meta-analysis of prevalence and determinants. *European Psychiatry: The Journal of the Association of European Psychiatrists, 53*, 74–99. https://doi.org/10.1016/j.eurpsy.2018.06.003

Ong, N. Y., Teo, F. J. J., Ee, J. Z. Y., Yau, C. E., Thumboo, J., Tan, H. K., & Ng, Q. X. (2024). Effectiveness of mindfulness-based interventions on the well-being of healthcare workers: A systematic review and meta-analysis. *General Psychiatry, 37*(3), Article e101115. https://doi.org/10.1136/gpsych-2023-101115

Padesky, C., & Kennerley, H. (2023). *Dialogues for discovery: Improving psychotherapy's effectiveness.* Oxford: Oxford University Press.

Palitsky, R., & Kaplan, D. M. (2021). The role of religion for mindfulness-based interventions: Implications for dissemination and implementation. *Mindfulness, 12*, 2076–2208. https://doi.org/10.1007/s12671-019-01253-0

Paller, K. A., Creery, J. D., et al. (2014). Benefits of mindfulness training for patients with cognitive decline and their caregivers. *American Journal of Alzheimer's Disease and Other Dementias, 30*(3), 257–267. https://doi.org/10.1177/1533317514545377

Pan, Y., Li, F., Liang, H., Shen, X., Bing, Z., Cheng, L., & Dong, Y. (2024). Effectiveness of mindfulness-based stress reduction on mental health and psychological quality of life among university students: A GRADE-assessed systematic review. *Evidence-based Complementary and Alternative Medicine: eCAM.* , Article 8872685. https://doi.org/10.1155/2024/8872685

Papola, D., Ostuzzi, G., Tedeschi, F., et al. (2022). Comparative efficacy and acceptability of psychotherapies for panic disorder with or without agoraphobia: Systematic review and network meta-analysis of randomized controlled trials. *The British Journal of Psychiatry, 221*(3), 507–519. https://doi.org/10.1192/bjp.2021.148

Pascoe, M. C., Thompson, D. R., Jenkins, Z. M., & Ski, C. F. (2017). Mindfulness mediates the physiological markers of stress: Systematic review and meta-analysis. *Journal of Psychiatric Research, 95*, 156–178. https://doi.org/10.1016/j.jpsychires.2017.08.004

Pascoe, M. C., Thompson, D. R., & Ski, C. F. (2017). Yoga, mindfulness-based stress reduction and stress-related physiological measures: A meta-analysis. *Psychoneuroendocrinology, 86*, 152–168. https://doi.org/10.1016/j.psyneuen.2017.08.008

Paul, G. L. (1967). Strategy of outcome research in psychotherapy. *Journal of Consulting Psychology, 31*(2), 109–118. https://doi.org/10.1037/h0024436

Pseftogianni, F., Panagioti, M., Birtwell, K., & Angelakis, I. (2023). Mindfulness interventions for obsessive–compulsive and related disorders: A systematic review and meta-analysis of randomized controlled trials. *Clinical Psychology: Science and Practice.* https://doi.org/10.1037/cps0000132

Qin, K., Yu, Y., Cai, H., Li, J., Zeng, J., & Liang, H. (2024). Effectiveness of mindfulness-based intervention in schizophrenia: A meta-analysis of randomized controlled trials. *Psychiatry Research, 334*, Article 115808. https://doi.org/10.1016/j.psychres.2024.115808

Querstret, D., Morison, L., Dickinson, S., Cropley, M., & John, M. (2020). Mindfulness-based stress reduction and mindfulness-based cognitive therapy for psychological health and well-being in non-clinical samples: A systematic review and meta-analysis. *International Journal of Stress Management, 27*(4), 394–411. https://doi.org/10.1037/str0000165

Quinn, C., Clare, L., & Woods, R. T. (2010). The impact of motivations and meanings on the wellbeing of caregivers of people with dementia: A systematic review. *International Psychogeriatrics, 22*(1), 43–55. https://doi.org/10.1017/S1041610209990810

Ramachandran, H. J., Bin Mahmud, M. S., Rajendran, P., Jiang, Y., Cheng, L., & Wang, W. (2023). Effectiveness of mindfulness-based interventions on psychological well-being, burnout and post-traumatic stress disorder among nurses: A systematic review and meta-analysis. *Journal of Clinical Nursing, 32*(11–12), 2323–2338.

Reid, C. E., Moss, S., & Hyman, G. (2005). Caregiver reciprocity: The effect of reciprocity, caregiver self-esteem and motivation on the experience of caregiver burden. *Australian Journal of Psychology, 57*(3), 186–196. https://doi.org/10.1080/00049530500141022

Roemer, L., & Orsillo, S. M. (2013). *The mindful way through anxiety: Break free from chronic worry and reclaim your life*. Guilford Press.

Rogers, C. (1980). *A way of being*. New York: Houghton Mifflin Company.

Rosenbaum, E. (2021). *The heart of mindfulness-based stress reduction: A MBSR guide for clinicians and clients*. New Harbinger Publications.

Rosenkranz, M. A., Davidson, R., MacCoon, D. G., Sheridan, J. F., Kalin, N. H., & Lutz, A. (2013). A comparison of mindfulness-based stress reduction and an active control in modulation of neurogenic inflammation. *Brain, Behavior, and Immunity, 27*, 174–184. https://doi.org/10.1016/j.bbi.2012.10.013

Roubinov, D. S., Epel, E. S., Coccia, M., Coleman-Phox, K., Vieten, C., Adler, N. E., Laraia, B., & Bush, N. R. (2022). Long-term effects of a prenatal mindfulness intervention on depressive symptoms in a diverse sample of women. *Journal of Consulting and Clinical Psychology*. https://doi.org/10.1037/ccp0000776. Advance online publication.

Russell, T., & Arcuri, S. (2015). A neurophysiological and neuropsychological consideration of mindful movement: Clinical and research implications. *Frontiers in Human Neuroscience, 9*. https://doi.org/10.3389/fnhum.2015.00282

Sabé, M., Kohler, R., Perez, N., Sauvain-Sabé, M., Sentissi, O., Jermann, F., Prada, P., Perroud, N., & Böge, K. (2024). Mindfulness-based interventions for patients with schizophrenia spectrum disorders: A systematic review of the literature. *Schizophrenia Research, 264*, 191–203. https://doi.org/10.1016/j.schres.2023.12.011

Sanada, K., Montero-Marin, J., Barceló-Soler, A., Ikuse, D., Ota, M., Hirata, A., Yoshizawa, A., Hatanaka, R., Valero, M. S., Demarzo, M., Campayo, J. G., & Iwanami, A. (2020). Effects of mindfulness-based interventions on biomarkers and low-grade inflammation in patients with psychiatric disorders: A meta-analytic review. *International Journal of Molecular Sciences, 21*(7), 2484.

Sapthiang, S., Shonin, E., Barrows, P., & Van Gordon, W. (2023). Authentic mindfulness within mindfulness-based interventions: A qualitative study of participants' experiences. *International Journal of Transpersonal Studies, 42*(2), 101–116. https://doi.org/10.24972/ijts.2023.42.2.101

Saragih, I. D., Batubara, S. O., Sharma, S., Saragih, I. S., & Chou, F. H. (2024a). A meta-analysis of mindfulness-based interventions for improving mental health and burden among caregivers of persons living with dementia. *Worldviews on Evidence-Based Nursing, 21*(2), 183–193. https://doi.org/10.1111/wvn.12690

Saragih, I. D., Batubara, S. O., Sharma, S., Saragih, I. S., & Chou, F. H. (2024b). A meta-analysis of mindfulness-based interventions for improving mental health and burden among caregivers of persons living with dementia. *Worldviews on Evidence-Based Nursing, 21*(2), 183–193. https://doi.org/10.1111/wvn.12690

Sauer-Zavala, S. E., Walsh, E. C., et al. (2013). Comparing mindfulness-based intervention strategies: Differential effects of sitting meditation, body scan, and mindful yoga. *Mindfulness, 4*, 383–388. https://doi.org/10.1007/s12671-012-0139-9

Schmidt, H., & Pilat, C. (2023). Effects of meditation on pain intensity, physical function, quality of life and depression in adults with low back pain - A systematic review with meta-analysis. *Complementary Therapies in Medicine, 72*, Article 102924. https://doi.org/10.1016/j.ctim.2023.102924

Schultz, R., & Beach, S. R. (1999). Caregiving as a risk factor for mortality. *JAMA, 282*, 2215–2219. https://doi.org/10.1001/jama.282.23.2215

Schultz, R., & Sherwood, P. (2008). Physical and mental health effects of family caregiving. *American Journal of Nursing, 108*(9), 23–27. https://doi.org/10.1097/01.naj.0000336406.45248.4c

Segal, Z. V., Williams, J. M. G., & Teasdale, J. D. (2013). *Mindfulness-based cognitive therapy for depression* (2nd ed.). Guilford Press.

Shah, M. K., Gandrakota, N., Cimiotti, J. P., Ghose, N., Moore, M., & Ali, M. K. (2021). Prevalence of and factors associated with nurse Burnout in the US. *JAMA Network Open, 4* (2), Article e2036469. https://doi.org/10.1001/jamanetworkopen.2020.36469

Shim, M., Tilley, J. L., Im, S., Price, K., & Gonzalez, A. (2021). A systematic review of mindfulness-based interventions for patients with mild cognitive impairment or dementia and caregivers. *Journal of Geriatric Psychiatry and Neurology, 34*(6), 528–554. https://doi.org/10.1177/0891988720957104

Shires, A., Sharpe, L., Davies, J. N., & Newton-John, T. R. O. (2020). The efficacy of mindfulness-based interventions in acute pain: A systematic review and meta-analysis. *Pain, 161*(8), 1698–1707. https://doi.org/10.1097/j.pain.0000000000001877

Singh, N. N., Lancioni, G. E., et al. (2020). Using mindfulness to improve quality of life in caregivers of individuals with intellectual disabilities and autism spectrum disorder. *International Journal of Developmental Disabilities, 66*(5), 370–380. https://doi.org/10.1080/20473869.2020.1827211

Singh, N. N., Lancioni, G. E., Karazsia, B. T., & Myers, R. E. (2016). Caregiver training in mindfulness-based positive behavior supports (MBPBS): Effects on caregivers and adults with intellectual and developmental disabilities. *Frontiers in Psychology, 7*, 98. https://doi.org/10.3389/fpsyg.2016.00098

Son, J., Erno, A., Shea, D. G., Femia, E. E., Zarit, S. H., & Stephens, M. A. P. (2007). The caregiver stress process and health outcomes. *Journal of Aging and Health, 19*(6), 871–887. https://doi.org/10.1177/0898264307308568

Steadman, P. L., Tremont, G., & Davis, J. D. (2007). Premorbid relationship satisfaction and caregiver burden in dementia caregivers. *Journal of Geriatric Psychiatry and Neurology, 2* (2), 115–119. https://doi.org/10.1177/0891988706298624

Stjernsward, S., & Hanson, L. (2018). Effectiveness and usability of a web-based mindfulness intervention for caregivers of people with mental and somatic illness. *Internet Interv, 12*, 46–56. https://doi.org/10.1016/jinvent.2018.03.004

Stjernsward, S., & Hanson, L. (2020). A qualitative study of caregivers' experiences, motivation and challenges using a web-based mindfulness intervention. *Community Mental Health Journal, 56*, 416–425. https://doi.org/10.1007/s10597-019-00477-7

Suleiman-Martos, N., Gomez-Urquiza, J. L., Aguayo-Estremera, R., et al. (2020). The effect of mindfulness training on burnout syndrome in nursing: A systematic review and meta-analysis. *Journal of Advanced Nursing, 76*, 1124–1140. https://doi.org/10.1111/jan.14318

Thomas, J. (2018). *Mindfulness and Christian spirituality: Making space for god*. SPCK Publishing.

Tilden, E. L., Holmes, L. R., Vasquez Guzman, C. E., Orzech, C. P., Seghete, K. M., Eyo, V., Supahan, N., Rogers, G. R., Caughey, A. B., Starr, D., DiPietro, J. L., Fisher, P. A., & Graham, A. M. (2022). Adapting mindfulness-based cognitive therapy for perinatal depression to improve access and appeal of preventive care. *Journal of Midwifery & Women's Health, 67*(6), 707–713. https://doi.org/10.1111/jmwh.13444

Treleaven, D. A. (2018). *Trauma-sensitive mindfulness: Practices for safe and transformative healing*. New York: W.W. Norton & Company.

Usset, T. J., Stratton, R. G., Knapp, S., Schwartzman, G., Yadav, S. K., Schaefer, B. J., Harris, J. I., & Fitchett, G. (2024). Factors associated with healthcare clinician stress and resilience: A scoping review. *Journal of Healthcare Management, 69*(1), 12–28. https://doi.org/10.1097/JHM-D-23-00020

Uusberg, H., Uusberg, A., Talpsep, T., & Paaver, M. (2016). Mechanisms of mindfulness: The dynamics of affective adaptation during open monitoring. *Biological Psychology, 118*(12). https://doi.org/10.1016/j.biopsycho.2016.05.004

Vaidya, A. D. B., & Vaidya, R. (2023). A century of 'The science of yoga' (1921-2021): Revival, renewal and renaissance. *Journal of Ayurveda and Integrative Medicine, 14*(1), Article 100613. https://doi.org/10.1016/j.jaim.2022.100613

van der Kolk, B. (2014). *The body keeps the score: Brain, mind, and body in the healing of trauma*. New York: Viking.

Vollbehr, N. K., Hoenders, H. J. R., Bartels-Velthuis, A. A., Nauta, M. H., Castelein, S., Schroevers, M. J., Stant, A. D., Albers, C. J., de Jong, P. J., & Ostafin, B. D. (2022). Mindful yoga intervention as add-on to treatment as usual for young women with major depressive disorder: Results from a randomized controlled trial. *Journal of Consulting and Clinical Psychology, 90*(12), 925–941. https://doi.org/10.1037/ccp0000777

Wang, C. W., Chan, C. H. Y., et al. (2014). Managing stress and anxiety through qigong exercise in healthy adults: A systematic review and meta-analysis of randomized controlled trials. *BMC Complementary and Alternative Medicine, 14*, 8. https://doi.org/10.1186/1472-6882-14-8

Weng, H. C., Hung, C. M., Liu, Y. T., Cheng, Y. J., Yen, C. Y., Chang, C. C., & Huang, C. K. (2011). Associations between emotional intelligence and doctor burnout, job satisfaction and patient satisfaction. *Medical Education, 45*(8), 835–842. https://doi.org/10.1111/j.1365-2923.2011.03985.x

Whitebird, R. R., Kreitzer, M., Crain, A. L., et al. (2013). Mindfulness-based stress reduction for family caregivers: A randomized controlled trial. *The Gerontologist, 53*(4), 676–686. https://doi.org/10.1093/geront/gns126

World Health Organization. (2018). *International classification of diseases for mortality and morbidity statistics (11th revision)*. Retrieved from https://icd.who.int/browse11/l-m/en.

World Health Organization. (2019). *ICD-11 for mortality and morbidity statistics*. Retrieved from https://icd.who.int/browse11_2019-04/l-m/en#/http%3A%2F%2Fid.who.int%2Ficd%2Fentity%2F129180281.

Yu, D. S. F., Cheng, S. T., & Wang, J. (2018). Unravelling positive aspects of caregiving in dementia: An integrative review of research literature. *International Journal of Nursing Studies, 79*, 1–26. https://doi.org/10.1016/j.ijnurstu.2017.10.008

Yu, J., Song, P., Zhang, Y., & Wei, Z. (2020). Effects of mindfulness-based intervention on the treatment of problematic eating behaviors: A systematic review. *Journal of Alternative & Complementary Medicine, 26*(8), 666–679. https://doi.org/10.1089/acm.2019.0163

Zhang, D., Lee, E. K. P., Mak, E. C. W., et al. (2021). Mindfulness-based interventions: An overall review. *British Medical Bulletin, 138*(1), 41–57. https://doi.org/10.1093/bmb/ldab005

Zhang, X., Ren, H., Wang, C., Zhang, Y., Zhou, Q., & Fan, J. (2024). The effect of mindfulness- based interventions on mental health outcomes and wellbeing of informal caregivers of people with mental illness: A systematic review and meta-analysis. *International Journal of Mental Health Nursing, 33*, 797–816. https://doi.org/10.1111/inm.13295

Index

'*Note*: Page numbers followed by "b" indicate boxes.'

9780443298219